WOODWORK

STEP BY STEP

WOODWORK

STEP BY STEP

CONTENT PREVIOUSLY PUBLISHED IN
*WOODWORK: A STEP-BY-STEP PHOTOGRAPHIC
GUIDE TO SUCCESSFUL WOODWORKING*

CONTENTS

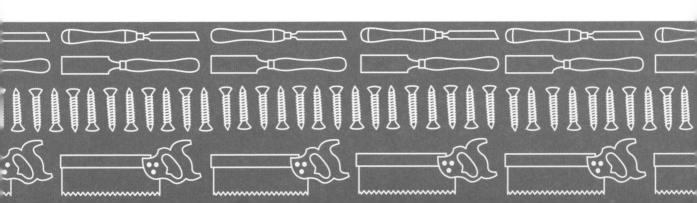

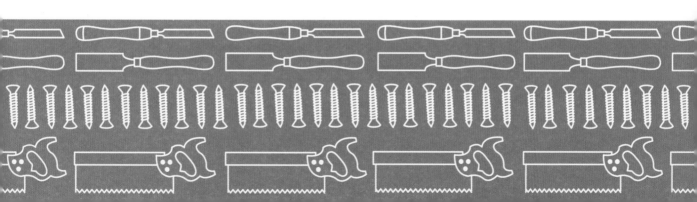

INTRODUCTION

Wood has been fundamental to the development and survival of humankind throughout history. Trees have provided us with the essentials for living—oxygen, food, warmth, medicine, and shelter—as well as offering the raw ingredients for key markers of cultural progress, such as paper, furniture, musical instruments, and works of art. Even today, in a world of sophisticated technology and materials, we use wood for much of our work on buildings and furniture because of its versatility, beauty, and availability.

Because of this long tradition, wooden furniture has a rich and diverse heritage of styles, while examples that are centuries old can be found all around us—in museums, antique stores, or galleries. This range of styles and sense of tradition and craftsmanship offers the modern woodworker an inspirational archive to draw upon, whether designing or constructing their own pieces.

Creating furniture by hand is a skill that has to an extent been supplanted by the development of power tools and machinery, yet the importance of using hand tools cannot be underestimated. Tools may have advanced in sophistication throughout history, but the fundamentals of woodworking have not changed significantly over the centuries, and this age-old craft is still the cornerstone of all furniture making. Of course, it is possible to make furniture entirely by machine, but this requires a large workshop and a very large wallet. By contrast, hand skills allow you to create furniture within a limited space and with a limited budget while experiencing the pleasure of working closely with wood to craft an object of your choice.

Woodwork Step by Step celebrates the joys of creating furniture. It provides a core grounding in the fundamental woodworking skills and techniques, and the use of both hand and power tools; showcases a catalog of the various types of timber available and their individual working properties; and supplies you with achievable, yet challenging, projects. Whether you are a novice or more experienced in the art of carpentry, *Woodwork Step by Step* is an essential addition to your bookshelf.

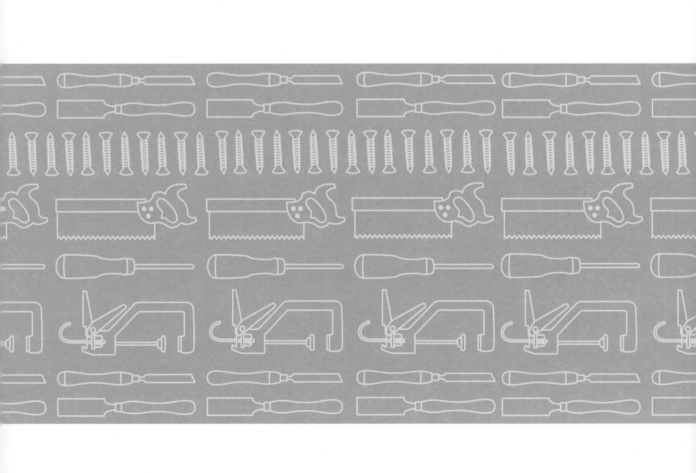

TOOLS

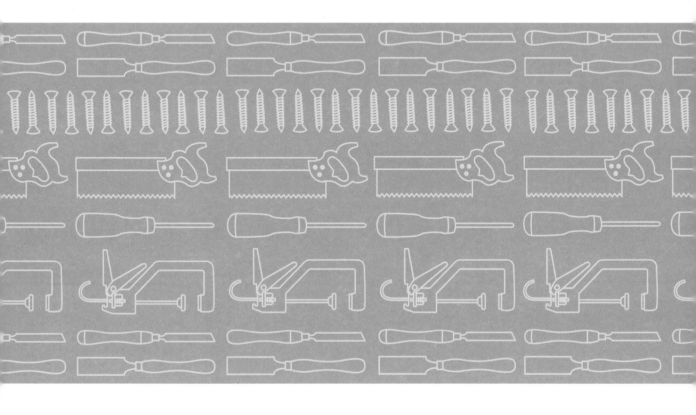

INTRODUCTION

Much of the pleasure of woodworking comes from the appreciation of the many tools used. Handling and using a metal hand plane, for example, should be enjoyable—the way the crisp wood shavings curl up from a workpiece is a pure delight to the woodworking devotee. Equally, a carving gouge should be a joy to work with, and even a hammer or a power drill are beautiful objects in their own right. That said, tools are only enjoyable (and safe) to use if they are well balanced and are kept clean and sharp. It is also important to always use the correct tool for the task at hand.

⚙ USING THE RIGHT TOOLS FOR THE JOB

You should avoid the temptation to simply browse a manufacturer's catalog and order a vast range of tools. When starting out in woodworking, it is best to carefully consider your first project—its size and shape, the materials and techniques required—and then visit a quality tool supplier and select the minimum number of tools necessary to complete the job. Once you start work, you may of course discover that you need more tools—a different plane or another clamp, for example—but at least these extra purchases will be guided by your actual needs. Another important issue to address when buying tools is whether to opt for power tools or hand tools. This decision depends on whether you want the job done quickly and easily—but with the noise, dust, setup requirements, and potential hazards associated with power tools—or whether you would prefer to work more slowly and enjoy the quieter, subtler pleasures of working with hand tools. If you are an absolute beginner and have concerns about your own abilities, the best way to seek advice and gain confidence is either to work alongside an experienced woodworker or join a woodworking group. If you are slight in stature or not particularly strong, for example, you will be able to discuss what you can and can't feasibly achieve in the workshop. Equally, if you have limited funds or your working space is restricted, you will be able to discuss your options. Above all, talking to and working with other woodworkers will inspire you to make the most of your newfound interest.

NEW OR SECOND-HAND TOOLS?

As a general rule, hand tools should last a lifetime, and power tools and machines are only as good as their electrical parts. When deciding between buying new or second-hand tools, the best advice is to buy new power tools and machines and consider buying some hand tools that are second-hand. The main advantage of buying second-hand tools is that it may be possible to acquire a complete set of tools—in their own dedicated storage chest—that have been lovingly cared for by the previous owner.

STORING TOOLS

You should treat the phrase "a place for everything and everything in its place" as a golden rule in the workshop. It is important that you know the location of every tool at all times. Your tools should also be close at hand. This will allow you to access each tool as required, quickly and safely. Carefully storing your tools will help prolong their life; make sure that they are clean, well oiled, and carefully stored in a dry box or chest or in a designated storage rack. The working area needs to be dry, well-lit, dust-free, and clean—for the benefit of both you and your tools. While woodworking should be a rewarding, even therapeutic, activity, these benefits will only be realized if the workshop is a safe, comfortable, and orderly place to work. This is true for all sizes of workshop, from the largest production workshop to the smallest garden shed.

Leather roll
A good way to store cutting tools like chisels is in a leather roll, which will keep the tools separate and protect the cutting edges.

WORK SAFELY

Tools can be very dangerous, so correct and safe use is crucial. The chart below outlines the hazards associated with common tools and the precautions that you should take. However, you should also refer to the manufacturer's instructions and seek formal training whenever possible. For information about personal protective equipment (PPE), see p.53.

HAND TOOLS	TOOL	HAZARDS	SAFETY PRECAUTIONS
Look after your hand tools. Keep them clean and well maintained—a dirty chisel, for example, is hard to hold steady, and the badly fitting head of a hammer may fly off. 　Keep your blades sharp. While a blunt cutting tool may inflict less damage than a sharp one, it is more dangerous to use—you will need to use more force, which means it is more likely to slip.	Hand saw; marking knife	• Cuts to hands	• Cover blade when not in use • Support workpiece • Never force the saw while cutting • Take extra care when starting a cut
	Plane	• Cuts to hands when handling blades	• Wear gloves when handling sharp blades
	Chisel and other cutting tools; screwdriver	• Piercing wounds	• Never place hand or body in front of blade

HANDHELD POWER TOOLS	POWER TOOL	HAZARDS	SAFETY PRECAUTIONS
Ensure that your handheld power tools are electrically safe and that all blades and bits are securely and correctly mounted on the tool. 　While these tools may seem small and unlikely to cause serious injury, they work at very high speeds and are powerful enough to cause considerable injury.	Drill	• Lacerations to hands	• Support the workpiece correctly (not with hands)
	Router	• Bit breakage • Lacerations to hands • Flying debris • Tool "jumping"	• Follow good practice; set router to correct speed • Support the workpiece correctly (not with hands) • Never start/stop tool while the bit is in contact with a surface • Make cuts in the correct direction • Mount the bit correctly
	Circular saw	• Cuts and lacerations	• Always use the safety guards • Support the workpiece correctly (not with hands)
	Sander	• Respiratory damage	• Wear PPE
	Jigsaw; joiner	• Cuts and lacerations	• Take general precautions (see below, left)
	Nail gun	• Piercing wounds	• Never hold the tip of the nail gun • Support the workpiece correctly (not with hands)

MACHINE TOOLS	MACHINE	HAZARDS	SAFETY PRECAUTIONS
These powerful machines are potentially very dangerous and should be treated with respect. This is not to say, however, that you should use them in a timid way; hold a workpiece firmly and feed it in a controlled—and deliberate—manner. **General precautions for machine tools** • Use push sticks to feed in a workpiece • Always use the blade guards • Always set the machine up correctly, especially the bit's speed and position • Never stand behind the workpiece in case of kickback (the workpiece being "thrown") • Do not wear loose clothing or jewelry; tie back long hair	Table saw	• Kickback (workpiece being "thrown")	• Adjust side fence correctly • Seek assistance to help keep the kerf (width of cut) open when machining thick boards
	Band saw	• Cuts and lacerations to hands	• Follow general precautions for machine tools
	Radial-arm saw	• Saw "climbing" the workpiece	• Use a negative-rake blade
	Jointer	• Kickback	• Ensure that the in-feed table is adjusted correctly
	Thickness planer	• Trapped fingers	• Ensure that the workpiece is fully on the roller
	Lathe; mortiser; drill press	• Cuts and lacerations to hands	• Follow general precautions for machine tools
	Router table	• Cuts and lacerations to hands	• Ensure bit guards are correctly positioned • Make several small cuts rather than one large cut

SAWS

Saw blades have serrated edges called "teeth" along one side, which are bent at an angle and set to alternate sides. When cutting through wood, the teeth create a slot, or "kerf," that is wider than the blade. This helps the blade move freely through the wood without getting stuck. There are many different types of saws, each designed for specific woodworking tasks. Western (or European) saws cut on the "push" stroke, whereas Japanese saws (see opposite) cut on the "pull" stroke.

PANEL SAWS

Panel saws are among the most commonly used of all saws. They have a long, flexible blade and are ideal for cutting boards and panels, as well as for ripping or cross-cutting solid timber (see below). Good-quality panel saws have blades that are ground to a taper to ease sawing.

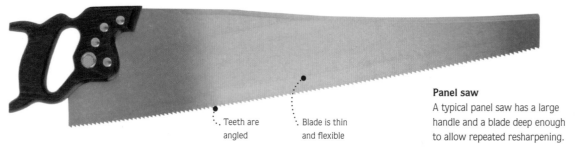

.. Teeth are angled

. Blade is thin and flexible

Panel saw
A typical panel saw has a large handle and a blade deep enough to allow repeated resharpening.

Ripping with a panel saw
To rip (cut down the grain) with a panel saw, hold the wood securely on two trestles and position yourself as comfortably as possible. As you saw closer to the trestle, move the wood forward carefully, ensuring that the other end does not drop down. When necessary, move the wood back and cut between the trestles. Finish the cut by working from the other end.

Focus eyes on the cutting line ....

Extend thumb to help guide saw ....

.. Balance posture

Place foot .... firmly on ground

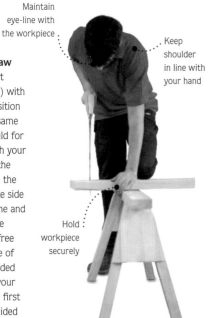

Cross-cutting with a panel saw
To cross-cut (cut across the grain) with a panel saw, position yourself in the same way as you would for ripping, but with your saw parallel to the end grain. Place the saw to the waste side of the cutting line and carefully rest the thumb of your free hand on the side of the blade for added stability. Move your thumb after the first few carefully guided strokes.

Maintain eye-line with the workpiece .

. Keep shoulder in line with your hand

Hold : workpiece securely

🪚 BACK SAWS

Used primarily for cutting tenons (see pp.91–107), the back saw gets its name from the piece of folded, or cast, metal that runs along its back edge, supporting the blade. This heavy metal spine keeps the saw steady when cutting through wood but limits the depth of your cut. Back saws have smaller teeth than panel saws, which results in a finer cut but at a slower pace. There are two types of back saw: the tenon saw and the dovetail saw.

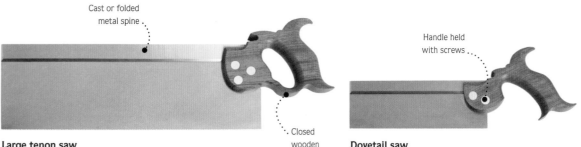

Cast or folded metal spine

Closed wooden handle

Handle held with screws

Large tenon saw
The large tenon saw has a long blade that cuts deep joints with ease. It has around 11 points, or teeth, per inch (or 4 per centimeter). Its larger size makes it slightly harder to handle than a small tenon saw.

Dovetail saw
Similar in appearance to a tenon saw, the dovetail saw is smaller with more teeth—approximately 18 per inch (7 per centimeter). These produce the fine cuts useful for cutting joints.

🪚 JAPANESE SAWS

The blades of Japanese saws are designed to cut on the pull stroke and are much thinner than their Western counterparts. The blades are kept steady by the pulling action, unlike those of Western saws, which depend on their thickness to prevent bending. The teeth of Japanese saws are sharp on all sides, which results in a clean, slicing cut.

Blade stiffened with steel spine

Small Japanese back saw
Similar to the dovetail saw, the small Japanese back saw produces very accurate cuts for fine joinery.

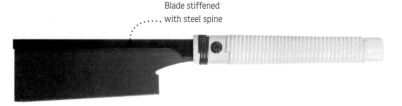

🪚 COPING SAWS

When performing tricky tasks, such as cutting curves or removing waste from joints, such as dovetails (see pp.116–121), a coping saw is indispensable. The blade is thin and narrow, which allows it to be turned easily. Use a fret saw, which is similar to a coping saw but has a finer blade, for intricate fretwork in thin board or veneer.

Frame provides tension

Two pegs hold blade in position. These can be twisted in unison to rotate blade

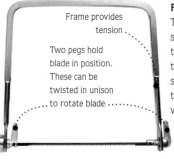

Fitting the blade
The blade of a coping saw must be fitted in the frame so that the teeth cut on the pull stroke. If fitted with the teeth pointing the wrong way, it might break.

Handle is turned clockwise to tension blade

SAW TEETH

Saw teeth are designed to enable the saw to perform certain tasks. Panel-saw teeth have an edge that is square to the blade, which acts like a chisel to chop the grain and prevent clogging. The teeth of cross-cut saws are sharpened to a point, helping them slice the grain. The three exposed sides of Japanese saw teeth are all sharp and produce a neat, slicing cut. All saw teeth have a certain amount of "set" (the amount by which the teeth are bent). Teeth along a blade are measured in points per inch (PPI)—the larger the PPI, the finer the cut, but the longer it will take.

PANEL-SAW TEETH

CROSS-CUT SAW TEETH

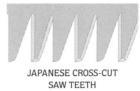

JAPANESE CROSS-CUT
SAW TEETH

SET OF TEETH—PLAN VIEW

HANDHELD POWER SAWS

Three types of saw are available: circular saws, jigsaws, and reciprocating saws, although the latter is more suited to DIY tasks than woodwork. Circular saws and jigsaws can perform most of the jobs that do not require more heavy-duty machine saws, such as table saws (see opposite) and band saws (see p.16). Both are ideal for carpentry work and cutting timber and manufactured boards to a rough size prior to machining or trimming with a plane (see pp.17–23) or router (see pp.38–43). Power saws can be either corded or battery-powered.

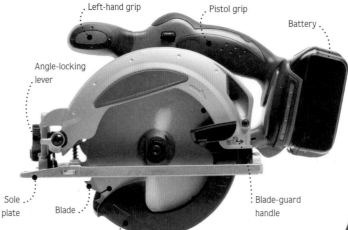

Left-hand grip

Pistol grip

Battery

Angle-locking lever

Sole plate

Blade

Spring-loaded blade guard

Blade-guard handle

Circular saws

There are two types of circular saw. The first type has a sole plate that is set to the desired depth and fitted before use; this type of saw is fed into the work from the edge. The second type has an adjustable sole plate. As the saw is lowered, the base plate stops moving once the blade reaches the preset depth. This type of saw performs plunging cuts, as well as standard cuts.

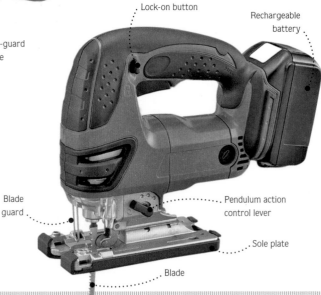

Lock-on button

Rechargeable battery

Blade guard

Pendulum action control lever

Sole plate

Blade

Jigsaws

Slower than other handheld power saws, jigsaws are best suited for cutting boards and thin sections of timber. Due to the narrow sizes of the blades used, jigsaws can be used to cut curves, as well as to make straight cuts. The blades of basic machines move straight up and down. However, jigsaws with an orbital or pendulum action cut into the work on the upstroke and away from it on the downstroke. This back-and-forth swinging action aids in chip removal. You can adjust the extent of the pendulum action to get the desired result.

TABLE SAWS

Consisting of a flat table through which a rotary saw blade protrudes, the table saw is the workhorse of the workshop. Mainly used for cutting solid timbers and flat boards, the size of the machine is defined by the size of the blade. A typical blade has a diameter of 10–17¹¹⁄₁₆ in (250–450 mm); the larger the blade, the deeper the cut it can make. A basic modern table saw has a side fence for guiding the workpiece and a blade that can be raised, lowered, or tilted. Most models have a sliding table which, combined with a tiltable blade, enables the woodworker to cut compound angles.

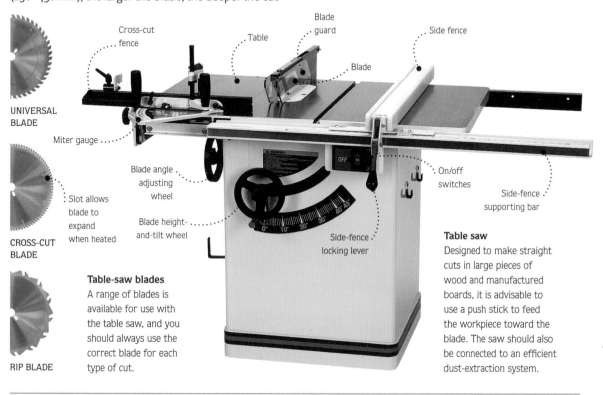

UNIVERSAL BLADE

CROSS-CUT BLADE

Slot allows blade to expand when heated

RIP BLADE

Cross-cut fence

Miter gauge

Blade angle adjusting wheel

Blade height-and-tilt wheel

Table

Blade guard

Blade

Side fence

Side-fence locking lever

Blade height-and-tilt wheel

On/off switches

Side-fence supporting bar

Table-saw blades
A range of blades is available for use with the table saw, and you should always use the correct blade for each type of cut.

Table saw
Designed to make straight cuts in large pieces of wood and manufactured boards, it is advisable to use a push stick to feed the workpiece toward the blade. The saw should also be connected to an efficient dust-extraction system.

WORK SAFELY
If used incorrectly, woodworking machines have the potential to be extremely dangerous. It is important that you are aware of the risks, take proper safety precautions, and undergo appropriate training—especially when using powered cutting tools. Always read the manufacturers' safety instructions before starting work. Follow the correct procedures at all times, and never be tempted to rush a job or take shortcuts.

Isolating switch
All table saws should have an isolating switch. This is used to disconnect, or isolate, the saw from its power source. Once the machine has been isolated, you are safe to make adjustments or carry out repairs.

Blade guard
A blade guard covers the top of the blade—you should never operate a table saw unless this guard is correctly in position. An extraction system sits on top of the blade guard to carry away excess dust.

BAND SAWS

Band saws are simple yet versatile cutting machines. They consist of a flexible steel blade that runs around two (or sometimes three) wheels in a continuous loop. The blade passes through a table that holds the workpiece. Available in a range of sizes, band saws can cut curves and perform deep ripping cuts—a task impossible on a table saw (see p.15).

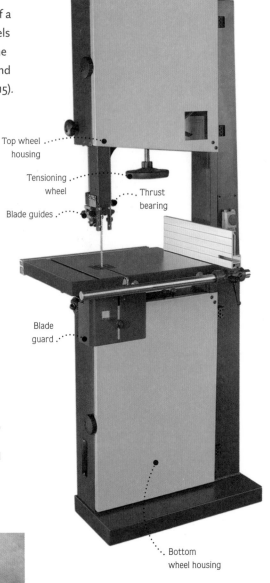

Top wheel housing

Tensioning wheel

Thrust bearing

Blade guides

Blade guard

Bottom wheel housing

Floor-mounted band saw
A more stable and powerful machine than the bench-mounted band saw, this machine is ideal for making heavy ripping cuts.

Using a band saw
Lower the blade guard as far down the blade as the fence allows. Start the machine. When the blade has reached full speed, start feeding in the workpiece, using the fence as a guide. As you reach the end of the cut, use push sticks to feed the workpiece safely onto the blade.

CUTTING CURVES WITH A BAND SAW

A band saw is useful for cutting curves in timber. Choose the widest possible blade for the tightest section of curve and use an off-cut (waste piece of timber) to guide you. Make a series of straight relief cuts perpendicular to the proposed curve. These relief cuts will reduce the tension between the board and blade and ease tension on the saw, thereby avoiding the need to withdraw the workpiece from the blade when cutting (which can pull the blade off its wheels). You will not be able to use a band saw to cut shapes (holes) in a sheet of timber—for that, you will need a jigsaw (see p.14).

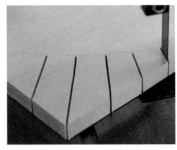

1 Draw the proposed curve on the workpiece with a pencil or marking knife (see p.27). Make a series of relief cuts at right angles to the curve, stopping very close to the line.

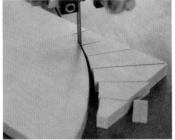

2 Start cutting along the curve. As you proceed, the waste will fall away as each relief cut is reached, making it easier for the band saw to move around the curved line.

PLANES

Planes are used to smooth, flatten, shape, or reduce the thickness of timber. As the plane glides over the wood, the angled blade shaves the surface to create a uniform finish. The thickness of the shaving can be controlled by adjusting the position of the blade within the body. The most common type of plane is the bench plane (see below); however, there is a large variety of planes available for different woodworking purposes.

BENCH PLANES

Most bench planes have a blade at a fixed angle, or "pitch," of 45 degrees, with the bevel facing downward. (If it were facing upward, the resultant pitch would be too great for general planing.) Planes with a pitch greater than 45 degrees (sometimes called a "York pitch") are used for hard timbers, whereas low-angle planes—with pitches of approximately 42 degrees—are useful for cutting end grains. Planes are also known as either "Bailey" or "Bedrock" types—the main difference centers around the "frog" (the sliding iron wedge that holds the blade at the correct angle). With Bailey planes, the blade must be removed before adjustments to the frog are made; with Bedrock planes, you do not have to remove the blade to make adjustments. Bench planes come in different body lengths: short lengths clean rough edges and smooth surfaces effectively, while longer lengths create very straight edges.

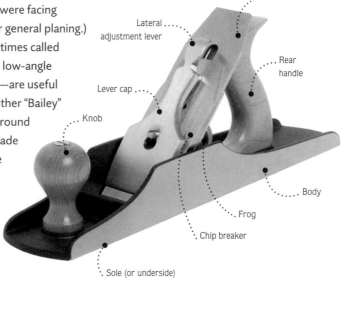

Blade

Lateral adjustment lever

Rear handle

Lever cap

Knob

Body

Frog

Chip breaker

Sole (or underside)

No. 4 plane
This size of plane is very easy to control and is an excellent choice for small, light work. The no. 4 bench plane is ideal for trimming surfaces and planing joints.

No. 5½ plane
Wider and longer than the no. 4 plane, the no. 5½ plane is also known as a "jack" plane. This is a general-purpose plane.

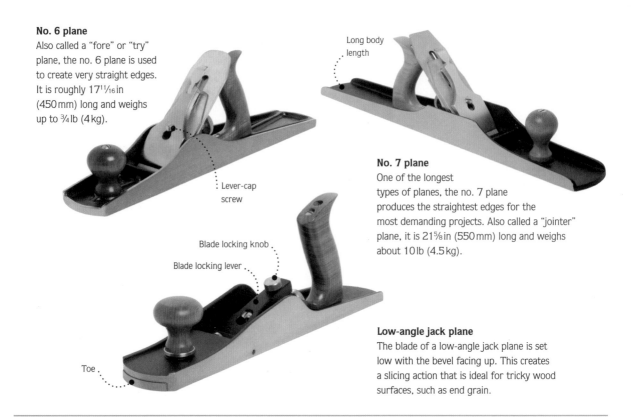

No. 6 plane
Also called a "fore" or "try" plane, the no. 6 plane is used to create very straight edges. It is roughly $17\frac{11}{16}$ in (450mm) long and weighs up to $\frac{3}{4}$ lb (4 kg).

Long body length

Lever-cap screw

No. 7 plane
One of the longest types of planes, the no. 7 plane produces the straightest edges for the most demanding projects. Also called a "jointer" plane, it is $21\frac{5}{8}$ in (550 mm) long and weighs about 10 lb (4.5 kg).

Blade locking knob

Blade locking lever

Low-angle jack plane
The blade of a low-angle jack plane is set low with the bevel facing up. This creates a slicing action that is ideal for tricky wood surfaces, such as end grain.

Toe

ADJUSTING A BENCH PLANE

In order to achieve the best results, it is important that you know how to adjust a plane. Use the frog-adjusting screw to change the size of the "mouth" (the gap between the face of the blade and the edge of the opening in the sole). A large mouth is used for coarse grain, while fine work requires a small mouth. To control the blade extension and set the depth of the cut, use the depth wheel at the back of the blade. Use the lateral adjustment lever behind the frog to make sure that the blade sits parallel with the sole.

CHECKING THAT THE PLANE IS TRUE

1 Check the flatness of the sole against the edge of a straight surface (such as a ruler). A very slightly concave sole is acceptable, but the sole must never be convex.

2 Use a combination square (see p.28) to check that the plane is square. This is helpful if the plane is to be used on a shooting board (a flat board with grooves used for guiding a plane).

REMOVING THE BLADE

1 Lift up the handle of the lever cap. If the cap does not move easily, loosen it with a screwdriver. Make sure you use the correct screwdriver (see p.36) for the job.

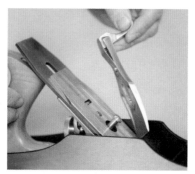

2 Remove the lever cap from the plane. The cap will lift off to expose the blade assembly. Unscrew the chip breaker that sits on top of the blade.

3 Carefully lift the blade off the frog. Hold it from behind and ensure you avoid bringing your hands too close to the sharp cutting edge of the blade.

ADJUSTING THE FROG

To adjust the frog on a Bailey plane, first remove the blade to bring the frog-locking screws into view. Loosen the screws, then move the frog in the required direction. Retighten the screws and fit the blade back onto the frog. Look along the sole of the plane and check the throat to ensure you have adjusted the opening to the desired measurement. On a Bedrock plane (pictured), the locking screws are located behind the frog, so you do not need to remove the blade to access them.

CHECKING THE CHIP BREAKER

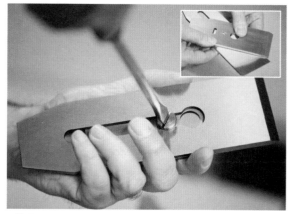

1 Undo the screw on the blade assembly to release the chip breaker. Slide the elements apart (inset). To make this task easier, turn the chip breaker away from the blade's edge.

2 Check the flatness of the chip breaker with a combination square placed first along its length, then its width. A gap between the blade and the chip breaker will result in chips getting trapped.

🔷 GRINDING THE BLADE

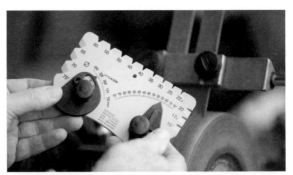

1 Fit the blade into the holder of a purpose-made jig. Slide it up firmly to the side stops and ensure that it is square.

2 Set the gauge to the size of the grinding wheel and fix the angle at which the blade is to be sharpened (usually 25 degrees).

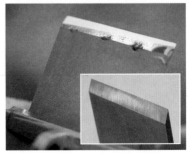

3 Set the blade on the grinding wheel (use a coarse benchstone if you want to grind by hand), place the gauge on top, and adjust the angle of the blade's cutting edge to match the gauge.

4 Fill the trough with water and start the grinder. During the grinding process, continuously move the blade back and forth over the grinding wheel.

5 Check the blade during grinding and ensure that the new edge is forming equally along the width of the blade. When the cutting edge is perfectly flat (inset), the blade is ready to be honed.

🔷 HONING THE BLADE

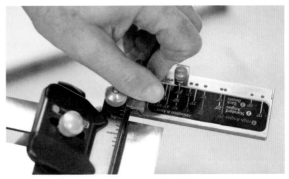

1 Use a diamond whetstone (1,000 grit) set in a stone holder to hone the blade. Secure this to the workbench. Flatten the back of the blade to remove any burr that has formed during the grinding process. Rub the blade, flat side down, across the whetstone (pictured).

2 Set the angle of the honing guide, which is used to keep the angle and flatness of the bevel edge consistent while sharpening. The honing angle for planes is usually 30 degrees.

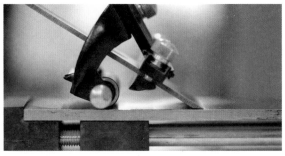

3 Set the width of the honing guide to the same width as the blade. Insert the blade and tighten the guide to secure it. Then place this assembly on the whetstone.

4 Starting with a backward stroke, hone the blade by working it back and forth with firm and even pressure. Use the entire surface of the whetstone to prevent any grooves from forming.

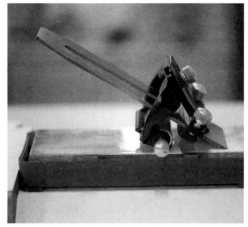

5 Rub the flat side of the blade to remove any burrs and continue rubbing until an even secondary bevel of about $\frac{1}{32}$–$\frac{1}{16}$ in (1–2 mm) has formed along the width of the blade.

6 Change to a stone of a finer grit, such as a 4,000- to 6,000-grit waterstone. Lubricate with water and repeat steps 3–5. Keep turning the stone from time to time as you work. For the finest "mirror" finish, repeat steps 3–5 with an 8,000-grit waterstone. To finish off, rub the flat side on the stone to remove any burrs.

REASSEMBLING THE PLANE

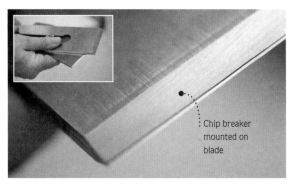

Chip breaker mounted on blade

1 Assemble the blade and the chip breaker (inset), so that the end of the chip breaker is aligned no more than $\frac{1}{32}$ in (1 mm) from the edge of the blade. This not only prevents the blade from chattering (vibrating) when cutting difficult timbers, but also supports the cutting edge as the level of grinding becomes thinner.

2 Slot the blade assembly onto the frog and ensure that the lateral adjustment lever, an adjusting lever located on the back of the frog, is central.

ADJUSTING THE CUT

1 Set the plane vertically on a piece of paper and look through the mouth. Turn the blade depth lever, located on the back of the frog at its base, until you can see the blade sitting squarely.

2 Adjust the lateral adjustment lever until the blade is parallel to the sole of the plane. When parallel, use the blade depth wheel to extend the blade back below the sole.

3 Place the plane on a piece of wood and continue extending the blade as you move it across the wood's surface. The blade is correctly set when it starts to remove a fine curl of wood.

BLOCK PLANES

Smaller than bench planes, block planes can be used with one hand. Their blades are mounted with the bevel facing up and can be of low-angle, rebate, or skewed-blade type. Block planes are used for cutting end grain, trimming dovetails (see pp.77–79, pp.116–121), fitting miters (see pp.85–90), and forming small chamfers (small beveled edges).

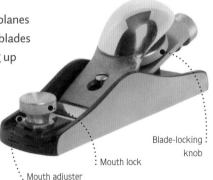

Blade-locking knob

Mouth lock

Mouth adjuster

LOOKING AFTER YOUR PLANE

To keep your plane in good working order, protect it from dampness and keep the blade sharp. Rub the sole of the plane with an abrasive block and apply tea seed oil. To avoid damaging the sole of the plane, always store the plane on its side or with one end raised.

CLEANING WITH AN ABRASIVE BLOCK

APPLYING TEA SEED OIL

WOODEN PLANES

Although metal planes are more widely used than wooden planes, wooden models are still popular in some countries. The body of a modern wooden plane is made from beech or pear and the sole (the base of the plane) is made from lignum vitae, a durable "self-lubricating" hardwood. The two wooden parts are joined using mortise-and-tenon joints. The blades of wooden planes are easy to adjust and produce excellent results.

WOODEN BLOCK PLANE

WOODEN SMOOTHING PLANE

SPECIALIZED PLANES

Bench planes and block planes are used for simple tasks, such as smoothing surfaces and creating straight edges over large, unrestricted surfaces. However, for more specific tasks, such as those in joinery work, it is useful to use specialized planes, such as rebate planes, router planes, plow planes, and spokeshaves.

Router planes
Specially designed to form and clean up housings, the blade of a router plane is suspended below the body. Blades for these planes are available in different shapes and sizes depending on the work being carried out.

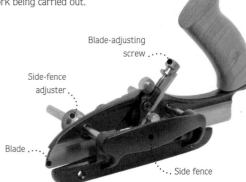

Blade-adjusting screw

Side-fence adjuster

Blade

Side fence

Plow planes
Designed with a narrow sole, plow planes are used to form grooves in the timber. Levers on plow planes can be adjusted to form grooves of desired depths, and the fence can be moved to create the groove at a specific distance from the edge.

Blade-locking knob

Blade

Scraping planes
The blade of a scraping plane is set so that it leans forward in the direction of the cut. These planes are used to finish a surface and are useful for tackling very difficult timbers or those with a coarse grain.

Blade

Blade-locking screw

Body

Handle

Shoulder planes
Shoulder planes are tall, with sides at right angles to their soles. This allows them to trim the shoulders of joints, such as tenons (see pp.91–107), squarely.

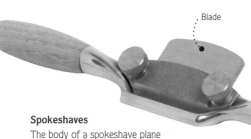

Blade-locking lever and handle

Rebate planes
These types of planes have blades that extend to the full width of the plane, which allows them to reach fully into the corners of rebate or shoulder joints. Rebate planes are used to create, clean, and adjust rebates.

Blade

Spokeshaves
The body of a spokeshave plane has a very short sole held between two handles. It is used to form curves or chamfers as it is drawn along the timber. Other types of spokeshave plane include the travisher and pullshave, which have convex blades for planing concave surfaces.

JOINTERS AND THICKNESS PLANERS

Jointers and thickness planers allow you to produce flat and square timber sections, which are a basic requirement for furniture making and joinery. Jointers are used to smooth faces and edges, while thickness planers shave off wood to produce sections of uniform thickness or width. To save space, a combination machine called a jointer-thickness planer has been developed. Jointing takes place on the upper section of the machine, which consists of "in-feed" and "out-feed" tables. The jointing tables can be lifted to reveal a lower thicknessing table. Converting the machine between jointing and thicknessing modes takes about two or three minutes.

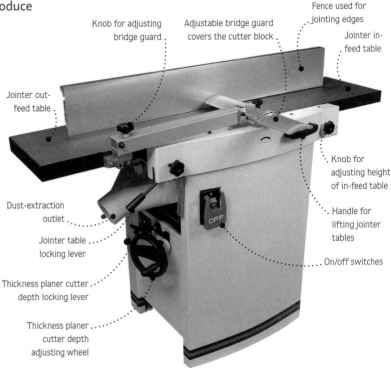

Knob for adjusting bridge guard

Adjustable bridge guard covers the cutter block

Fence used for jointing edges

Jointer in-feed table

Jointer out-feed table

Knob for adjusting height of in-feed table

Handle for lifting jointer tables

Dust-extraction outlet

On/off switches

Jointer table locking lever

Thickness planer cutter depth locking lever

Thickness planer cutter depth adjusting wheel

Jointer-thickness planer in jointer position
When jointing, ensure that the tables are locked down. Unsecured tables are a safety hazard and may result in uneven work.

⬤ USING A JOINTER

The main function of a jointer is to produce smooth, flat faces and edges on wood stocks. These smoothed surfaces act as a reference for subsequent work, helping you achieve parallel surfaces. Unlock the in-feed table, adjust the depth of cut (the amount of wood you want to remove), and then relock the table. You will have to pass the stock across the jointer a number of times to achieve a smooth surface. Never joint stock smaller than $17^{11}/_{16}$ in (450 mm) in length; stock with lengths shorter than this is difficult and dangerous to work with.

Jointing a face
At the first pass, set the cutters to take off no more than $^1/_{16}$ in (5 mm) of wood. Set the bridge guard to approximately $^1/_{32}$ in (1 mm) above your work.

Jointing an edge
Adjust the bridge guard to the thickness of your stock. Always ensure that the fence is square to the bed of the jointer or at the desired angle to create a bevel.

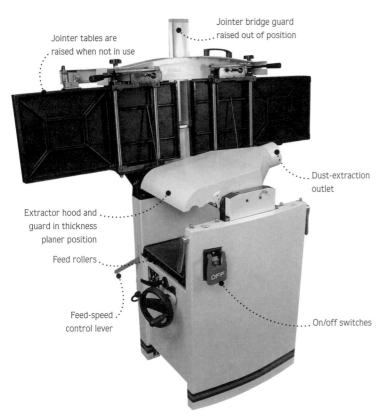

Jointer bridge guard
raised out of position

Jointer tables are
raised when not in use

Extractor hood and
guard in thickness
planer position

Feed rollers

Feed-speed
control lever

Dust-extraction
outlet

On/off switches

Jointer-thickness planer in thickness planer position
For thicknessing, the jointer tables are raised and the extraction hood, which also acts as a guard, is flipped over the cutter block. Most machines have a microswitch that breaks the electric circuit if the cutters are exposed—the machine will only operate if the guard is in position.

BENCHTOP THICKNESS PLANERS

A small version of the industrial machines found in large workshops, the benchtop thickness planer is an ideal machine for use in the home workshop because it can be easily mounted on a bench or sawhorses. However, keep in mind that the benchtop thickness planer is only designed for cutting workpieces to the required thickness. If you need to joint your workpieces first, you will have to consider purchasing a dedicated jointer machine.

USING A THICKNESS PLANER

Set the height of the thicknessing table to the desired thickness. Check that the feed rollers are in gear. (Most machines have a lever that engages the drive mechanism.) Feed the piece in smoothly from the left-hand side of the machine, pressing its flat face down onto the table. Once the feed rollers grip the workpiece, let it go and allow the rollers to take it through.

Thicknessing a face
As for jointing, do not use stock that is smaller than 17^{11}/$_{16}$ in (450 mm) in length. After feeding in the stock, move to the other side of the machine to support the workpiece as it emerges, keeping it level.

Thicknessing an edge
Feed the stock smoothly, with the flat edge on the bed of the table. Always stand to the side of the machine while working in case the stock bounces back or chips of wood fly out.

CHISELS

Chisels are probably the most important cutting tools used by woodworkers. Comprised of a steel blade with one end sharpened and the other mounted in a handle, they can cut with, across, or along the grain, removing large amounts of wood or the thinnest of shavings. Chisel blades are sharpened on one side only. The slope that forms on the sharpened edge is normally at an angle of 30 degrees to the flat surface. The variety of chisels available is very large due to their many different uses.

Bevel-edged chisels
The most common of all chisels, bevel-edged chisels get their name from the bevels running down on both sides of the blade. The blades of these chisels taper toward the cutting edge, and the sides have a small surface area. This allows them to reach easily into corners and joints, unlike chisels with rectangular blades.

Mortise chisels
As their name suggests, the main function of mortise chisels is to chop mortises. They have large-section blades and very robust handles, which means they can be struck with a mallet repeatedly without any risk of damage.

Japanese chisels
The blades of Japanese chisels are sometimes made from the same type of steel used to make samurai swords, which allows them to be sharpened to a very fine edge. The backs of these chisels are also ground hollow, which reduces the friction when paring and also speeds up the process.

Paring chisels
Although they look like bevel-edged chisels, paring chisels have longer, thinner blades. They are used, flat side down, for taking off small amounts of timber. These chisels are especially useful for smoothing out roughly chopped joints, for example, when you need to clean out the sides of a mortise joint.

Skewed chisels
A variation of the bevel-edged chisel, skewed chisels have a cutting edge that is at an angle to the blade. They are used to clean out joints where the point of the cutting edge will easily trim into tight corners. Left- and right-handed versions of skewed chisels are available for ease of use.

SHARPENING A CHISEL
Using a sharp chisel means that you will not have to exert as much force as you would with a blunt chisel. A sharp chisel will also improve the quality of your work. There are many ways to sharpen chisels, but using a water-cooled grindstone with specially made jigs is a popular method. This technique ensures that only a small amount of metal is removed to form the final bevel. It also allows you to fix common settings, which is helpful in saving time, especially when several chisels have to be sharpened together. You will need a jig to hold the chisel in place, a measuring device to set the angle of the cutting edge, and a grindstone for sharpening. For honing, you will need a honing guide and whetstones ranging between 1,000–8,000 grit.

MEASURING AND MARKING TOOLS

Measuring and marking tools are essential for producing accurate work. They can be divided into three main groups: measuring tools, tools for marking the wood (such as a bradawl), and directional or guiding tools (such as a combination square).

◗ BASIC MEASURING TOOLS

Having access to a good selection of measuring tools is important for producing accurate work.

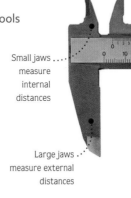

Rulers
Choose steel rulers with a matte surface—unlike rulers with polished surfaces, they do not reflect light and can be read accurately. Rulers reach up to 39⅜in (1,000mm) in length.

Dividers
Dividers are spring-loaded and can be adjusted by means of a knurled knob running on a threaded rod—keep the points sharpened and cover them when not in use.

Small jaws measure internal distances

Large jaws measure external distances

Vernier caliper
These have two jaws—one for measuring external distances (such as the width of wood) and one for internal distances (such as a mortise)—and a scale for taking readings.

Retractable tape measure
The most common tape measures are 9¾ft (3m) or 16½ft (5m). Use the end hook only for rough measurements because it is often inaccurate. To get an exact measurement, measure from the 1in, 1ft, or 100mm mark and deduct this from the reading.

◗ BASIC MARKING TOOLS

Pencils are indispensable for marking guiding lines on workpieces. For more accurate work, use V-point marking knives or Japanese marking knives. Bradawls can be used to mark points for screw fittings.

Bradawl
A pointed bradawl is useful for marking positions and making holes for screws. Bradawls also come with a chisel-like tip to cut across the grain.

Pointed tip easily cuts through wood

Long chisel-like edge

Japanese marking knife
The blade of a Japanese marking knife is extremely hard and sharp, which means that it marks wood precisely and is ideal for fine woodworking.

V-point marking knives
The two chisel-like blades of V-point marking knives differentiate them from Japanese marking knives (see left), which only have one.

Pencil
Choose a pencil with a hard lead, such as a 2H pencil. These are tough and work well on wood, leaving a dark, precise line to follow.

SQUARES AND DIRECTIONAL TOOLS

Metal blades or "scales," fitted in wood or steel-based stocks, are called squares and are used for measuring and marking right angles, as well as checking for squareness.

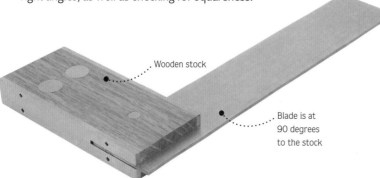

Wooden stock

Blade is at 90 degrees to the stock

DOVETAIL MARKERS

Simple yet useful, dovetail markers are tools that are set at the angles required to mark out dovetail joints. They are available in different measurements and can be used with both softwood and hardwood.

SLIDING BEVELS

The adjustable blades of sliding bevels, held in a timber stock, are used for measuring and marking angles. Locking mechanisms maintain their position, so it is easy to transfer consistent angles onto a number of pieces of wood.

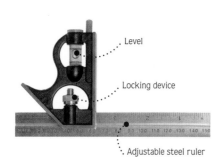

Level

Locking device

Adjustable steel ruler

Combination squares

They are so called because the stock has a 90-degree face, as well as one at 45 degrees, which is useful when marking and checking the two halves of miter joints (see pp.85–90), for example. A precise instrument capable of accurate work, combination squares have an adjustable ruler that slides through the stock and is held in place by a spring-loaded locking device.

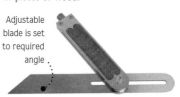

Adjustable blade is set to required angle

MARKING GAUGES

These adjustable tools are used to transfer precise measurements onto wood and are useful for tasks such as marking out hinge rebates and joint housings. Always retract the pin into the stock when not in use.

Wooden marking gauge

The gauge has a recess for the pin, which is not only safe, but also allows the pin to sit very close to the stock. A variation of this type of gauge is a mortise gauge, which has two pins—one fixed, one adjustable—so they can scribe the two edges of a mortise simultaneously.

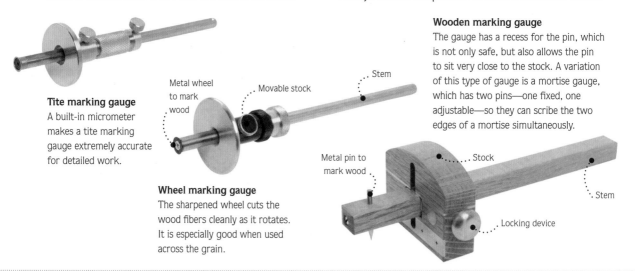

Tite marking gauge

A built-in micrometer makes a tite marking gauge extremely accurate for detailed work.

Metal wheel to mark wood

Movable stock

Stem

Metal pin to mark wood

Stock

Stem

Locking device

Wheel marking gauge

The sharpened wheel cuts the wood fibers cleanly as it rotates. It is especially good when used across the grain.

CLAMPS

Clamps are tools that hold pieces of wood in place. A woodworker will need a large number and variety of clamps, in different sizes, to complete projects successfully. Clamps are used to hold pieces in position while work is being carried out and to clasp joints while the adhesive dries.

C-clamps
Available in many sizes, C-clamps are probably the strongest clamps available. They are considered essential by many woodworkers, with a threaded bar that can be adjusted to the required jaw size. However, using too much force on the tommy bar can damage the clamp.

Tommy bar

Hand clamps
A selection of small hand- or spring-operated clamps are available for clamping small joints and for holding items during construction and assembly.

Bar

Jaws

Spring-controlled hinge

Protective cover

Rod

Adjustable jaw

Ratchet

Ratchet lever

Operating trigger

Strap

Bar

Screw handle

RATCHET STRAP CLAMP

Rod-release lever

Band and ratchet strap clamps
Useful for holding frames and coopered work, such as barrels or casks, band clamps are tensioned around the workpiece and exert their load inward. Ratchet strap clamps are similar to band clamps but are intended for heavier mechanism and can exert a greater load.

Speed clamps
Capable of being operated with one hand, speed clamps are useful to quickly hold two items together. They cannot exert a large clamping load, so they should only be used for small gluing operations.

F-clamps
Much quicker to adjust to the required size than C-clamps, F-clamps also have a greater reach into the workpiece. However, they cannot exert as much load as a C-clamp.

Sash clamps
Sash clamps have a tommy bar to tighten the screw-operated jaw; the adjustable jaw is secured with a pin that can be inserted into holes on the bar.

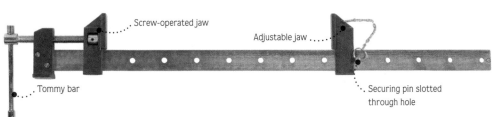

Screw-operated jaw

Adjustable jaw

Tommy bar

Securing pin slotted through hole

STRIKING TOOLS

Striking tools, such as hammers and mallets, are used when fitting pieces of wood together. Steel-headed hammers are used for striking nails and pins, wooden mallets are used for tapping chisels, and soft-headed rubber mallets are used for assembling jointed components. The handles of these tools are generally made of an impact-resistant timber, such as hickory. Striking tools are available in a variety of styles, weights, and materials depending upon their intended use. Woodworkers most often use cross pein and Japanese hammers.

Domed face

Flat face

Japanese hammers
All Japanese hammers are generally of the same design: one flat face for striking nails and another slightly domed face for the final blow to ensure that the nail finishes slightly below the timber surface.

Cross pein

Cross pein hammers
These are small, light hammers with a wedge-shaped extension on one side, called a "cross pein." This is useful for starting pins in wood before driving them in fully with the flat side. Pin hammers are small cross pein hammers.

Wooden mallet
The head of a wooden mallet is often made of a soft timber, such as beech.

Rubber mallet
The soft head of a white rubber mallet does not dent or mark the wood when assembling joints.

Magazine

NAIL GUNS
For some projects, it can be a good option to swap hammer and nails for a nail gun. Used for tasks that involve the insertion of a large number of nails or pins, nail guns can be gas-, compressed air-, AC-, battery-, or hand-powered. Always take extreme care when operating a nail gun, because it can be a dangerous tool. Be very careful when working with thin materials, because there is a danger that the nail will pass straight through the workpiece. While nail guns can be used with a range of nail sizes, they will not take every size of nail. It is important that you choose the correct machine for your needs. Some nail guns, such as the one pictured, have a magazine that holds the nails in a long strip.

SHARPENING TOOLS

All woodworkers need to keep their tools sharp, and investing in a grinding wheel, for example, or a selection of sharpening stones could be a wise investment. Motorized grinders are used to grind the blades of tools, such as planes (see pp.17–23) and chisels (see p.26). To remove large amounts of metal, you will need a high-speed grinder. However, for general resharpening, a motorized whetstone is preferable.

SHARPENING STONES

Bladed tools must be kept sharp, so you will need a variety of sharpening stones made from either natural stone or synthetic materials, which are generally more affordable. Most stones should be lubricated before use: as the names suggest, oilstones are lubricated with oil, and waterstones (also called whetstones) with water.

Single 1,000-grit whetstone
Man-made oilstones and waterstones of various grits are available. A 1,000-grit stone is coarse and used for initial honing or restoring an edge.

Combination oilstone
Used by most woodworkers, oilstones come in different qualities, the best being Novaculite ("Arkansas") and cheaper versions made from silicon carbide.

Diamond whetstone
While very expensive, diamond whetstones are far more efficient to use than other stones, because they need no lubricant and stay flat. The steel plate is coated with diamond grit and the holes in the plate capture the swarf.

MOTORIZED WHETSTONE

The slower speed of this machine makes it easy to control, and the grindstone is cooled by water, which prevents overheating and helps preserve a blade's temper.

Blade-holding jig
Leather strop wheel
Grindstone
Water reservoir
Angle-setting jig

SCRAPER BURNISHER

To sharpen a cabinet scraper (see p.32), you will need to use a dedicated tool called a scraper burnisher. This sharpening tool has a cylindrical blade made of a particularly hard steel, which is not marked or damaged by the sharp edge of the cabinet scraper.

HONING GUIDES

Used for holding a blade at the correct angle while it is being sharpened, a honing guide will also help preserve a blade's beveled edge. This means that it will require less regrinding, increasing its lifespan. This guide can be seen in action on pp.20–21.

Blade clamp
Bevel angle-setter
Blade registration system squares blade in guide

CABINET SCRAPERS

Used to remove fine shavings from the surface of timber, a cabinet scraper is a thin, sharp-edged sheet of tempered steel. Standard rectangular scrapers are used for flat surfaces, while goose-neck and concave/convex models are suited to moldings and shaped work. You should keep a variety of scrapers, especially because you will want to have a replacement available if one you are using becomes blunt. (A scraper that produces dust instead of wood shavings needs to be sharpened—see Sharpening a cabinet scraper, below.)

GOOSE-NECK CABINET SCRAPER

All edges are used for scraping

Curved edges are used for scraping

Long edge is used for scraping

STANDARD CABINET SCRAPER

CONCAVE/CONVEX CABINET SCRAPER

Cabinet scrapers
Cabinet scrapers are available in a range of standard shapes, which are capable of dealing with the demands of most projects. If necessary, however, it is possible to reshape a scraper as required.

SHARPENING A CABINET SCRAPER

A cabinet scraper takes fine wood shavings off the surface of timber, and it is a burr running along the edge of the scraper that does the cutting work. This burr is created and angled by a scraper burnisher. To sharpen a cabinet scraper, you must first remove the old burr and prepare its edges. You will know when a scraper needs to be sharpened because it will form dust instead of shavings when drawn across timber. The edge of the cabinet scraper must be straight and the corners must be square before it is sharpened. This sharpening technique takes practice.

1 Hold the scraper vertically and rub it along the surface of a sharpening stone to flatten the edges of the scraper.

2 Place the scraper flat to the stone and rub it back and forth in order to remove the remains of the old burr from each side.

3 Place the scraper on the edge of the workbench and run the burnisher along the long edges of the scraper. Angle the burnisher downward slightly to raise the burr.

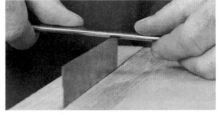

4 Place the scraper in a vise and run the burnisher along the edge in order to "turn" the burr. The burr should be angled at approximately 90 degrees to the flat sides.

ABRASIVES

Sandpaper, which is also called abrasive paper (although sand is no longer used as an abrasive), is one of the most commonly used general-purpose abrasives. Papers are available in a range of grit sizes (see below) for preparing wood to varying degrees of quality. Steel wool, another popular abrasive, is used for both applying and stripping finishes.

Sandpaper backing
The abrasive grit on sandpaper is bonded onto backing paper, which can be folded or cut to size to suit the timber being finished. The type of bonding agent and the weight of paper used vary according to the intended use.

Aluminum oxide paper
This type of abrasive paper is available in sheet form for sanding by hand, as well as in disk or belt form for use with sanders (see p.44). Grit sizes range from a very coarse 40, to 240, which is suitable for creating a final finish.

Abranet
As the name implies, this sandpaper consists of a fine abrasive net or mesh. The mesh allows for easy dust extraction, which makes Abranet particularly resistant to clogging. It is available in various grit sizes.

Available in a range of grit sizes

Webrax
A commercial web-like material, Webrax is highly flexible, which makes it ideal for use on contoured timber. It does not easily clog up with dust and is also available in a nonabrasive form for applying finishes.

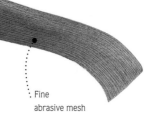

Fine abrasive mesh

GRIT SIZES
The coarseness of sandpaper is determined by the size of the abrasive particles bonded to the paper. A paper's coarseness is measured in grit sizes:

GRIT SIZE	TYPICAL USES
100–120 (Coarse)	• Initial sanding of timber that will be finished with oil or wax. • Final sanding of timber that will be finished with paint.
150–180 (Medium)	• Improving the surface of timber that will be finished with oil or wax. • Final sanding of timber that will be finished with varnish.
240–320 (Fine)	• Final sanding of timber that will be finished with oil or wax.
360+ (Very fine)	• Final sanding of timber that will be finished with the very finest finishes, such as French polish.

SANDING BLOCK
Sandpaper should be used in conjunction with a sanding block. Ready-made sanding blocks are available to purchase, but you can easily make one in the workshop. Cork is the preferred material, because it is more comfortable to work with than hardwood and offers the right amount of resilience during use. Cork is available in tile form, which can be glued to a backing board (this increases the overall depth of the block) and cut to size.

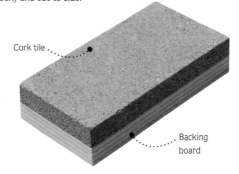

Cork tile

Backing board

DRILLS AND DRIVERS

A drill is an essential tool for creating holes in wood to accommodate screws (see p.36) and other fittings. Various drill bits are available, the most useful being lip-and-spur bits and forstner bits. Equally, the job of driving in screws once a hole has been drilled has also been made easy with the introduction of powered drivers, although a selection of hand-held screwdrivers (see p.36) is still a must in every toolbox. There are two main types of drills: hand-operated drills and power drills. Power drills come in two forms: those that are connected to a power-supply cable and cordless, battery-operated models. Drills adapted to hold a screwdriving bit are called drivers.

POWER DRILLS

- Speed selector
- Keyless chuck
- Torque control setting
- Trigger
- Pistol grip
- Rechargeable battery

CORDLESS DRILL-DRIVER

Modern power drills typically have variable-speed controls and chucks that can take shank sizes of up to $\frac{3}{8}$ in (10 mm) or more. With the improved efficiency of modern batteries, cordless drills are increasing in popularity. Tools that perform the dual task of drilling and driving are known as drill-drivers. These can also be found in power-supply cable and cordless varieties. Cordless drill-drivers with batteries ranging between 9.6-volt and 18-volt are adequate for general-purpose use.

HAND DRILLS

Single- or double-pinion hand drills are useful for simple drilling operations. Being hand-operated, they can be used for delicate drilling tasks—for example, where the drilled hole must not exceed a certain depth. Hand drills can also be used in areas that are inaccessible to a power drill.

DRILL PRESSES

A drill press is a heavy-duty machine that is used for drilling very precise holes. While there are many different ways to drill holes in timber, it is sometimes necessary to produce work that is particularly accurate. This is especially important when drilling deep holes, large-diameter holes, or those that must be drilled at a specific angle. To produce such precise work, a drill press is the most appropriate machine to use.

- Start/stop toggle switch
- Chuck guard
- Chuck
- Depth gauge and stop wheel
- Pillar or cylindrical post
- Adjustable drill table

BENCH-MOUNTED DRILL

- Driving wheel rotates drill

DRILL BITS

Three of the most useful drill bits are high-speed steel (HSS) bits, lip-and-spur bits, and forstner bits. HSS bits are for use with a variety of materials, from steel to timber. Lip-and-spur bits are for accurate drilling in timber. Forstner bits are used for drilling large-diameter, clean-sided, flat-bottomed holes. Other bits include the combination counterbore bit, which is used to cut all of the holes needed for counterboring in one operation.

Special coating aids durability

HIGH-SPEED STEEL BIT

Spur

LIP-AND-SPUR BIT

Bit enlarges hole's opening so screw can sit flush with the wood

COUNTERSINK BIT

Bit cuts the wood plug used to fill a counterbore hole

PLUG CUTTER BIT

Sharp edges prevent chipping

FORSTNER BIT

COMBINATION COUNTERBORE BIT

COUNTERSINKING

The best way to achieve a neat finish on your workpiece is to ensure that the screw's head is flush with the surface. This is achieved by using a special drill bit called a countersink bit. It drills out a conical space from the top of the clearance hole. The screw's head then fits into this space.

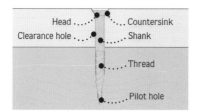

Head — Countersink
Clearance hole — Shank
— Thread
— Pilot hole

1 Mark the position where the screw needs to be inserted. Drill a pilot hole if necessary. Using a drill bit that matches the shank size of the screw, drill a clearance hole.

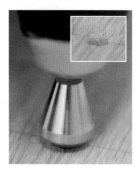

2 Change to a countersink bit and drill to the depth required. Be sure to place the drill directly over the clearance hole. The countersink bit will drill a conical space over the hole. Insert the screw into the clearance hole using a driver. The head of the screw should sit in line with, or slightly below, the surface of the workpiece (inset).

COUNTERBORING

Counterboring is a technique that recesses the head of a screw. Use a drill bit with a diameter that is larger than the head of the screw being inserted to drill a hole on the same line as the pilot and clearance holes. This counterbore allows a shorter screw to be used and the hole can be plugged with wood to completely hide the screw head if needed.

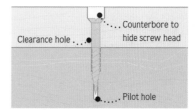

Clearance hole — Counterbore to hide screw head
— Pilot hole

1 Fit a drill bit that is larger than the screw head. Set the required depth using masking tape (inset). Drill the counterbore into the top piece of timber to the depth indicated by the masking tape (pictured). Drill a straight hole, keeping the drill in an upright position.

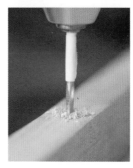

2 Use masking tape to mark the required depth for the pilot hole (use a small diameter bit) and the clearance hole (use a bit big enough to prevent the screw from gripping the wood). Using the masking tape as a guide, drill the pilot hole into both pieces of timber. Finally, drill the clearance hole through the top piece of wood only.

FASTENERS

Metal fastenings are a quick and simple means of holding pieces of timber together when joints or connectors are not appropriate. Available in a wide variety of shapes and sizes, they vary in terms of purpose and quality. Some are purely functional, while others have an esthetic quality that makes them attractive enough to be visible on the finished work.

SCREWS

Screws are an excellent choice when a mechanical fastening is needed to join timber. Screws come in various lengths and diameters and have heads in different designs to suit the project. When using traditional woodscrews, it is advisable to drill both a pilot and a clearance hole so that they are easier to drive in. This also prevents the timber from splitting. The choice of head depends on the desired look and the pieces being joined together.

Brass slot-headed screws
Used predominantly when appearance is an important factor, these metal screws are relatively soft. They are therefore easily damaged if used with a screwdriver of the wrong type or size. Brass screws are also liable to break if the pilot hole is too small.

Brass round-headed screws
Brass round-headed screws are typically used to fasten metal objects, such as name plates and escutcheons, onto a timber surface.

Steel slot-headed screws
These traditional screws can be difficult to use with a power driver but, used with both a clearance and pilot hole, will fit very tightly.

Chipboard screws
The thread extends over most of the shaft (useful for gripping the rough fibers of chipboard) and the heads are shaped for countersinking (see p.35).

Pozidriv screws
Used with power drivers, these screws are cross-headed with extra divisions between the cross's slots. This makes the driver less likely to slip.

SCREWDRIVERS
Woodworkers typically use two types of screwdrivers: slot-headed drivers and cross-headed drivers, such as Phillips and Pozidriv. Cross-headed drivers fit into the screw head more securely and, therefore, are now used for most jobs. A stubby screwdriver is useful for driving screws when space is tight, and an electric screwdriver makes it easier to drive screws in awkward places. Always use a screwdriver that matches the size and shape of the screw; this will help prevent damage to the screw and driver.

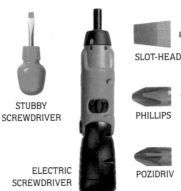

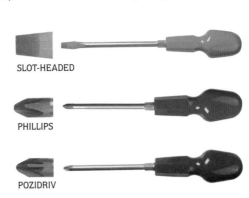

STUBBY
SCREWDRIVER

ELECTRIC
SCREWDRIVER

SLOT-HEADED

PHILLIPS

POZIDRIV

NAILS AND PINS

Used for basic fastenings in which the extra strength of a screw is unnecessary, nails are an easy way of holding pieces of timber together. Most, however, will become loose if there is any movement in the pieces being joined. Pins are thinner with smaller heads.

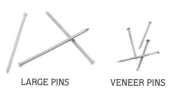

LARGE PINS   **VENEER PINS**

Pins
Popular when making temporary fittings, pins cause minimal damage to timber. The thinnest types are used to hold veneers.

KNOCK-DOWN FITTINGS

These are used when a joint may need to be taken apart some time after its assembly, such as in the case of "flat pack" furniture or large woodworking projects such as a bed. However, they are also useful when working on difficult materials, such as chipboard.

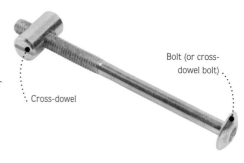

Bolt (or cross-dowel bolt)

Cross-dowel

CROSS-DOWEL AND BOLT

HINGES

Used to attach two components together that still need to move relative to each other, hinges are available in a wide range of styles and sizes. Always use the correct hinge for the job, such as a table hinge for a drop-leaf table, and check for quality—for example, each one of a pair should be exactly alike and move smoothly on the pivot.

Brass butt hinge
A common fastening, brass butt hinges are an attractive and traditional option. The screws should fit flush with the surface of the hinge leaf.

Scissor hinge
These hinges (so called because of the design) fit onto the top and bottom edges of a door. They are less noticeable than brass butt hinges.

Table hinge
The leaves of table hinges are of different lengths, which allows the fastening screws sufficient depth of timber on drop-leaf tables.

Soss hinge
Hidden completely from view when the door is closed, soss hinges are designed to be fitted with the use of a router (see pp.38–43).

Soss barrel hinge
Similar in operation to standard soss hinges, soss barrel hinges are held in place with a tensioning mechanism rather than screws.

Concealed hinge
Available in different styles, concealed hinges are invisible from the outside and allow for a range of opening angles and thicknesses of material.

ROUTERS

A router is a power tool that routs (mills) channels, holes, and profiles in timber. The versatility and relative affordability of a router allows the woodworker to produce complex joints and carry out advanced techniques quickly and easily. The tool consists of a basic electric motor (with a speed of 20,000–25,000 rpm) connected to a tapered collet (chuck or metal collar), which holds a cutter. Router tables (see below), in which the router is mounted beneath a benchtop, are also available.

HAND-HELD ROUTERS

There are two main types of hand-held router: the fixed-base router, which is popular in the US; and the plunge router, which is more widely used in Europe. On a fixed-base router, a screw mechanism fixes the cutter depth before use; on a plunge router, the cutter is lowered into position during use. Routers are available in a range of sizes (specified by the diameter of the collet), with the most common being ¼ in (6 mm) and ½ in (12 mm). An array of cutters is also available; it is this diversity of cutter types and sizes that makes a router so versatile.

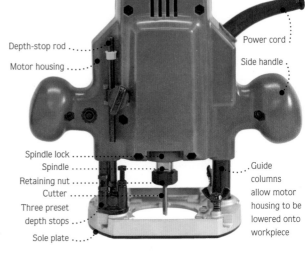

Depth-stop rod
Motor housing
Power cord
Side handle
Spindle lock
Spindle
Retaining nut
Cutter
Three preset depth stops
Sole plate
Guide columns allow motor housing to be lowered onto workpiece

¼ in (6 mm) plunge router
Ideal for general-purpose use, this router has enough power (typically 1,000–1,400 watts) and weight to tackle most jobs without being too heavy or cumbersome. A dust extractor (not shown) is usually fitted as standard.

Fixed-base router
The position of the cutter is set prior to use and remains fixed until all cutting at the set depth is complete. This ensures consistency of depth across the whole cut.

Power cord
Side handle
Toggle on/off switch
Motor housing
Sole plate

ROUTER TABLE

Proprietary router tables consist of a table side fence and sliding fence with provision for mounting a router upside down beneath the table with the cutter protruding through the surface. The workpiece is fed into the cutter (instead of the router being moved across the workpiece). Using a router table makes it easier to control the cut because both hands are free to feed in a workpiece and the cutter is clearly visible.

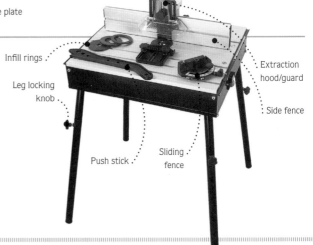

Infill rings
Leg locking knob
Push stick
Sliding fence
Extraction hood/guard
Side fence

ROUTER CUTTERS

Most cutters have hard tungsten carbide cutting edges. Cutters are available in a range of shapes and sizes. The following cutters will enable you to carry out the majority of routing tasks.

GROOVE CUTTERS

V-groove/Chamfer cutter
Cuts V-shaped grooves; if a fence is attached to the router, cuts chamfers (bevels) on the edges of a workpiece.

Dovetail groove cutter
Cuts dovetail housings (see pp.82–83); note that the cutter will remove the sides of the dovetail as it is plunged in and out.

Straight groove cutter
Used to cut straight, square-section grooves and housings; can be used to cut out mortises (see pp.91–92).

EDGE CUTTERS

Roundover cutter
Used together with bearings of different sizes to cut ovolo and roundover (types of convex) moldings.

Cove cutter
Used for cutting concave moldings; the bearing acts as a guide along the edge of the wood.

Flush-cut cutter
Used with a bearing to trim laminates flush with the edge of a board; also used to cut templates.

CLEANING AND SHARPENING A CUTTER

Resin will accumulate on the router cutter, particularly if you are working with softwood. To prolong a cutter's life, you will need to clean it periodically. While denatured alcohol will do the job, there are more effective and environmentally friendly cleaning agents available.

1 After brushing off any loose dust, apply the cleaning agent. If several cutters need to be cleaned, it may be easier to stand them in a small pot of the cleaning agent.

2 Leave the cleaning agent to work for a few minutes until the resin is soft enough to remove. An old toothbrush is ideal for removing the softened resin.

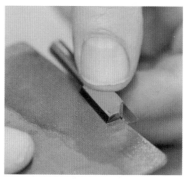

3 Sharpen the inside edge of the cutting blades using a diamond "credit card" sharpening stone. Do not work on the outside edges or you may alter the dimension of the cut.

🪚 INSERTING A COLLET AND CUTTER

A router is sometimes supplied with more than one collet but, if the model type permits, you may be able to insert a number of different collets to further increase the tool's versatility. You will need to remove a collet occasionally to clean it—and to clean the housing into which the collet fits. (Always clean the housing when changing a collet.) Be aware that a collet can be damaged if it is not holding a cutter when the retaining nut is tightened. When fitting a cutter, however, ensure that the retaining nut is firmly tightened—this removes the risk of the cutter working itself loose during use.

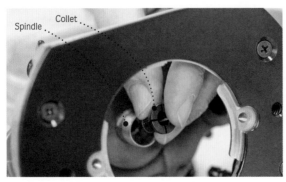

1 Ensure that the openings in both the spindle and collet are clean and free of obstructions. Insert the collet into the opening until it locks into position. (Do not force it.)

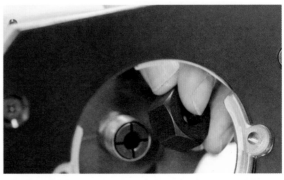

2 Fit the retaining nut onto the spindle and twist it several times to ensure that the thread is fully engaged. Do not tighten the nut onto the collet itself.

3 Slot the cutter into the collet so that three-quarters of the cutter's shank is inserted. Do not allow the shank to touch the far end of the spindle.

4 Lock the spindle (using its button- or lever-operated locking mechanism) to prevent it from freely rotating. Using a wrench, fully tighten the retaining nut.

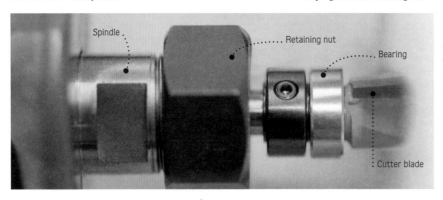

5 Closely inspect the cutter to ensure that it does not sit too close to the collet or retaining nut, either of which may restrict its movement.

⚙ ADJUSTING THE DEPTH OF THE CUT

All plunge routers have a system for controlling the depth of cut. Typically this consists of an adjustable depth-stop rod attached to the motor housing. This rod is aligned with one of the depth stops mounted on a revolving turret on the sole plate of the router. By setting the gap between the end of the rod and the stop on the turret, the downward travel of the motor housing is halted at a predetermined point.

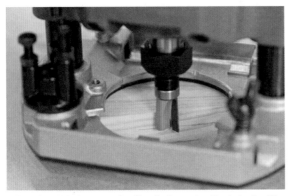

1 Ensuring that the power is off, grip the router firmly by its side handles. Plunge down the router until the cutter touches the surface of the workpiece.

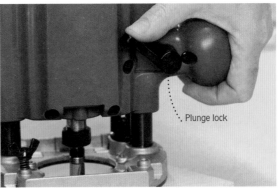

Plunge lock

2 Lock the motor housing into this position by depressing the plunge lock—usually located on the back of one of the handles.

Depth stops

Depth-stop rod

3 Set the depth-stop rod so that the gap between the rod and the stop matches the required depth of cut; make fine adjustments by screwing the stop either slightly up or down.

Screwdriver

4 If required, adjust the height of the remaining stops using a screwdriver; this will allow you to make different depths of cut without having to reset the depth-stop rod.

5 Make trial cuts for each depth of cut setting in off-cuts of wood. Measure the results and make any further adjustments to the router as necessary.

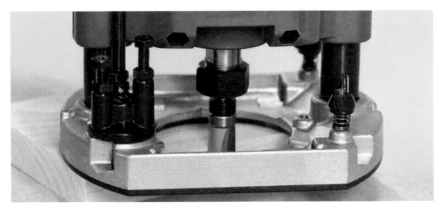

CUTTING A STRAIGHT LINE

To accurately cut a straight line, you will need to either fit a side fence or, as shown, use a straight piece of timber as a guide. This is useful in situations in which you need to cut a groove or housing so far in from the edge of a workpiece that a fence will not reach. Position the timber guide so that it is on the left-hand side of the router cutter's clockwise rotation—this helps prevent the router from moving off the line. Place the flat part of the router's sole plate against the timber guide.

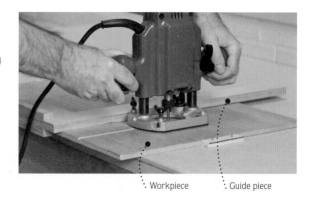

.·. Workpiece   .·. Guide piece

SETTING THE FENCE

The side fence is a guide that determines how far in from the edge of a workpiece the cutter will sit. It also guides the router in a straight line along a workpiece. If the router's cutter rotates in a clockwise direction, the side fence should be attached to the left-hand side of the router. This will ensure that the fence is pulled in flush to the edge of the workpiece as the router is moved along the timber, keeping the router on its line and preventing it from running away from you.

1 Fix a short length of smooth timber to the fence. This timber will butt up against the workpiece and, being smooth, will glide easily along its surface.

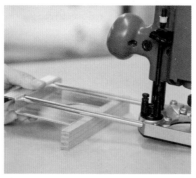

2 Slide the fence into the holes in the router's sole plate. Remember to attach it to the correct side of the router to allow for the direction in which the cutter rotates.

3 Place the router on the workpiece with the cutter in the correct position to make the cut. Slide the fence up to the edge of the workpiece and lock it into position.

CUTTING A GROOVE

The best way to cut a straight groove is to use a side fence. Mark out the position of the groove and place the router on the workpiece, aligning the cutter with the groove markings. Slide the fence up to the edge of the workpiece and lock it in place. Use an off-cut of timber to cut a trial groove to check that the fence is set correctly; adjust if necessary. Never start or stop the router when the cutter is in contact with the workpiece.

1 Position the router and fence on the workpiece. When steadied, switch on the power. Plunge the cutter to the required depth and make the first cut, moving the router along the workpiece.

2 Release the plunge lock after making each cut. Allow the router to fully rise and the cutter to clear the workpiece before switching off the power. Repeat the process until the groove is finished.

CUTTING A PROFILE

When cutting a profile on the edge of a workpiece, make sure you have a support timber at both the front and back of the workpiece to act as a "lead on" and "take off" support. This will help you achieve a cleaner finish to the cut. Use a bearing-guided cutter to cut a profile—while it is possible to use an ordinary cutter and a side fence for straight lines, a bearing guarantees perfect alignment and can also be used on curved outlines.

CUTTING A PROFILE WITH A
BEARING-GUIDED CUTTER

Support timber

Bearing

Profile

CROSS-SECTION OF WORKPIECE

CUTTING TO A TEMPLATE

By cutting a template of the finished shape and positioning it either on top of or underneath (pictured) an oversized workpiece, you can use a bearing-guided cutter to trim either straight or curved edges. You will need to create a template of the required shape from a board material such as MDF. (As the bearing needs a smooth edge along which to run, MDF is particularly appropriate.) The cutter length depends on the thickness of the edge you are cleaning up. You should not trim more than ⅛in (3mm) of material off the edge of the workpiece.

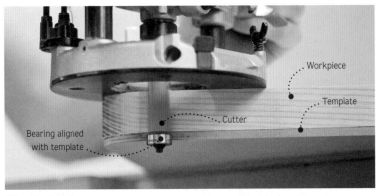

Workpiece

Template

Cutter

Bearing aligned with template

Align the bearing

Ensure that the bearing is positioned to run on the template and that the cutter covers the full thickness of the workpiece. It is especially important to accurately position the bearing if the template is very thin. Cutters are also available with the bearing mounted at the top.

FITTING A DUST-EXTRACTION SYSTEM

All routers are fitted with a dust-extraction system. Although these systems differ from model to model, most routers have a transparent plastic hood that fits over the sole plate and encloses the cutter. This hood contains the dust and waste produced while routing; it is attached to the hose of a vacuum extractor, which extracts and collects the waste. Many vacuum extractors are automatically activated when the router is switched on, and turn off approximately 10 seconds after the router is switched off.

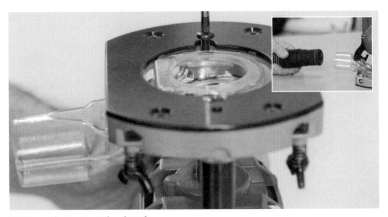

Fitting a dust-extraction hood

Screw the base of the dust-extraction hood into position on the sole plate (pictured). Some models allow for the hood to be clipped into place. It is important to ensure that there is a tight seal between the hood and the vacuum extractor hose (inset).

SANDERS

Power sanders make the often laborious task of sanding quick and easy. In addition to hand-held power sanders, there are a number of bench-mounted sanding machines available that are suited to the home workshop.

Random orbital sander

A random orbital sander is used for sanding large areas of wood. The sandpaper is held in place with a Velcro system. A soft pad can also be attached to turn the sander into a polishing tool.

On/off switch

Power cord

Dust bag

Vent carries dust from wood surface to bag

Orbiting disk

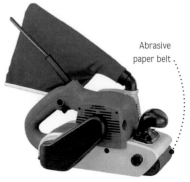

Abrasive paper belt

Belt sanders

A belt sander is comprised of two rollers, around which runs a loop, or belt, of sandpaper. They are used to smooth large wooden surfaces, such as floors, decks, and porches. Belt sanders remove waste very aggressively, so you should always take great care when using this tool. You can choose between hand-held and bench-mounted models, in a range of sizes.

On/off switch

Power cord

Dust bag

Palm sander

A palm sander is a smaller version of the random orbital sander. It is used on small wood surfaces and finishing work. The sandpaper is held in place with a lever clamp and is easy to change.

Sanding pad

Lever clamp

Spindle sanders

Using a spindle sander is the best way to sand curved edges and other shaped woodwork. These machines are ideal for smoothing complex surfaces, such as the inside edges of concave curves. Spindle sanders use replaceable spindles, or bobbins, for the sanding operation. Spindles are available in a range of sizes depending on the job.

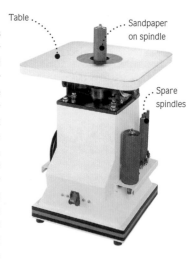

Table

Sandpaper on spindle

Spare spindles

MORTISERS

A mortiser is a machine used to cut out mortises (see pp.91–95). While you can adapt alternative tools to do the same job—such as a drill press (see p.34) or router (see pp.38–43)—a mortiser is better suited because it produces clean, square-cornered mortises. Mortisers are available in either bench- or floor-mounted models. A floor-mounted mortiser is used to chop large mortises in large pieces of timber. A bench-mounted mortiser is used for relatively small jobs, such as mortises measuring approximately ⅝ in (16 mm) in size.

On/off switches

Movable head

Mortiser bit

Chuck

Fence

Clamp

Bench-mounted mortiser
Ideal for the home workshop, the bench-mounted mortiser is used for more precise work than floor-mounted models.

MORTISER BITS
There is a wide range of mortiser bits available, with each one consisting of a square outer chisel, which cuts the wood, and an inner auger, which removes the waste.

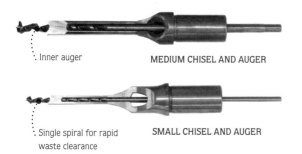

Inner auger

MEDIUM CHISEL AND AUGER

Single spiral for rapid waste clearance

SMALL CHISEL AND AUGER

USING A MORTISER
A mortiser removes waste from the workpiece much faster than is possible by hand. However, you should avoid plunging the machine too quickly because this can lead to the chisel overheating and becoming damaged. Adjust the height of the chisel to give clearance for large timbers and to place the handle at a convenient height—you can even sit down for some types of work. To ensure your own safety, check that the chisel is secure and remember to wear protective goggles.

1 To make the first cut, align the chisel with the markings on the surface of the workpiece, which indicate the intended position of the mortise. Lower the chisel into the timber, but do not cut too deeply.

2 After making the first cut, take the chisel out of the mortise and move the timber sideways to make a new cut. Space the cuts so that the last one is made using the full width of the chisel (inset).

COMMERCIAL JOINING SYSTEMS

Dowel, pocket-hole, biscuit, and domino joining systems are effective and discreet methods of connecting timbers. They are used when it is not possible or desirable to use conventional woodworking joints, or when basic connectors, such as nails and screws (see pp.36–37), are not up to the job. Jigs and joiners are available for aligning and cutting the holes and slots into which the relevant connectors are fitted.

DOWEL-BASED SYSTEMS

In a dowel-based system, the dowel acts as a loose tenon; dowel systems have many of the same attributes of the conventional mortise-and-tenon joint. The design of the dowel affects the performance of the joint, so it is important to choose the correct type. Dowels can be used individually or in multiples, and it is important to correctly align each side of the joint for an effective and attractive connection. Use a center point to align the holes for a single-dowel joint or a dowel jig to align the holes for a multiple-dowel joint.

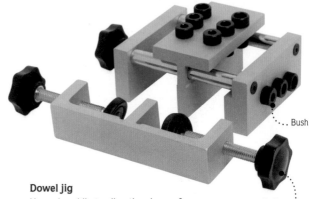

Bush

Dowel jig
Use a dowel jig to align the pieces of timber to be connected. Use a power drill (see p.34) to drill through each bush to create a series of holes for the dowels.

E-clamp keeps timbers correctly spaced

POCKET-HOLE SYSTEMS

A pocket-hole system is used when it is necessary to hide a screw head or when it is not possible to drill from the outside of a joint. A Kreg jig is used to make the acute-angled, pocketed (counterbored, see p.35) holes necessary for this type of joint. The jig simplifies this process and ensures accuracy. The stepped drill bit allows both the pocket and the pilot hole to be drilled in one operation.

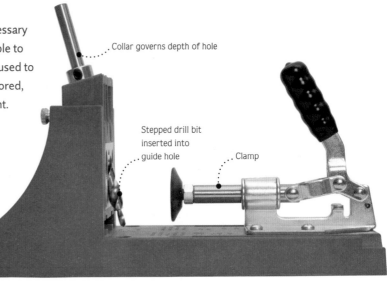

Collar governs depth of hole

Stepped drill bit inserted into guide hole

Clamp

Kreg pocket hole jig
The Kreg drill allows a series of pocketed screws to be drilled into a workpiece at the required angle. A clamp holds the workpiece in position.

BISCUIT-BASED SYSTEMS

A biscuit is a thin, oval-shaped piece of compressed wood that acts in the same way as a loose tenon in a conventional mortise-and-tenon joint. A biscuit joiner is used to cut the circular slot into which the biscuit is fitted. The joiner's depth stop ensures that the slots are of the correct depth for the size of biscuit being used. The fence can be adjusted for different thicknesses of timber and to match the angle of the joint face.

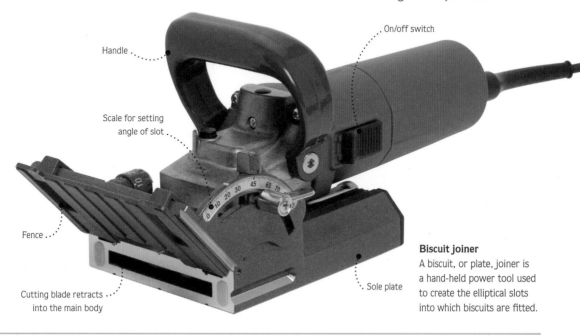

Handle

On/off switch

Scale for setting
angle of slot

Fence

Cutting blade retracts
into the main body

Sole plate

Biscuit joiner
A biscuit, or plate, joiner is a hand-held power tool used to create the elliptical slots into which biscuits are fitted.

DOMINO-BASED SYSTEMS

Domino joints are similar to small mortise-and-tenon joints (see pp.91–95). The slot, or mortise, is formed by a cutter that both rotates and oscillates laterally. The cutter can be set to the required depth and width, while the fence can be set square or angled. Attachments help with awkward shapes or for making a series of cuts.

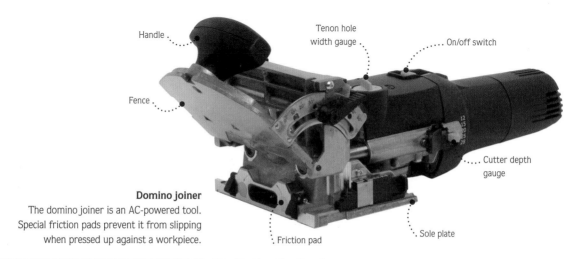

Handle

Tenon hole
width gauge

On/off switch

Fence

Cutter depth
gauge

Domino joiner
The domino joiner is an AC-powered tool. Special friction pads prevent it from slipping when pressed up against a workpiece.

Friction pad

Sole plate

LATHES AND CUTTING TOOLS

Known as "turning," the most effective method of shaping round or cylindrical objects—such as knobs or table legs—is to use a powered machine called a lathe. The lathe spins the workpiece around a central axis of rotation at a constant speed. You can then shape or sand the workpiece symmetrically by holding a hand-held cutting tool or abrasive paper against it.

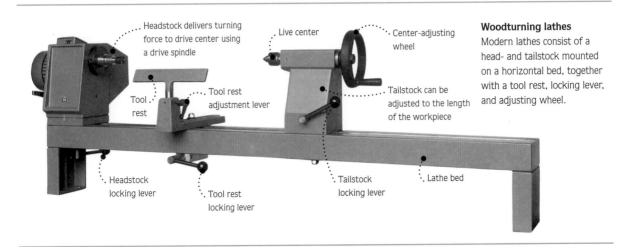

Headstock delivers turning force to drive center using a drive spindle

Live center

Center-adjusting wheel

Tool rest

Tool rest adjustment lever

Tailstock can be adjusted to the length of the workpiece

Headstock locking lever

Tool rest locking lever

Tailstock locking lever

Lathe bed

Woodturning lathes
Modern lathes consist of a head- and tailstock mounted on a horizontal bed, together with a tool rest, locking lever, and adjusting wheel.

CUTTING TOOLS

Lathe cutting tools can be divided into three main categories: gouges, parting tools, and scrapers. There are also specialized lathe tools for more advanced woodworking; for example, beading tools, specialized scrapers that have the shape of a bead formed on the blade's tip, are used to form grooves and beads.

ROUGHING GOUGE

SMALL PARTING TOOL

Flat tip

FLAT-NOSED SCRAPER

Angled tip

SKEWED CHISEL

Gouges
Roughing gouges are used for the initial stages of turning square stock into a cylinder. Spindle gouges, often used next, are thinner with a rounded tip, and are useful for forming coves.

Parting tools
Used for cutting grooves and recesses, parting tools are also capable of forming shoulders, beads, and other convex curves.

Scraper tools
The main purpose of scraper tools is to remove marks left by other tools before sanding. Their shallow cutting angle leaves a smooth finish on the workpiece.

Skewed chisels
Also used as a general cutting tool (see p.26), skewed chisels are used to form beads and to make V-cuts.

CALIPERS
To measure the diameter of a piece of work, use calipers. When turning a workpiece, use outside calipers for measuring the diameter of spindles and inside calipers for measuring the internal diameter of bowls and other hollows. Spring-loaded calipers are best because they cannot be altered easily by mistake.

OUTSIDE CALIPERS

MOUNTING A WORKPIECE ON A LATHE

The height at which a lathe should be positioned is a matter of personal comfort, but a good rule of thumb is to fit it so that the center line of the workpiece is at elbow height. When working between the drive and live centers, you can use the same basic technique to mount a workpiece, although there are several types of center to cope with different shapes and sizes of workpieces. The most basic arrangement involves a 2- or 4-prong drive center in the headstock and a standard 60-degree live revolving center in the tailstock.

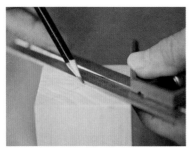

1 Find the center of one end grain by drawing diagonals between the corners. Use a center-finder for round-section material.

2 Drill a hole ³⁄₁₆in (4mm) in diameter and ³⁄₁₆in (4mm) deep into the marked point. Repeat steps 1–2 on the other end grain of the workpiece.

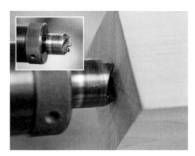

3 Insert the appropriate drive center into the headstock (inset). Fit the workpiece by placing one of the end-grain centerholes on the drive center.

4 Hold the workpiece parallel to the lathe bed and slide the tailstock up until its live center engages with the other hole (inset). Lock the tailstock (pictured).

5 Advance the tailstock center by rotating the wheel until the workpiece fits onto the drive center (pictured). Lock the tailstock center in place (inset).

USING LATHE TOOLS

When using a gouge or parting tool, always position its handle lower than the tool rest. The handle of a scraper should be angled slightly above the tool rest or roughly horizontal. Your dominant hand should hold the handle and your other hand should hold the blade against the tool rest—either above the tool (for rough-cutting) or below it (for delicate work). Maintain this steady contact to ensure good control.

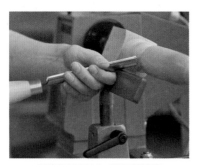

CUTTING TOOLS—UNDERHAND

CUTTING TOOLS—OVERHAND

SCRAPERS—ANGLED UP

WORKBENCHES AND WORK SUPPORTS

Most woodworkers will need a workbench—either bought or self-built—that is tailored to his or her own needs. The bench should be as sturdy as possible, which will prevent movement during use and will allow it to withstand heavy impacts, such as those caused by a mallet (see p.30). The most important item on any workbench is the front vise, which is used to hold a workpiece securely in position. Other useful features include a second vise (end vise), which is usually located at one end of the bench. Together with "bench dogs" (securing pegs), this second vise allows long workpieces to be held in place.

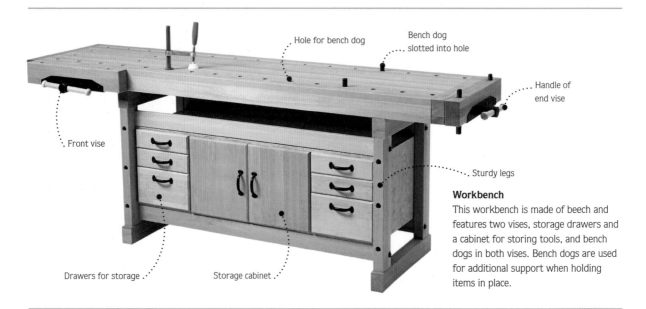

Hole for bench dog

Bench dog slotted into hole

Handle of end vise

Front vise

Sturdy legs

Workbench
This workbench is made of beech and features two vises, storage drawers and a cabinet for storing tools, and bench dogs in both vises. Bench dogs are used for additional support when holding items in place.

Drawers for storage

Storage cabinet

BENCH VISES

A vise is an important part of any workbench, making the task of firmly gripping a workpiece quick and easy. Cast-iron vises should be used with wooden "cheeks," which prevent a workpiece from slipping or becoming damaged.

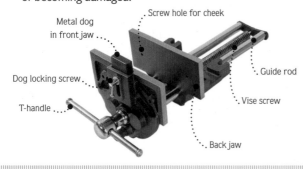

Metal dog in front jaw

Screw hole for cheek

Dog locking screw

Guide rod

T-handle

Vise screw

Back jaw

COMMERCIAL WORKBENCHES

Small, commercially available workbenches can also be used. These are portable and can be folded away. Despite their small size, they carry a considerable load when locked in the open position. The user can increase the bench's stability by placing a foot on the step. Controlled by handles, the rear half of the benchtop acts as a vise. Plastic pegs fit into holes to help support a workpiece.

Holes for plastic pegs

Folding frame

Sturdy steel step

BENCH HOOKS

A bench hook is used to hold timber in place on a workbench. It is a useful addition to any bench and can be bought or easily constructed by the woodworker. It consists of either a solid board or piece of plywood, with a cross timber or square of wood attached at each end on opposite sides. These cross timbers allow it to be hooked over the edge of the workbench. Sizes vary, but a typical bench hook measures 10 x 10 in (250 x 250 mm).

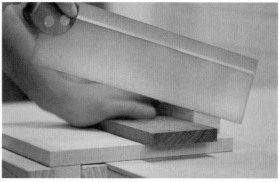

Setting up a bench hook
Hook the front cross timber over the edge of the bench or, as shown here, hold it in a vise. Using a vise is preferable, as it eliminates movement and leaves one hand free to hold the workpiece.

Using a bench hook
Slide the workpiece forward until it rests against the back cross timber of the bench hook. Hold it in place with the heel of one hand while using the thumb of the same hand to guide the edge of the saw.

SHOOTING BOARDS

Shooting is the process of taking a few shavings from the edge or end of a board in order to correct an angle, straighten an edge, or clean up its surface. Similar in nature to a bench hook, a shooting board is designed to hold a workpiece in position, although a shooting board has an additional board attached to its underside. It is along this board extension that a plane (see pp.17–23)—which must be turned on its side—is run. The plane then trims the edge of the workpiece.

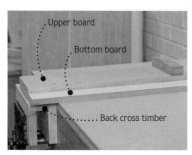

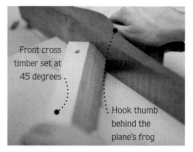

Setting up a shooting board
Hook the back cross timber over the edge of the bench, or grip it in a vise (shown above). Check that the front cross timber is square to the upper board.

Using a shooting board
Rest the side of the plane on the bottom board. Press its sole against the upper board. Push the workpiece up to the front cross timber and against the plane.

Using a shooting board at 45 degrees
The front cross timber can be set at an angle of 45 degrees to allow for the trimming of a miter (see pp.85–90). The best way of checking that the cross timber is set to the correct angle is to trim two off-cuts. When these off-cuts are placed together, they should form a right angle.

SAFETY CLOTHING AND FIRST AID

Power tools and machines can be hazardous—many are noisy; create large amounts of dust; and have sharp, fast-moving blades. However, as long as you wear the correct safety clothing and take the necessary precautions (see p.11 for the safe use of tools), woodworking should be a safe and rewarding occupation. A well-stocked first aid kit must be the first fixture in your workshop. Learn first-aid techniques, seek training in the correct use of all tools and equipment, and always follow the manufacturer's instructions. Remember also that timbers can be heavy, so research and use the correct lifting techniques and protect your hands and feet by wearing gloves and safety boots.

BASIC FIRST AID KIT

Always keep a well-stocked first aid kit in your workshop. Use an easily identifiable cabinet and place it in a conspicuous place. (Someone unfamiliar with the layout of your workshop may need to access it.) A basic first aid kit should contain the following items:

- Bandages
- Butterfly bandages
- Scissors
- Tweezers
- Safety pins
- Antibiotic ointment
- Antiseptic ointment
- Iodine or similar prep pads
- Alcohol prep pads
- Gauze pads
- Medical adhesive tape
- Pain relievers
- Eye drops
- Burn medication

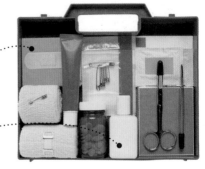

Keep your kit orderly—items need to be quick and easy to retrieve in an emergency

Replace medications before they exceed their expiration dates

WORK SAFELY

Wearing the correct personal protective gear is a basic requirement—you must also follow safe working practices, seek appropriate training, and keep your tools well maintained. Keep in mind the following safety advice as you work (see also p.11).

- **Work neatly and don't rush:** Tripping is one of the most common causes of injury in the workshop. To reduce the risk, always work in a neat manner, carefully stowing all tools, equipment, and workpieces; if your workshop is tidy and well-organized, you will be able to move around it more safely and freely. Plan your work schedule so that you are never tempted to rush a job or cut corners; following safety procedures correctly and thoroughly takes time.
- **Working with hazardous materials:** All wood dust poses a risk if inhaled or caught in the eyes, and some woods can be harmful to handle. Adhesives and finishes are also potentially harmful. You should research all potential dangers and take necessary precautions, such as wearing a dust mask, safety goggles, and protective gloves.
- **Working with machines and power tools:** Machines and power tools can cause severe injury if used incorrectly. Always follow the manufacturer's instructions and never attempt operations beyond your experience or ability. Always disconnect the power supply before removing or handling blades or cutters. Regular maintenance will keep machines and tools safe and in good working order. For information about the safe use of specific tools, see the chart on p.11.

TRAINING CLASSES

As a woodworker, you will need to acquire a huge amount of information in order to work safely and to the best of your ability. As such, you should consider attending formal training classes—of which there are many to choose from. Your first priority should be to seek training in first aid and the correct and safe use of machines and power tools. You may then wish to move on to training classes that focus on more specialized woodworking techniques. The advantages of attending dedicated training classes include keeping up-to-date with the latest practices and techniques and receiving personalized advice from expert woodworkers.

⬡ PERSONAL PROTECTIVE EQUIPMENT (PPE)

A term that encompasses all of the clothing and equipment used to protect an individual's body, PPE includes items as diverse as jumpsuits and body armor. While not every item of PPE will be needed by the woodworker, those shown below should be considered essential. It is important that PPE is worn or used correctly, looked after properly, and replaced before it becomes worn out. Because you will often have to wear several items of PPE at the same time—such as a dust mask, safety goggles, and acoustic earmuffs (ear defenders)—choose items that complement each other and do not cause discomfort. While many hazards can be avoided by the wearing of protective clothing, inappropriate clothing in itself can be hazardous. For example, loose clothing should be avoided because it can become entangled in the rotating parts of a machine or power tool. For the same reason, don't wear loose jewelry, and if you have long hair, tie it back.

STEEL TOE–CAPPED SAFETY BOOTS

Steel toe cap · Slip-resistant sole

Protecting your feet
If a large workpiece were to slip from your grasp and fall on your feet, it could cause serious injury. Safety boots or shoes with steel toe caps will protect your toes; many boots also have steel insoles to protect the soles of your feet should you step on a nail. Boots must be comfortable and have slip-resistant soles.

Protecting your hands
It is essential to wear tough protective gloves when changing or handling blades and cutters; these will prevent cuts and loss of grip. When handling timber, gloves will protect your hands from splinters and increase your grip when maneuvering large workpieces. However, be aware that gloves will reduce your level of control when operating machines and power tools, so they should be avoided in these circumstances. Wear rubber gloves and apply barrier ointment when working with toxic finishes.

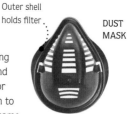

Extra layer of protection · Cotton back

Stiff cuff · Absorbent padding on palm

PROTECTIVE GLOVES

Protecting your ears
As a general rule, if you cannot understand normal speech from a distance of 3 ft (1 m) with a machine switched on, you need to wear ear protection. You may decide to wear ear plugs, which are inserted into your ears, or headphone-style ear defenders, which sit over your head and cover the outside of your ears.

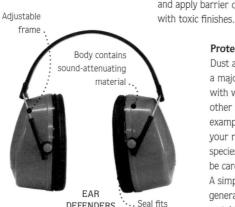

Adjustable frame ·

Body contains sound-attenuating material ·

EAR DEFENDERS

Seal fits over ears ·

Protecting your lungs
Dust and noxious fumes are a major hazard when working with wood, glue, varnish, and other active agents. Dust, for example, will cause irritation to your respiratory tract (and some species of wood, such as blackbean, produce dust that can be carcinogenic), so it is vital to protect your nose and mouth. A simple dust mask with a filter will provide adequate general-purpose protection, while full-face respirators with cartridges designed to filter specific particles are available for use with more harmful substances.

Outer shell holds filter ·

DUST MASK

Impact-resistant lens · Side protection ·

SAFETY GOGGLES

Ventilation prevents fogging ·

Protecting your eyes
It is essential that you protect your eyes from dust and from any flying objects or particles, such as a disintegrating router cutter. Safety goggles are rated by the level of impact resistance they offer; if in doubt, use a higher resistance than seems necessary. Goggles should also offer protection to the side of your face. If you wear glasses, look for safety goggles that have plenty of ventilation, which will prevent fogging; goggles with prescription lenses are available.

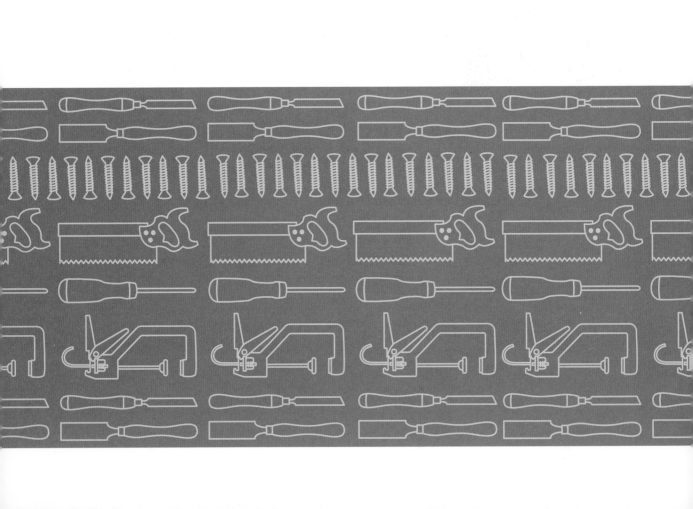

TECHNIQUES

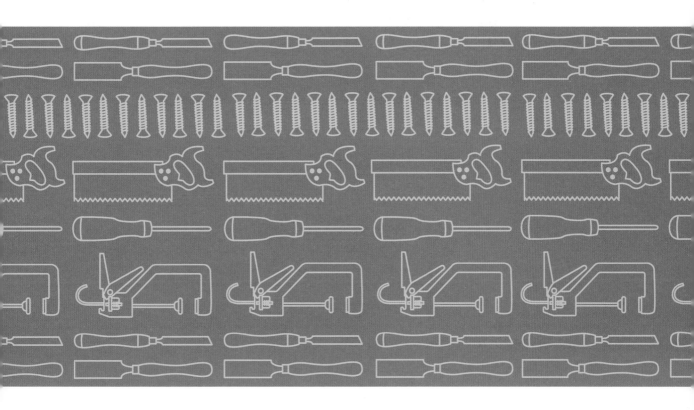

INTRODUCTION

This section details the core woodworking techniques that, with practice, will enable you to complete all of the projects in the Projects chapter (see pp.166–215). In effect, any woodworking project is simply the sum of many different, well-executed techniques. There is often more than one way of working to achieve the same result. For example, wood can be sawn and planed by hand using a hand saw and plane or by machine using a table saw and planer. The same principle applies to cutting joints. This book explains both hand and machine techniques in detail so that you can choose your preferred way of working.

LEARNING THE TECHNIQUES

Woodworking techniques are best developed by using a practical, methodical approach. There is plenty of material available to help you with this. As well as using practical manuals (such as this one), there are instructional DVDs and online demonstrations. Ideally, you could back this up with some hands-on instruction by attending a college course or a workshop or, in a perfect world, work alongside an experienced woodworker who can show you first-hand how best to work. Whatever combination of instructions you choose, you will only really improve by constant practice. Once you understand the anatomy of a technique, such as how a carefully maintained tool can be used to make a predictable mark or cut, then the only way to perfect that technique is to practice it repeatedly.

WORKING ACCURATELY

Accurate woodworking relies on two main considerations: the position of the cutting lines you've marked and the position of your tool in relation to that line. While this may sound obvious, if your line is not exact or your cut is a fraction over or under the line, you will end up with a sloppy joint or a component part that is less than perfect.

To avoid this, mark out all cutting lines with the flat side of a marking knife. Once you have made a crisp knife cut, and you have established which side of the cutting line will go to waste, then you can run the tool to the waste side of the cutting line in the confident knowledge that your cut cannot go wrong. As well as this, the success of any woodworking technique is dependent on the quality of the tools that you are using. For good, accurate work, ensure that your tools are in good condition before you begin.

Cutting accurately to the waste side ensures precision.

BEFORE YOU BEGIN

When working on wood for the first time, you are likely to encounter various problems and difficulties. There are a few basic rules that you can bear in mind to help keep any setbacks to a minimum:

- **Read it through**: Make sure you read through every step of the instructions in full before you start working on the wood. It is important to know what you are trying to achieve; otherwise, you may not notice if you have done something wrong along the way.
- **Equipment**: Assemble all the equipment you'll need in advance of starting a project. (This is listed in the Tools and Materials panel on each project.) You don't want to get halfway through and realize you don't have a vital tool.
- **Patience**: Learning to craft and shape wood can be time-consuming and at times tricky, but don't let this put you off. Patient practice is the only way to build up your skills and proficiency.
- **Off-cuts**: It is more than likely that your skills will take time to hone, so make sure that you practice on off-cuts until you feel fully confident. Mistakes on large pieces of wood can prove expensive.
- **Unfamiliar terminology**: The glossary (see pp.216–219) will explain any unfamiliar terms that you may encounter in the instructions.

PREPARING WOOD

In mass-produced furniture, you will often see mismatched colors, defective areas, and bland or clashing grain patterns, whereas handmade furniture should avoid these mistakes and instead display the strength and beauty of the wood. This section describes how to select timber and how to convert rough-sawn planks and manufactured boards into accurately sized components.

SELECTING TIMBER

Timber varies not only in species (see pp.146–163), but also in quality. Grain or figure, color, and "defects" (see below) are the main aspects that define each piece both structurally and visually. The exception is manufactured boards, which are intentionally uniform in quality.

Rough-sawn planks
When planks are purchased, they are often in a rough-sawn state and may be green (wet), air-dried, or kilned. Choose planks with an attractive figure and check for defects (see right).

WOOD DEFECTS

Defective wood can be ugly and, worse still, it may fail structurally. Common imperfections in boards are knots, worm holes, and stains or rot caused by fungi. All knots weaken the lumber, especially "dead" knots, where a branch has died and become encased; these often fall out when the plank is dried or planed, leaving a hole. Softwood that has no dead knots is called "clear." Different parts of the world use different grading terms for hardwoods, but always buy the best grade possible. Grain that runs diagonally across the face of the board is a defect due to poor conversion and will limit its use. (Grain that runs diagonally across the thickness may be unusable.) An extremely warped plank may be due to poor seasoning or storage and will only be useful for very small components.

ROUGH SIZING

Work out the most efficient way to cut the components needed from the rough-sawn boards that are available. The board must be flat and about ¼ in (6 mm) thicker than the finished thickness. Large components that take up a whole board are easy to mark out, as there are no choices to make regarding placement. Mark out the length of these with a tape measure, straight edge, and carpenter's pencil, avoiding defects and sapwood. Midsize components (over 15¾ in/400 mm long) need careful placement and, where possible, should be cut from the same plank as shorter components to make use of the whole length. Small components (under 15¾ in/400 mm long) should not be rough-sized at this stage, but rather marked out as groups of components that are planed first and only cut later. Keep in mind that some components should have matching grain. As a general rule when cutting short pieces, cross-cut first and rip second.

PLANING A FACE AND EDGE

The techniques on the following pages describe the method by which roughly sized components are planed to make a rectangular-section component with flat and smooth sides. The piece is first planed flat on one face (across the width) and then planed flat on an adjacent surface (the edge), ensuring that it is 90 degrees to the face. The remaining rough face and edge are then planed smooth and parallel with the first face and edge. Planing by hand may not be necessary if you have machines to do the work for you (see p.63 for the machine method), but nevertheless it is a good planing exercise.

CREATING A FACE AND EDGE BY HAND

Planing the first and widest surface by hand is usually performed with a no. 5½ plane (also called a "jack" plane, see p.17), which has a sole about 15 in (380 mm) long. For boards wider than 5⅞ in (150 mm), consider using a no. 7 plane (also called a "joiner" or "try" plane, see p.18) with a sole about 21⅝ in (550 mm) long, as this will produce a flatter surface. The plane should be set to a coarse cut and used at a slight angle to the direction in which it is pushed (a shearing angle). If the board is greater than 5⅞ in (150 mm) wide, work the plane at an angle to the grain and then follow up with an opposing angle. This levels the board across the width, after which you can proceed to planing the edge. In all cases, ensure that you are working the plane in the direction that lays the grain to produce a smooth surface. If the grain tears, try working from the opposite end. Keep the pressure on the front of the plane as you begin a stroke, then transfer the pressure to the back of the plane as you complete the stroke. This avoids rounding over at the ends.

SQUARING UP

When planing, the "face side" is the first and widest surface to be planed flat. It is often also selected as the most attractive surface that will be most visible. After planing, it is marked with a loop. The second, adjacent surface is called the "face edge" and is planed at 90 degrees ("squared up") to the face side and marked with a V-shaped arrowhead.

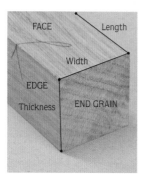

CREATING A FACE SIDE

1 Choose the face side, then assess where the high points are and which direction to plane in order to lay the grain.

2 Place the wood in the vise and start planing with a bench plane. Concentrate on the obvious high points first and work at a slight angle to the grain. Continue planing until the rough sawn surface and the "shadows" of the saw have been removed and the surface is clean, flat, and smooth.

3 Use winding sticks to check if the surface is flat and that you are planing square. Place a stick at each end of the face side of the piece of wood. Sight across the sticks with your eyes at the level of the closest stick and compare their position. If they are exactly parallel, then the surface is flat.

4 A long, straight edge such as a metal ruler turned on its edge is used to assess the flatness of the face side from end to end in various positions, both straight and diagonally. Sighting along the ruler with your eyes at its level will help you spot defects.

5 Complete the face side, planing with the no. 5½ plane set for a fine cut, until the surface is perfectly flat and smooth. Annotate it with a standard face-side mark that points to what will be the face edge.

WINDING STICKS

A winding stick consists of two pieces of light and dark wood glued together to form a straight stick about 23⅝ in (600 mm) long. Used in pairs and placed at each end of a piece of wood, they give a visual indication of flatness or of winding ("wind"), which is a twist along the length. Because the sticks are longer than the width of the board they extend and exaggerate any twist, making it easier to spot.

Far winding stick is placed the other way up from the near stick, with the dark wood on top

STICKS PLACED AT EITHER END

Brown wood of far stick is visible above the pale wood of the near stick, meaning the surface is not flat

WINDING STICKS NOT PARALLEL

CREATING THE FACE EDGE

1 Plane the face edge flat and square (at 90 degrees) to the face side (inset). Check the squareness with a carpenter's or combination square (pictured).

2 Mark any locations that are out of square and require further planing.

3 Plane the face edge again, concentrating on the marked locations. Continue planing until all of the pencil marks have been removed.

4 Check the squareness again. Holding the piece of wood at eye level against the light helps reveal any discrepancies.

5 Use a metal ruler to check the end-to-end flatness in the same way as for the face side (see step 4, p.59). If the face edge is a similar width to the face side, check for twisting using the winding sticks (see p.59).

6 When the face edge is flat and smooth, use a pencil to annotate it with the standard face-edge mark, pointing to the face-side mark.

MARKING THE THICKNESS

1 Having prepared the face side and the face edge, all subsequent measurements should be taken from these surfaces. Measure with a ruler (pictured) and then set the marking gauge to the desired thickness of the face edge (inset).

2 Place the marking gauge against the face side and score the thickness along the face edge.

3 Use the marking gauge to score the thickness along the other edge and both ends of the piece. A standard wooden marking gauge with a pin (see p.28) can be used, but this often fails to mark a clean line on the end grain.

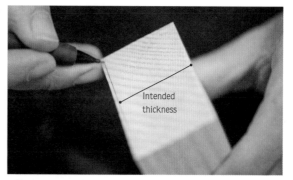

Intended thickness

4 If necessary, make the line easier to see by drawing into the scored line with a fine pencil.

CUTTING THE THICKNESS

Intended thickness

1 Ascertain how much material needs to be removed to get down to the desired thickness. If ¼in (6mm) or more, consider sawing off the bulk of the waste. If less than ¼in (6mm), remove the excess material from the nonface side with a plane.

2 During planing, routinely check the relative position of the scored line all around the piece.

3 Continue planing until you have reached the scored line denoting the thickness and the surface is smooth. This nonface surface is now square to the face edge.

MARKING AND CUTTING THE WIDTH

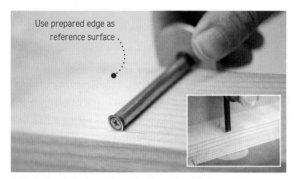

Use prepared edge as reference surface

1 Mark the desired width on the face side with the marking gauge (pictured). Mark both sides of the wood. Small amounts (less than ¼in/6mm) can be planed. Larger reductions need to be sawn—either by hand (using a rip saw) or, more commonly, with a band saw. Cut the width with a band saw using a fence, making a test cut before continuing (inset). Always "undercut" to allow for hand-finishing by plane to the exact width.

2 Use the no. 5½ plane to remove the excess material on the remaining rough edge. As you work, check the relative position of the scored line all around. Continue until you have reached the line and achieved a smooth, flat surface.

⚙ FACING AND EDGING BY MACHINE

This procedure describes planing the face side and the face edge flat and smooth using a jointer (a process called jointing when using this machine). The purpose of this is to establish two good flat surfaces that are perfectly square to each other, which can be used to work from when "thicknessing." (Thicknessing creates the two remaining surfaces that establish the thickness and width of the component.) Never machine-plane stock that is less than 17¹¹⁄₁₆ in (450 mm) in length, as the rollers will not grip it properly. The jointer is an extremely dangerous machine if used incorrectly. See p.11 and pp.24–25 for information on how to use the jointer safely, and always ensure you follow the manufacturer's guidelines.

USING A JOINTER

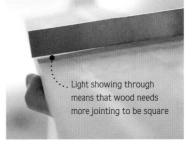

Light showing through means that wood needs more jointing to be square

1 Take off only the minimum amount of the rough-sawn face side to achieve a flat, smooth, and clean surface. Set the cutters to take off no more than ¹⁄₁₆ in (1.5 mm) of wood at a time.

2 Check that the fence is set to 90 degrees using a square. Press the face side of the piece against the fence and joint the face edge.

3 Use a square to check that the finished jointed edge is 90 degrees to the face. If it is not, the fence may be out of square or you may not be holding the wood firmly against the fence.

USING A THICKNESS PLANER

1 Use a caliper to find and measure the thickest part of the piece (inset). Bear in mind, a warped plank may be substantially thicker in the central area. Adjust the thickness planer to the caliper measurement minus ¹⁄₃₂ in (1 mm). Pass the wood through the planer face-side down in the direction that lays the grain (pictured). If the machine motor sound indicates that it is struggling, quickly (but safely) release the bed lock (if it has one) and wind down the bed. Avoid allowing the motor to grind to a halt. Reset the machine to a greater thickness and try again. Continue, reducing the thickness by ¹⁄₃₂ in (1 mm) increments or less for hardwoods, and ¹⁄₁₆ in (2 mm) or less for softwoods, until the desired thickness is achieved.

2 Measure the width with a caliper (pictured). If the piece needs reducing by more than ³⁄₈ in (10 mm) to achieve the desired width, saw off the bulk of the waste first. Set the thickness planer to the desired reduction and pass the wood through the machine face-edge down in the direction that lays the grain. Continue reducing the width by small increments (as in step 1) until the desired width is reached.

CUTTING TO FINAL SIZE

When components have been planed square to the correct thickness and width, they can be cut to the precise finished length on a table saw (or radial-arm saw, see below right). Check on an off-cut that the machine is producing precise 90-degree cross-cuts, then make the necessary adjustments before proceeding. On a table saw, adjust the height of the blade to give the best results (see below). If the component first requires cutting along the grain to reduce its width, this procedure can be carried out on the table saw using a short-rip fence.

CROSS-CUTTING TO FINAL SIZE USING A TABLE SAW

Ensure that the teeth of the blade are above the surface of the wood

1 For the best results, adjust the blade height so that the teeth are about ⅜ in (10 mm) above the surface of the board or the base of the uppermost tooth is just above the surface of the wood. This will result in a cleaner cut than if the blade were set higher.

2 Cut off the rough end of the piece. Hold the wood against the cross-cut fence and cut off the minimum amount to leave a clean, square end.

3 Set the cross-cut end-stop scale for cutting the piece to the desired length, then make the cut. Use the same setting for cutting identical length components.

RADIAL-ARM SAW

A radial-arm saw consists of a circular saw attached to a movable arm. Most commonly used for cross-cutting, it is a highly versatile tool (although not all radial-arm saws are designed to make rip cuts, which can be very dangerous). For example, its head can be raised to make partial cuts when kerfing (producing a curve) or tilted for angled cuts. You can also rotate the arm to cut the wood at a variety of angles.

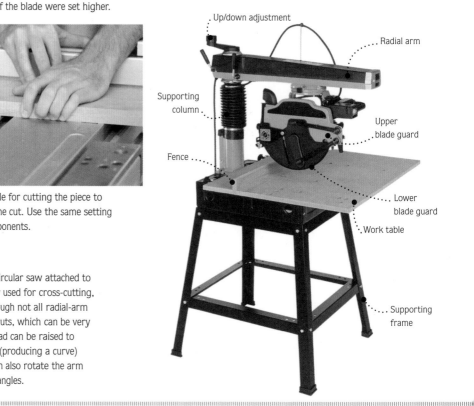

Up/down adjustment

Radial arm

Supporting column

Upper blade guard

Fence

Lower blade guard

Work table

Supporting frame

CUTTING SHEET MATERIALS

It is often necessary to cut a 96 in x 48 in (2,440 mm x 1,220 mm) sheet of plywood or MDF into smaller pieces. Many hobby-rated table saws cannot accommodate this size of sheet, in which case one of the methods illustrated below can be used. If a large table saw can be used, ask for help to maneuver the board. To cut the piece accurately, you must ensure that there is adequate support for the board as you saw, using extending supports or saw horses, and the person helping you, if possible. Manufactured boards are "inert" and therefore will not trap the table

saw blade—this means that it is safe to use the full extent of the rip fence when "rip" sawing. Vertical panel saws are the ultimate solution for cutting up sheets, but they are not usually found in small workshops. Breakout (splintering) is often a problem with plywood or veneered boards, especially when cutting across the grain. An effective technique to obtain the best results is to cut $\frac{1}{32}$–$\frac{1}{8}$ in (1–3 mm) short of the finished line with the saw (the amount depends on the extent of the breakout) and then cut back to the finished size using a router and guide (see p.42).

CUTTING SHEETS BY HAND USING A PANEL SAW

1 Support the board on trestles. Measure and mark the cut line with a square or straight edge and pencil. Double-check the measurements.

2 Position yourself over the line of cut, using your body weight to hold the board still. Use your thumb to guide the first few carefully aligned strokes to the waste side of the line (inset), and once the start of the cut is established, move your thumb away and continue sawing.

CUTTING SHEETS USING A CIRCULAR SAW

1 Mark the position of the cut in pencil as described in step 1, above. Ensure the board is fully supported on either side of the cut line. (Otherwise, when you complete the cut, the waste will fall down or swing up, or you could lose your balance, resulting in an accident.)

2 Mark the position of a fence on the stock (nonwaste) side of the cutting line to align the saw blade with the marked cutting line.

3 Clamp a fence in position (inset), then use a square to ensure that the fence is square to the cutting line. Saw through the wood with the circular saw (pictured), placing the edge of the saw up against the fence and using your weight to steady the board on the supporting trestles as you cut.

CHOOSING A JOINT

Joints are an integral part of woodwork—they literally hold a piece together—so the joint you choose and where it fits in the piece are both critical to the strength and longevity of the overall construction. The joint should be selected according to the type of wood, the function and esthetics of the item, and the role that the joint will play within it.

🪚 JOINT STRESSES

When selecting a joint, bear in mind that various stresses and strains will affect it throughout the life of the piece. There are four main types of joint stress—tension, shear, racking (also known as bending), and compression—each of which affect the joint in a different way.

RESULT

Tension

Occurring when the forces on a joint combine to pull it apart, tension is commonly found on a drawer front when pulling the drawer open. The physical force applied to the joint is increased by the weight of the drawer contents, increasing the tension. Dovetails, which have an inherent mechanical strength, are used in drawer fronts to counteract the tension.

RESULT

Racking

Common in chairs, tables, frames, or carcases that are unsupported, racking (or bending) can be resisted in a number of ways. A wedged through tenon or twin tenon can be used, or another shoulder can be added to a stub tenon. Gluing in a carcase back reduces racking potential, while a deeper rail or additional stretcher rail can reinforce a table or chair.

RESULT

Shear

Occurring when pressure is applied to a joint line, shear can cause the joint to fail. For example, a scarf joint or butt miter, which rely on glue to hold them together, could shear due to the lack of mechanical lock. Modern glues are very strong, but it is always good practice to reinforce a joint by pegging or using a loose tongue, or even screwing.

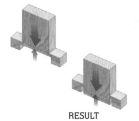

RESULT

Compression

Occurring when a joint is subject to down-force, compression is counteracted by choosing a joint that will resist load. The weight of a sideboard carcase on a mortise-and-tenoned plinth is a good example of this kind of stress, so in addition to ensuring that the joints and rails are deep enough, inserting glue blocks into the corners can also help.

JOINT TERMS

Woodworkers describe the shapes created when cutting joints using the terminology shown here. Other terms are "groove" (a narrow housing), "tongue" (created by two rebates), and "dovetails" and "pins" (parts of an interlocking "dovetail" joint employing tapered shapes).

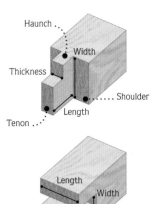

Haunch
Width
Thickness
Shoulder
Tenon
Length

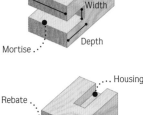

Length
Width
Mortise
Depth

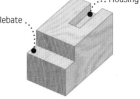

Housing
Rebate

JOINT NAME	STRENGTHS	WEAKNESSES	USES AND EXAMPLES
Butt joint	Modern glue makes the joint stronger than the wood itself.	On thick sections, it may need to be reinforced with a tongue.	All flat carcase sections, panels, and table tops.
Loose tongue-and-groove joint or spline	Makes locating boards easier and increases gluing area.	The joints can be weak if the tongue and grooves are too wide.	Constructing a carcase and panels.
Fixed tongue-and-groove joint	Increased gluing area increases strength; very versatile.	Time consuming to make and can be weak if joints are too big.	Decorative paneling for the back of pieces such as bookcases and floorboards.
Cross-halving joint	Stronger than corner halving and with a good resistance to racking.	No real weakness, but joints need careful cutting to look good.	Often used in stretcher rails and lattice frames.
Corner-halving joint	A simple and quick joint to make.	Relies on glue only and can be subject to racking.	Basic frames.
Dovetail half-lap joint	Capable of resisting pull-out and sideways racking.	No great weakness; this is the strongest of the lapped joints.	Any type of framing, carcase pieces, and rails for drawers.
Dado joint	A simple joint that has no strength in tension but good load capability.	Needs careful cutting, or the joints can look shoddy.	Used in bookcases and chests of drawers.
Dovetail housing joint	Strong, resists racking, and does not suffer from pull-out.	No weaknesses. Requires careful work to achieve a tight fit.	Bookshelves, carver chairs, bed frames, or for joining a stiffening rail to any frame.
Butt-miter joint	Quick to make and looks attractive.	Not very strong, even when glued up.	Picture frames and coffee table tops; used a lot in veneered work.
Mitered half-lap joint	An attractive joint with a good gluing area.	No strength until glued.	Frames and panels; most useful for tops.
Keyed miter joint	This is a strong and attractive joint.	No mechanical resistance against tension unless keys at opposing angles.	Picture frames and boxes.
Loose-tongue miter joint	Easy to adapt for various situations and very strong.	Has none of the weaknesses of the butt joint.	Attractive and can be used in any frame construction.
Basic mortise-and-tenon joint	Good against racking if used with top and bottom shoulders.	Only weak if the tenon is not made thick enough.	The staple joint of furniture making, used in almost any construction.
Haunched-tenon joint	The haunch increases the gluing area, making the joint stronger.	The haunch remains visible and is not always attractive.	Good for frame and panel work where the groove runs all the way through.
Secret haunched-tenon joint	Extra gluing area, but haunch remains hidden.	The joint can be fragile if not cut correctly.	Classy joint often used for front chair legs.
Wedged through mortise-and-tenon joint	Extremely strong, this joint cannot be withdrawn.	No weaknesses. Requires careful work to achieve an attractive result.	Chairs, chests of drawers, or any carcase piece that needs extra support.
Knock-down tenon joint	Joint easy to disassemble or knock-down.	The end of the tenon can split if the piece is subjected to racking.	Large pieces of furniture, such as bookcases and beds.
Drawbore tenon joint	A strong joint that does not require any glue.	The quality of modern glues means this joint is no longer used as often.	Decorative features; lends a traditional feel to furniture.
T-bridle joint	Very strong joint that is resistant to racking.	Requires great accuracy, especially when used in curved tables.	Used in the middle of rails.
Corner-bridle joint	Increased gluing areas, particularly if used in multiples.	Like an open topped mortise, not very strong until glued up.	Sometimes used double or even triple on chairs; very strong joint used in this way.
Comb joint	Its large gluing surface means that, once glued, it is very strong.	Little mechanical strength.	Boxes and carcase pieces.
Through-dovetail joint	One of the strongest woodwork joints there is, it resists load well.	No weaknesses. Requires careful work to achieve an attractive result.	Used decoratively in boxes and carcase pieces.
Biscuits	Very quick to make for a huge variety of joints; can be used in most situations.	No real mechanical strength until the joint is glued.	Used for attaching frames to carcases, making carcases, and mitered frames.
Dominos	A version of the loose tenon, a piece which is quick and easy to make.	Can only be used where there is room for a mortise in both sections.	Can be used just about anywhere there is a tenon, even for chair making.
Dowels	A quick method of construction—very easy to use in the home workshop.	Many areas used with this joint are end grain and harder to glue.	Can be used in most carcase work in multiples and as a mortise and tenon.

BUTT JOINT

The butt joint—also known as the edge-to-edge joint—is the most basic joint in woodworking, and it is also one of the most important. Without it, almost nothing could be made, since it allows individual boards to be joined together to create pieces wider than the width of wood available straight from a tree.

TOOLS AND MATERIALS

Bench plane
Pencil
Sash clamps
Masking tape
Wood glue and brush
Rubber mallet

PARTS OF THE JOINT

The individual boards that make up the butt joint must be perfectly square and true. To minimize warping, lay the boards so that the grain lies in alternate directions. Longer joints should have a slight hollow of approximately 1/64 in (0.5 mm) in the middle, which creates a sprung tension at the ends that prevents any shrinkage from pulling the joint apart.

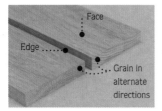

Face
Edge
Grain in alternate directions

🪚 PREPARING THE JOINT

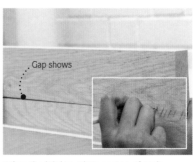

Gap shows

1 Place the first piece of wood in a vise with the edge to be joined uppermost (inset), then tighten the vise. Plane along the edge with a bench plane (pictured) to create a flat surface for the joint. Repeat this step for the second piece of wood.

2 Lay the joining edges on top of each other to check for gaps (pictured), which reveal an area that needs to be planed again. Use a pencil to mark any excess that needs to be planed further to level off the joining edges (inset).

3 Plane the marked area with a bench plane, removing a little at a time (pictured). Be sure to check the edge against the other piece to avoid removing too much material. Continue planing until the edges fit together closely with no gaps between the two pieces of wood.

4 Mark the exact position of the pieces in relation to each other when joined by drawing a V-mark in pencil.

ASSEMBLING THE JOINT

1 Set up the clamps before gluing the joint. Insert the two pieces of wood and adjust the clamps to the correct width.

2 Protect the wood from staining by sticking masking tape to the bars of the clamps that will be in contact with the wood.

3 Apply wood glue to one surface of the joint, spreading it evenly along the full length of the edge with a brush.

4 Place the pieces together with the V-mark aligned. Clamp the two pieces in position. Gently tap along the joint with a rubber mallet (pictured) to ensure that the edges are flush with each other.

5 Tighten the clamps, being careful to check that the two pieces remain perfectly aligned with each other.

6 Wipe away any excess glue with a rag and leave to dry for several hours or, ideally, overnight.

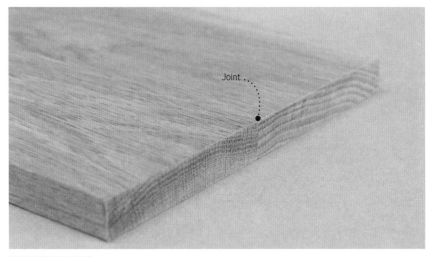

Joint

THE FINISHED JOINT

VARIATIONS OF THE BUTT JOINT

There are several joints that are related to the butt joint, such as the loose tongue-and-groove joint (see pp.70–71) and the fixed tongue-and-groove joint (see pp.72–73), as well as joints formed by biscuit joiners (see pp.122–123) and domino joiners (see pp.124–125). These methods incorporate additional features to improve the accuracy with which the pieces are joined, and also add to the strength of the joint.

LOOSE TONGUE-AND-GROOVE JOINT

Although termed "loose," the tongue is actually glued into place in the grooves of the two connecting boards. It can be used in either a single-tongue form (described here) to join standard-width boards or in a double-tongue assembly to join thicker boards.

When marking up a loose tongue-and-groove joint, it is essential to achieve the right ratio between the thickness of the tongue and the thickness of the board. A general guideline is that the tongue needs to be less than a third of the thickness of the board.

TOOLS AND MATERIALS

Bench plane
Mortise gauge
Plow plane
Ruler
Pencil
Band saw or circular saw
Wood glue and brush
Clamps

PARTS OF THE JOINT

The joint is formed by cutting a groove in each of the joining edges of the two pieces. A separate tongue of wood is inserted in the grooves and glued in place to hold the pieces together. Plywood is the usual material for the tongue, and since it is supplied in a standard thickness, the width of the grooves will always be the same, simplifying the cutting process.

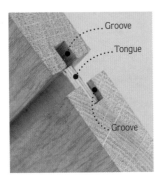

Groove
Tongue
Groove

PREPARING AND MARKING OUT THE GROOVE

1 Flatten the edges of both boards by planing them with a bench plane, as if preparing for making a butt joint (see pp.68–69).

2 Set a mortise gauge to the width of the blade of the plow plane. The choice of blade is determined by the thickness of the tongue.

3 Use the mortise gauge to scribe the width of the groove centrally on one edge of each of the two pieces.

SETTING THE PLANE AND CUTTING THE GROOVE

1 Adjust the fence of the plow plane to align the blade within the scribed groove marks.

2 Set the plow plane to the depth of the groove required. Usually, this is a little more than the width of the groove. Use the plow plane to cut the grooves on the edges of both of the pieces being joined (pictured).

MAKING THE TONGUE

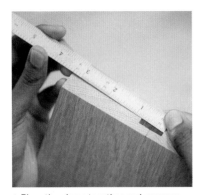

1 Place the pieces together and measure the combined width of the grooves in order to calculate the width of the tongue.

2 Cut the tongue to the length and width required using a band saw (pictured) or a circular saw. The width should be about $1/16$ in (2 mm) less than the combined measurement of both grooves.

3 Test-fit the tongue in the grooves. Mark the joining position on the faces of the pieces to be joined (see Marking the joint, below left).

GLUING THE JOINT

MARKING THE JOINT
Before you glue the joint, it is a good idea to mark the exact position of the two pieces of the joint. You can then dismantle the joint for gluing with the assurance that it can easily be reassembled in the desired position.

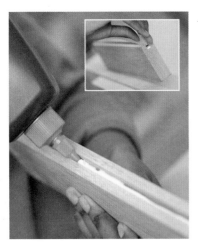

1 Apply a generous amount of wood glue into the grooves of both of the pieces that are to be joined (pictured). Insert the tongue into the groove of the first piece (inset), then clean any excess glue from the end grain.

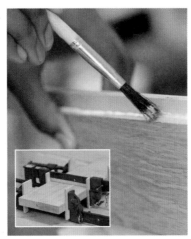

2 Brush glue onto the joining edge of each piece (pictured), then assemble the joint by placing the second piece over the tongue. Clamp and leave to dry (inset). When the glue is dry, plane the surface of the assembled pieces flush.

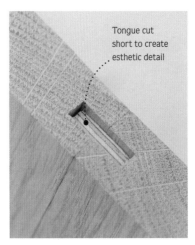

Tongue cut short to create esthetic detail

THE FINISHED JOINT

FIXED TONGUE-AND-GROOVE JOINT

This is a versatile butt joint that has many applications. It is most commonly used as a decorative feature for the back of pieces such as bookcases or bureaus; for floorboards or paneling; or simply to join boards together, although the strength of modern glues means that this usage has become less common.

TOOLS AND MATERIALS

Plow plane
Ruler
Rebate plane
Double-sided tape
Hammer and nails
Spare strips of wood
Wood glue and brush
Clamps

PARTS OF THE JOINT

A fixed tongue-and-groove has an integral tongue created by a double rebate on one piece that marries with the groove on the joining piece. The timber must be very flat for this joint to work, as it is easy to misalign the groove. The groove must be cut slightly deeper than the tongue in order to allow space for the glue.

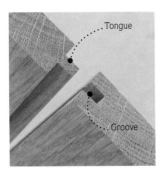

Tongue

Groove

CUTTING THE GROOVE AND SETTING THE PLANE

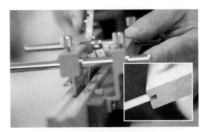

1 Prepare the edge and use a plow plane (pictured) to cut a groove of the required dimensions, as for the loose tongue-and-groove joint (see pp.70–71). Measure the depth of the groove to determine the length of the tongue (inset), which will be cut with a rebate plane.

2 Set the fence of the rebate plane to 1/32 in (1 mm) less than the depth of the groove to allow space for the glue. (The fence governs the width of the rebate.)

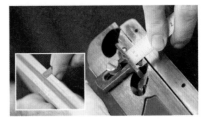

3 Set the foot of the plane (pictured) to the same measurement as that of each side of the groove (inset). (The foot governs the depth of the rebate.)

CUTTING THE TONGUE

Strips of wood nailed to the bench stop the piece from moving

1 Secure the tongue piece to the bench face uppermost, using double-sided tape and strips of wood to hold it firmly in place (pictured) as you plane the rebate. Use the rebate plane to cut along one side of the tongue piece until you have achieved the desired depth of rebate (inset).

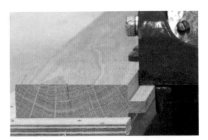

2 Turn the piece over and secure it to the bench, then plane the second rebate to create the tongue.

1 Check the fit of the tongue in the groove. Make any necessary adjustments to the pieces by further planing.

2 When you are sure that the fit of the tongue into the groove is satisfactory, squeeze a generous amount of wood glue into the groove and along the joining edges of both elements of the joint.

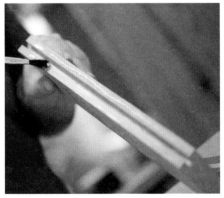

3 Spread the glue with a brush to distribute the adhesive evenly on all of the surfaces to be joined.

4 Assemble the glued elements and clamp together with clamps placed at regular intervals along the length of the joined pieces.

5 Wipe away any excess glue with a damp cloth and leave the joint to dry, ideally for several hours.

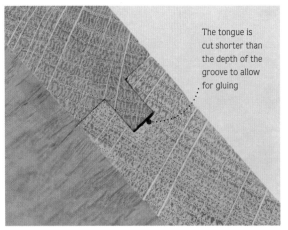

The tongue is cut shorter than the depth of the groove to allow for gluing

THE FINISHED JOINT

CROSS-HALVING JOINT

The cross-halving joint (sometimes called a cross-halved lap joint or center lap) is one of a family of joints, known as lap joints, that are useful whenever it is necessary to join two pieces of wood that cross each other. The cross-halving joint is commonly used in various types of building joinery and furniture construction—for example, on a range of basic carpentry frames and on stretcher rails for tables and chairs.

TOOLS AND MATERIALS

Pencil
Combination square
Marking gauge
Marking knife
Small tenon saw
Clamp
Bevel-edged chisel
Hand router (optional)
Wood glue and fine brush

PARTS OF THE JOINT

The cross-halving joint consists of two pieces with exactly half of their material removed to create four shoulders that cross each other. The fit of the components must be perfect; otherwise, the joint will be sloppy and unsightly. Although the amount of material removed incurs a risk of weakness, once the two parts are glued together, it is a very strong joint.

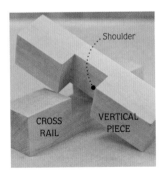

Shoulder

CROSS RAIL

VERTICAL PIECE

🪚 MARKING UP THE JOINT

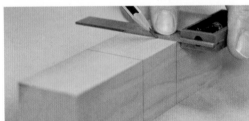

VERTICAL PIECE

CROSS RAIL

1 Mark the position of the joint on the cross rail by marking the width of the lap with a line on either side of the vertical piece.

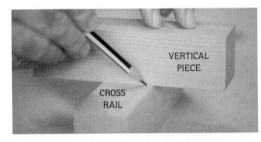

2 Extend the marks around three sides of the cross rail using a combination square and pencil or a marking knife.

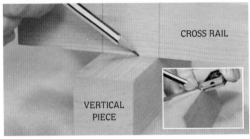

CROSS RAIL

VERTICAL PIECE

3 Reverse the pieces and mark the shoulders on the vertical piece, using the cross rail as a guide. Square the marks onto three sides of the vertical piece (inset).

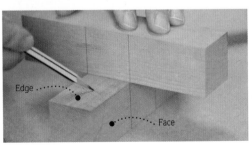

Edge

Face

4 Position the pieces in the desired position and mark the faces (see Squaring up, p.58).

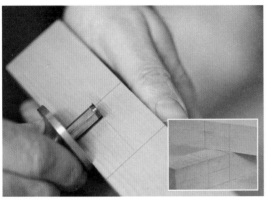

5 Set the marking gauge to half the thickness of the stock and mark the depth of the lap between the shoulder lines on the edges of both pieces. With the pieces aligned so that the faces that will be cut to create the laps are touching, mark the waste for removal (inset).

6 Scribe the edges of the waste on both pieces with a marking knife to ensure a clean cut across the grain.

CUTTING AND FITTING THE JOINT

1 Using a small tenon saw, cut on the waste side of the vertical marks until you reach the depth mark. Make a series of relief cuts vertically through the waste, being careful not to cut through the depth mark (pictured).

2 Remove the waste with a bevel-edged chisel, chopping horizontally from one edge of the piece (pictured). Reverse the piece in the vise and chop away the remaining waste (inset), working horizontally from the other edge.

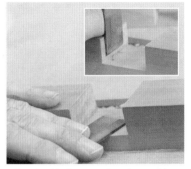

3 Use the chisel to pare the edges and base of the lap to the marks and to create a smooth finish (pictured). Alternatively, use a hand router if available. Remove the waste from the second piece in the same way (inset), using a tenon saw, chisel, and hand router if available.

4 Check the fit of the two pieces and adjust by paring further if necessary. When the fit is good, glue the joint, clamp it, and leave to dry.

THE FINISHED JOINT

CORNER-HALVING JOINT

One of the simplest types of joint, the corner-halving joint has no mechanical lock or resistance to racking or twist, so it should not be subjected to lateral strain. It has large gluing surfaces and relies on glue for its strength, but it can be reinforced with screws or dowels.

TOOLS AND MATERIALS

Pencil
Square
Marking gauge
Marking knife
Tenon saw
C-clamp
Bevel-edged chisel
Wood glue and brush
Bench plane or block plane

PARTS OF THE JOINT

This joint utilizes components of equal thickness, and each piece is a mirror image of the other. Each long-grain piece is half the width of the stock and mates against the end-grain shoulder of the opposite piece.

MARKING OUT AND CUTTING THE JOINT

Extra length

1 Mark the position of the joint on the first piece using the thickness of the other piece, aligned approximately 1/16 in (2 mm) from the end grain, as a guide.

2 Extend the mark around three sides with a square. With the marking gauge set to half the width of the wood, scribe around the two marked sides and the end (inset).

3 Score the lines with a marking knife (pictured), then cut the waste with a tenon saw. Make sure you cut to the waste side of the scored line. Clean up the joint with a bevel-edged chisel (inset), then follow steps 1–3 to cut a joint in the second piece of wood.

FINISHING THE JOINT

Test-fit to ensure the faces are flush and form a 90-degree angle (although the ends of the joint should protrude beyond the edges). Adjust by paring further if necessary. Once a good fit has been achieved, apply glue to the joint and clamp with a C-clamp (inset). Recheck the angle, wipe off excess glue, and leave it to dry. Once the glue has dried, use a bench plane or block plane to remove the excess length from the ends of the joint to achieve a flush finish on both edges.

THE FINISHED JOINT

DOVETAIL HALF-LAP JOINT

The dovetail half-lap is capable of resisting pull-out and sideways racking, so it is mechanically the strongest of all lap joints. It can be used on any type of framing and is often utilized on carcase pieces, particularly for top drawer rails and back rails, since it can be easily inserted into an existing frame.

TOOLS AND MATERIALS
Pencil
Square
Marking gauge
Marking knife
Dovetail marker
Tenon saw
Bevel-edged chisel
Bench plane

PARTS OF THE JOINT
As with all half-lap joints, the tail piece of the dovetail half-lap will measure half the thickness of the piece of wood, and in most cases the socket piece, into which it is to be fitted, will measure the same width and thickness. However, in some instances, the socket piece can be of a different thickness.

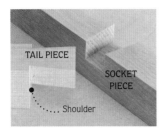

MARKING OUT THE TAIL

1 Set the socket piece on top of the tail piece, with the end grain of the tail piece protruding by up to 1/16 in (2 mm). Mark a line on either side of the socket piece and extend the lines onto all four sides of the tail piece with a square (inset).

2 Mark the position of the lap on the socket piece, using the tail piece as a guide. Square the measurements around all four sides.

3 Decide on the depth of the lap (see Parts of the joint, left) and scribe this measurement around the edges and end grain of the tail piece (inset). Scribe with a marking knife to reinforce the shoulder lines on both edges and on the underside (the waste side) of the tail piece (pictured).

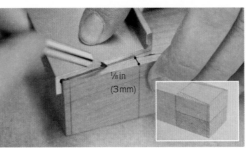

4 Using a dovetail marker as a guide, mark the tail from the end grain to the shoulders on the face side of the tail piece. Set the marker at least 1/8 in (3 mm) from the edge at the shoulder. Mark the waste (inset).

1 Secure the tail piece in a vise at an angle and cut the waste from the back of the tail using a tenon saw. Saw diagonally through the end grain to the shoulder.

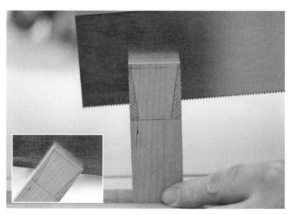

2 Turn the piece in the vise and saw diagonally from the other direction (inset). Finally, saw vertically to the shoulder (pictured).

3 Using a bevel-edged chisel, cut a V-groove along the shoulder line at the back of the tail.

4 Release the waste by cross-cutting along the shoulder line with a tenon saw.

5 Clean up the shoulder and edges with a chisel.

6 Scribe across the end grain from the marks made in step 4 of Marking out the tail (see p.77) with a marking knife and square.

7 Set the tail piece in the vise so that the line marking one side of the tail is vertical. Cut down the end grain to the shoulder with a tenon saw. Repeat to cut the other side of the tail.

8 With the tail piece secured in a vise, chisel a V-groove along the shoulder line on the edges of the tail.

9 Release the waste by sawing down the shoulder line on each edge and the back face. Clean up the shoulders with a chisel (inset).

MARKING OUT THE SOCKET

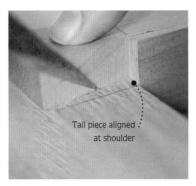

Tail piece aligned at shoulder

1 Set the tail in position over the socket piece, aligned at the shoulder. Scribe around the tail with a marking knife. Square the marks onto the edges.

2 Mark the depth of the socket on both edges using the marking gauge as previously set (inset). Use a tenon saw to cut the edges of the socket to this depth.

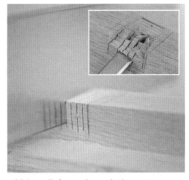

3 Make relief cuts through the waste. Chop horizontally with a chisel (inset) to release the waste. Clean up the base and edges with a chisel.

4 Test the fit of the joint and adjust as necessary. Saw off the excess length of the tail and plane flush to the edge of the socket piece using a bench plane (inset).

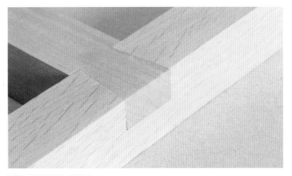

THE FINISHED JOINT

DADO JOINT

Among the most basic types of joint, the dado (or housing) joint consists of a groove—the "housing"—into which the end grain of the joining piece of wood—the "tenon"—is inserted. Ideal for making shelves for bookcases and plinths for pieces such as sideboards, it may also be used to make carcase furniture, such as desks and chests of drawers.

TOOLS AND MATERIALS

Marking knife
Square
Ruler
Appropriately sized chisel
   (slightly smaller than the
   thickness of the housing)
Marking gauge
Pencil
Tenon saw
Wooden mallet
Rubber mallet
Wood glue and brush
Clamps

PARTS OF THE JOINT

The housing is made to the exact thickness of the tenon piece and extends across the full width of the housing piece and into both edges. The depth of the housing is usually one third of the thickness of the housing piece, and certainly no more than half—any more than this will weaken the overall structure of the piece.

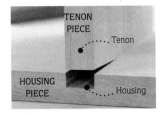

TENON PIECE
········ Tenon

HOUSING PIECE
········ Housing

MARKING OUT THE HOUSING

1 Score a single line on the face of the housing piece with a marking knife and square to mark the position of the housing.

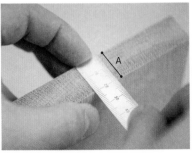

2 Measure the width of the end grain of the tenon piece (A) to determine how wide you will need to cut the housing.

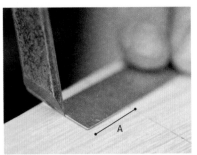

3 Mark the width of the tenon (A) on the housing piece. This defines the width of the housing.

4 Square this line across the face of the housing piece, using the marking knife and square.

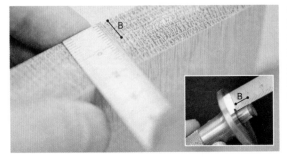

5 The thickness of the housing piece determines the housing depth (pictured). Set the marking gauge to between one third and one half of this measurement (B) (inset).

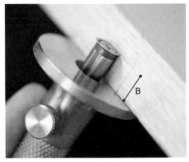

6 Extend the width marks around the edge of the housing piece on both edges, using a pencil and square.

7 Use the marking gauge to scribe the depth of the housing between the width marks on both edges.

8 Score along the width marks that you have made in pencil, using the marking knife and square.

CUTTING THE HOUSING

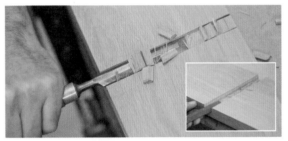

1 Use a chisel to make a V-groove along each of the housing lines on the face of the housing piece (pictured). Cut along the grooves with a tenon saw to the depth indicated by the edge markings (inset). Loosen the waste with a chisel by making vertical cuts along the width of the housing.

2 Use a chisel and wooden mallet to remove the bulk of the waste from the housing by chopping horizontally (pictured). Trim the base and edges with the chisel, smoothing off any loose cuts, splinters, and rough edges (inset).

ASSEMBLING THE JOINT

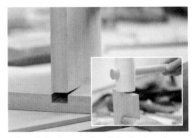

No light should show through between square and wood

1 Insert the tenon piece into the housing, taking care not to damage the edges as you bring the two pieces together. Use a rubber mallet to lodge the tenon in place (inset)—the fit should be snug. If the fit is too tight, adjust the width of the housing by paring with a chisel.

2 Check that the fit is square by holding a square against the joint. When you are satisfied with the accuracy of the joint, glue and clamp the joint.

THE FINISHED JOINT

DOVETAIL HOUSING JOINT

The dovetail housing is the strongest type of housing joint—it resists racking and does not suffer from pull-out, thanks to its shape. It is useful for carcase constructions where strength is important—such as open bookshelves, arm-to-side-rail joints on carver chairs, bed frames, or for joining a stiffening rail to any frame.

TOOLS AND MATERIALS
Squares
Pencil
Marking gauge
Hand-held router with straight and dovetail cutters
Chisel
Table-mounted router
Wood glue and brush

PARTS OF THE JOINT
The housing depth can be from a third to half the thickness of the stock, and the tail angle should be at the standard 1:8 ratio for hardwood (1:6 ratio for softwood). The shoulders of the tail produce a very neat joint. The tail piece is usually cut and driven in from the back of the carcase, so the housing is often stopped at the front.

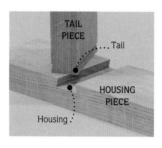

⬤ MARKING OUT THE HOUSING

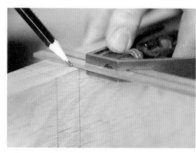

1 Draw a pencil line square across the housing piece to define the position of the housing. Mark the housing width (A) approximately ¼ in (6 mm) less than the thickness of the tail piece.

2 Square the marks onto both edges of the housing.

⬤ CUTTING THE HOUSING

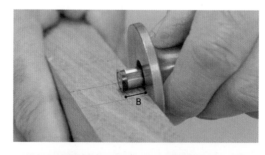

1 Mark the depth of the housing (B) on both edges with a marking gauge. The depth should be about one third of the thickness of the housing.

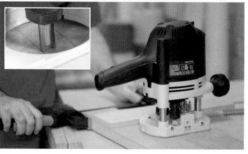

2 Use a hand-held router and straight cutter to cut the housing. Secure a fence to guide the router (see p.42) square to the housing (pictured) in order to align the cutter to one of the marks that define the edge of the housing (inset).

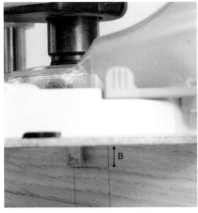

3 Set the router to the same depth as the housing (B).

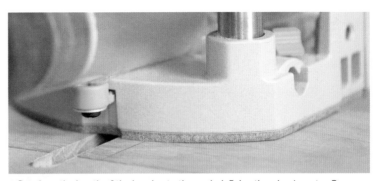

4 Cut along the length of the housing to the mark defining the edge (see step 2, Cutting the housing, opposite). Do not attempt to cut the full depth of the housing in one pass—instead, make several passes of the router until you reach the desired depth. Note that the waste material on either side of the workpiece helps support the router and contains breakout.

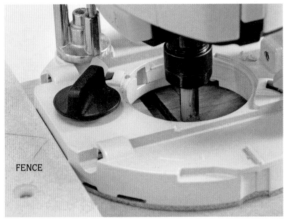

FENCE

5 Move the fence and router so that the cutter is aligned to the other marked edge of the housing, then make a further pass of the router.

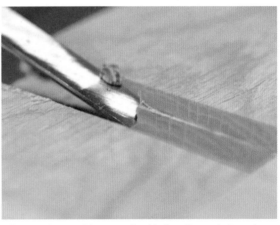

6 Remove the remaining waste by chiseling. Alternatively, make additional passes of the router until all the waste is removed.

7 Insert a dovetail cutter in the router. Adjust the fence to align the upper part of the cutter with one edge of the housing, so that a dovetail profile is cut without increasing the width at the top of the housing. Cut along the edge to the full depth (B).

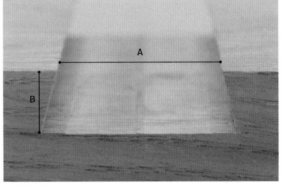

8 Adjust the fence to set the dovetail cutter against the other edge. Cut along this edge, then clean up the base and both edges with a chisel.

1 Mark the width of the top of the housing (A) onto the edge of the tail piece. Ensure that you center this measurement within the thickness of the piece.

2 Set a marking gauge to the depth of the housing (B), then scribe this measurement onto the edge of the tail piece.

3 Scribe the line around all four sides of the tail piece to mark the length of the tail.

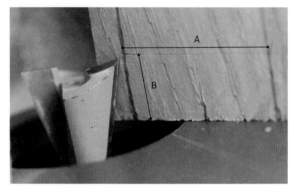

4 Use a table-mounted router to cut the tail. Set the depth of the cutter to the tail-length mark (B), then set the fence so that the outer tips of the cutter are aligned to the housing-width lines (A).

5 Cut both sides of the tail on the router. Check the fit within the housing, make any necessary adjustments, and refit. Glue the joint, check it is at a 90-degree angle, and then wipe off any excess glue.

THE FINISHED JOINT

BUTT-MITER JOINT

Possibly the most common joint, the butt miter is instantly recognizable as the joint frequently used to make wooden picture frames and is an attractive way of adding a frame to a table top or a panel. It is simply a 45-degree butt-jointed end grain. Reliable and accurate methods of cutting this joint include using a miter block, a compound miter saw, or a miter trimmer.

TOOLS AND MATERIALS

Combination square
Marking knife
Suitable clamp
Bench hook
Tenon saw
Bench plane
Shooting board
Wood glue and brush

PARTS OF THE JOINT

This simple joint consists of two pieces of wood of the same width and thickness, joined at the end grain. These joining end grains are cut to an angle of 45 degrees. There is no mechanical reinforcement, and this joint instead relies on glue for its strength. Accurate cutting of the miter is essential for a successful joint.

Mitered end grain ....

MARKING AND CUTTING THE JOINT

1 Use a combination square and marking knife to score a line at a 45-degree angle across one face of the first piece of wood.

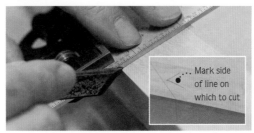

... Mark side of line on which to cut

2 Square the mark across the two adjacent edges, then mark a line at 45 degrees across the remaining face. Make a V-mark on the side of the line on which you will make the cut (inset).

3 Clamp the piece to a bench hook to secure it for cutting. Cut along the angle drawn with a tenon saw.

4 Plane the cut surface smooth, using a 45-degree shooting board for accuracy. Cut the second piece in the same way. Check the fit of the pieces, apply glue, and clamp.

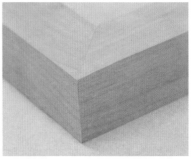

THE FINISHED JOINT

MITERED HALF-LAP JOINT

The principal advantage of the mitered half-lap over a conventional corner lap is the attractive appearance of the finished joint—it leaves a neatly mitered face with only one of the end-grain areas exposed. It could be argued that it is weaker than a conventional corner lap or straight butt miter, due to the smaller gluing and end-grain contact area; however, the glued area and lap part of the joint lend it greater strength.

TOOLS AND MATERIALS

Pencil
Combination square
Marking gauge
Marking knife
Tenon saw
Bevel-edged chisel
Wood glue and brush
Suitable clamp
Block plane

PARTS OF THE JOINT

As with other lap joints, the components of each joining piece must be of exactly the same dimensions. The lap is exactly half the thickness of each piece, and a simple miter is cut on the top face of each piece. The two pieces are cut in slightly different ways and are referred to as piece A and piece B for clarity.

MARKING THE PIECES

1 Position piece A over piece B close to the end grain, and mark the width on piece B, allowing an extra 1/16 in (2 mm) at the end grain. Reverse the pieces to mark piece A.

2 Square the marks onto all sides of both pieces. Then use a combination square set to 45 degrees to mark the angle of the miter between the marks on both pieces.

3 Mark the lap on the end grain and edges of both pieces with a marking gauge. Use a marking knife to extend the line of the miter onto the edge, then mark the waste (insets).

⬛ CUTTING THE PIECES

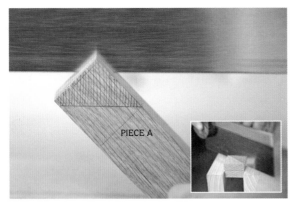

1 Cut the lap of piece A with a tenon saw until you reach the shoulder and the line marking the end of the miter. Saw along the line of the miter to release the waste (inset).

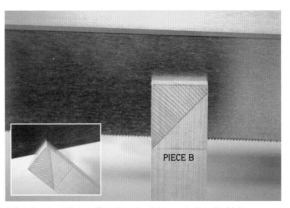

2 Cut the lap of piece B to the shoulder mark (inset). Make a cut through the other corner and then cut vertically to the shoulder (pictured).

3 Set piece B in the vise, unmitered section of waste uppermost. Chisel a V-groove along the shoulder, then saw to the marked depth. Saw along the line of the miter to release the remaining waste (inset).

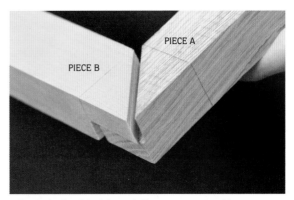

4 Check the fit of the joint and, if necessary, pare with a bevel-edged chisel.

5 Glue and clamp the joint, then once the glue has dried, use a block plane to cut the joint flush to the edge.

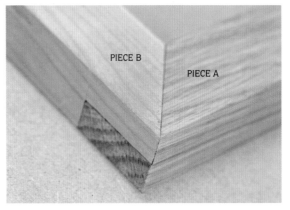

THE FINISHED JOINT

KEYED MITER JOINT

This is a strong and attractive joint that can be used on any miter with a small section—such as a picture frame—but is most commonly used for boxes. Its strength comes from the veneer keys, which are inserted into slots cut in the glued miter. You can make a decorative feature of the keys by using sections of veneer in a contrasting color to the miter. You could even choose different colors for different keys.

TOOLS AND MATERIALS
Veneer
Tenon saw
Square
Pencil
Scalpel
Marking knife
Wood glue and brush
Chisel or flush-cut saw
Sandpaper

PARTS OF THE JOINT
The basic construction is that of a simple butt-miter joint (see p.85). Cuts are made through the corner of the joint, into which the veneer keys are inserted. The placing of the keys is purely esthetic, but they are usually equally spaced on the stock.

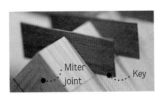
Miter joint   Key

MARKING OUT AND CUTTING THE JOINT

1 Join two pieces in a butt-miter joint (see p.85).

2 Use a tenon saw that has a kerf of the same width as the veneer, or cut the veneer to suit your saw. Make a test cut on spare wood with your saw to check the fit of the veneer within the kerf.

3 Mark the thickness of each piece square across both edges of the miter, and square the marks across the outside faces of both pieces to provide a guide for the depth of cut required.

4 Mark the positions of the keys on the corner of the joint, and extend the lines to the depth of the cut guides on the faces.

5 Secure the joint in a vise with the corner uppermost, and use your chosen saw to cut the slots to the depth of the cut guides marked in step 3, opposite.

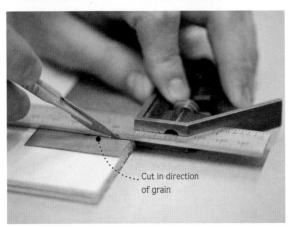

⋯⋯ Cut in direction of grain

6 Cut the required number of keys from the veneer with a scalpel. Cut the pieces oversize, and with one straight edge along the direction of the grain.

7 Test-fit the keys in the slots. Adjust if necessary and glue in place. Clean off any excess glue and leave to dry.

8 Score the keys flush with the surface using a marking knife. Then use a chisel (pictured) or flush-cut saw to pare away the excess. Sand smooth to finish (inset).

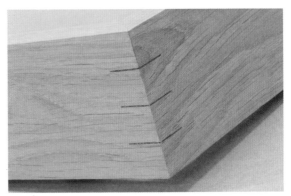

THE FINISHED JOINT

LOOSE-TONGUE MITER JOINT

A mechanically strong joint, the loose-tongue miter is far more versatile than the simple butt-miter joint (see p.85): useful for framing, it resists racking and twist and provides a larger surface gluing area. This joint is quick to build, and the basic construction process is the same as for a butt-miter joint.

TOOLS AND MATERIALS

Pencil
Square
Ruler
Mortise gauge
Clamp
Mortise chisel
Band saw or tenon saw
Wood glue and brush

PARTS OF THE JOINT

Mortises in the joining end grains hold the loose tongue. The best material to use for the tongue is ¼ in (6 mm) birch plywood, since it is strong and uniform in thickness. It should be square to provide the maximum gluing area.

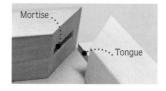

Mortise
Tongue

◢ MARKING OUT AND CUTTING THE JOINT

1 Miter two pieces as described for the butt-miter joint (see p.85). Mark the length of the mortise across the end grain with two horizontal lines (inset). Set the mortise gauge to the width of the chisel, which should be selected to match the thickness of the plywood used to make the tongue. Using the mortise gauge, mark the width of the mortise centrally between these lines (pictured). Repeat on the second piece.

2 Cut the mortise with the chisel. The slot should be triangular in section, with a vertical edge running from the upper end of the mortise and a horizontal edge from the lower end. Repeat on the second piece.

3 Measure the depth of the mortise, which will determine the dimensions of the tongue (see step 4).

4 Cut a square plywood tongue, using a band saw (pictured) or a tenon saw. The sides of the tongue should be the same length as the depth of the mortise. Insert the tongue into one of the mortises and test-fit all three elements of the joint. Adjust as necessary to achieve a tight fit, then glue and clamp.

THE FINISHED JOINT

BASIC MORTISE-AND-TENON JOINT

The mortise-and-tenon is one of the most commonly used joints. It has been used for many centuries in a wide range of woodwork, including the frame-and-panel furniture (such as linen chests, cabinets, and dressers) of the Middle Ages and the Tudor period, as well as in the construction of buildings. Today, it is still used for many of these pieces, as well as for doors, windows, and chairs.

It is important to remember that tenons are weak in tension and are therefore easy to pull out, but drawboring (pinning with a dowel), for example, is one of a number of methods of preventing this (see Drawbore tenon joint, pp.106–107). The basic joint described here is a stopped mortise-and-tenon joint (see Parts of the joint, below) that has a shoulder around all four sides of the tenon.

TOOLS AND MATERIALS

Ruler
Pencil
Square
Mortise gauge
Mortise chisel or mortiser
Marking knife
Masking tape
Wooden mallet
Marking gauge
Tenon saw or band saw
Bevel-edged chisel
Dovetail saw (optional)
Bench hook
Wood glue and brush

PARTS OF THE JOINT

The mortise is a slot—either stopped (as here) or extending through the thickness of the wood—into which a matching tenon fits. The tenon sides are called cheeks and the end grain faces are called shoulders. The tenon thickness should be between a third and half that of the mortise piece—too thick and the joint will be weak, too thin and the tenon is weakened.

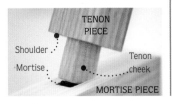

⬤ MARKING OUT THE MORTISE

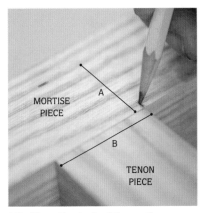

1 Decide on the depth of the mortise (A) and mark this measurement on the edge of the mortise piece. Mark the width of the tenon piece (B) on the mortise piece to provide a guide for the position of the mortise.

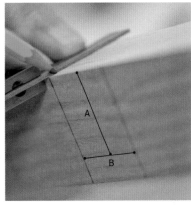

2 Use a square and pencil to extend the lines marking the width of the tenon piece (B) across the face and onto both edges.

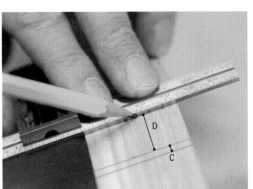

3 Mark the shoulder (C) on the face of the mortise piece inside both of the tenon width marks. Extend these marks across the face. The distance between the shoulder marks is the length of the mortise (D).

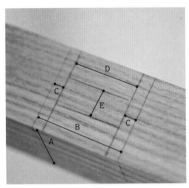

4 Set the pins of the mortise gauge to the width of the mortise chisel, which should be chosen to match the planned mortise width (E) (see step 2, Cutting out the mortise, below).

5 Set the fence of the mortise gauge to the mortise width (E) in the desired position between the shoulder marks within the mortise length, then scribe.

6 Reinforce all scribed lines in pencil. Then mark the waste within the mortise for removal.

CUTTING OUT THE MORTISE

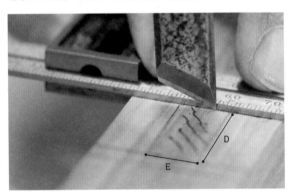

1 Use a marking knife and a square to reinforce the scribed marks defining the length of the mortise across the grain.

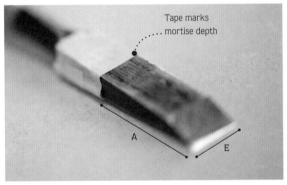

Tape marks mortise depth

2 Using the mortise chisel selected to match the width of the mortise (E) (see step 4, Marking out the mortise, above), mark the desired mortise depth (A) on the chisel with tape.

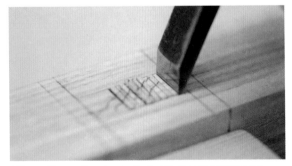

3 Secure the mortise piece to the bench, then make V-shaped cuts along the length of the mortise with the chisel and wooden mallet to release the waste.

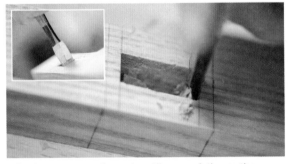

4 Continue to remove the waste until you reach the mortise depth marked on the chisel (inset). When you have reached the required depth, use the chisel to pare the sides and ends of the mortise precisely to the marked dimensions (pictured).

USING A MORTISER

Cutting a mortise by machine is usually done using a hollow chisel (of a gauge selected according to the width of mortise required) with an auger bit running through the center (see Mortisers, p.45). The auger drills as the chisel cuts with a downward plunging action. The machine is set to a repeatable position and depth. Once one mortise has been marked out, the others can all be cut using the same setting, so there is no need to mark out the other mortises fully. This considerably speeds up the process of making identical mortises on several pieces.

MARKING UP THE TENON

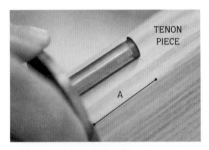

1 Set the marking gauge to the depth of the mortise (A). Mark the shoulder of the tenon on the face of the tenon piece.

2 Extend and deepen the scored lines around all four sides of the tenon piece using the square and marking knife.

3 Use the mortise gauge as previously set to mark the thickness of the tenon (E) on the face (pictured). Extend the marks around the end grain and nonface side.

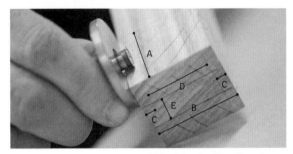

4 Set the marking gauge to the width of the shoulder (C) and scribe this measurement adjacent to both edges of the face, and across the end grain of the tenon.

CUTTING THE TENON CHEEKS

1 Secure the tenon piece in a vise at an angle, then saw along the tenon cheek with a tenon saw. Cut until you reach the depth mark on the edge closest to you.

2 Turn the wood so that you can saw in the same cut from the other side, until you reach the depth mark on that edge.

3 With the wood secured vertically in the vise, saw horizontally through the same cut. Repeat steps 1–3 on the other tenon cheek.

4 Secure the tenon piece in the vise with the face uppermost. Use a bevel-edged chisel to cut a groove along the shoulder line to create a clean sawing line.

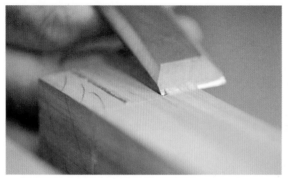

5 Cut a groove along the lines marking the edges of the cheeks, then chisel grooves on the other face and edge in the same way.

6 Use a small tenon saw or dovetail saw to cut along the groove in the first face to release the waste. Turn the tenon piece and saw off the other cheek.

CUTTING TENON CHEEKS USING A BAND SAW

To cut the tenon on a band saw, set up the fence to the marked lines on the end grain of the tenon piece. When satisfied that the settings are correct, cut the width of the tenon, then cut the small shoulders to trim the length of the tenon. Remove the cheeks by carefully setting the fence to the waste side of the marked lines. Cut to the lines, stopping well before the shoulder line. Once the first cheek is cut, the same setting should work for the other cheek. Finally, cross-cut to the waste side of the marked lines of the shoulders, taking care not to cut into the tenon itself.

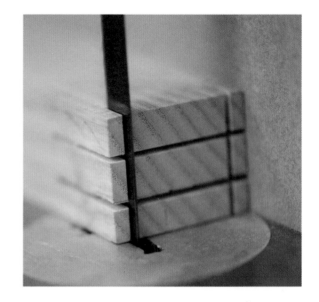

☼ CLEANING UP THE SHOULDERS

1 Insert the tenon piece in the vise with the tenon uppermost and a block alongside, level with the shoulder mark. Carefully chisel away the shoulder, using the block as a guide (pictured). Check the squareness of the shoulders with a square (inset), then adjust it by careful chiseling if necessary.

2 Square the line marking the width of the shoulder (C) from the end grain down the newly cut face of the tenon, using a marking knife (pictured). Cut down the shoulder line with a tenon saw to remove the waste (inset), then saw along the shoulder to release the waste. Repeat on the other side.

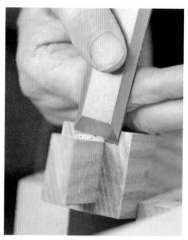

3 Use a bevel-edged chisel to pare accurately back to the scored line and neaten any rough edges left by sawing.

☼ FINISHING AND FITTING THE MORTISE AND TENON

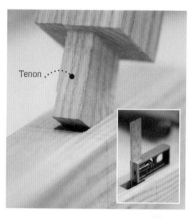

Tenon

1 Test the fit of the tenon in the mortise (pictured). It should be snug—pare with a chisel to ease the fit if necessary. Check the depth of the mortise and the length of the tenon (inset) to calculate how much material to trim from the tenon to create space for the glue in the joint.

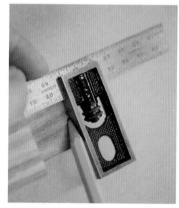

2 Mark a line on the face of the tenon to allow $\frac{1}{16}$in (2mm) between the end of the tenon and the base of the mortise, then extend the line around all four sides.

3 Holding the tenon piece on a bench hook, cut along the marked line with a tenon saw to remove the excess length from the end grain of the tenon.

4 To ease the fit, chamfer the edges of the tenon with a chisel. When you are happy with the fit, glue, assemble, check the joint is square, and clamp it.

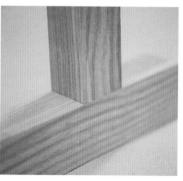

THE FINISHED JOINT

HAUNCHED-TENON JOINT

The haunched tenon is a variation of the basic (blind) mortise-and-tenon joint (see pp.91–95). It evolved from frame-and-panel carcasing, in which the groove holding the panel runs the whole length of the stile. The haunch fills and therefore strengthens the end of the groove. This joint allows extra tenon width near the shoulder without adding extra depth to the entire mortise, thus providing additional strength.

TOOLS AND MATERIALS

Mortise gauge
Mortise chisel
Tenon saw
Wood glue and brush
Clamp
Block plane

PARTS OF THE JOINT

The joint consists of a mortise that is cut to a reduced depth at one end. The haunch in the tenon is cut to fit this shape. In the example on this page, the full depth of the mortise extends through the thickness of the wood.

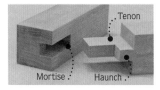

🪚 MAKING THE MORTISE AND THE HAUNCH

1 Mark the length and width of the mortise in the position required (see pp.91–92). Mark the length of the haunch (A) across the mortise width. The haunch should be around one third of the mortise length.

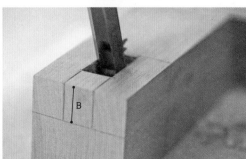

2 Extend the marks around the end grain and mark the depth of the mortise and the haunch (B). Cut the full-depth part of the mortise using a mortise chisel.

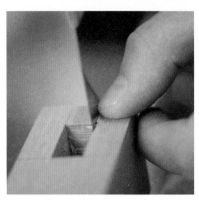

3 Cut the haunch, using a tenon saw to cut through the end grain to the marked depth.

4 Remove the waste with the chisel.

MAKING THE TENON

1 Cut the tenon to the full mortise width and depth (see pp.93–94). Mark the length (A) and depth (B) of the haunch on the tenon.

2 Cut the haunch from the tenon with a small tenon saw, taking care not to exceed the marked lines.

3 Test-fit the joint and pare with the chisel to adjust if necessary. Glue and clamp. When the glue is dry, plane both edges flush with a block plane.

THE FINISHED JOINT

SECRET HAUNCHED-TENON JOINT

Although the strength of modern glues has diminished its necessity, the secret haunched-tenon joint is nevertheless useful when an extra-strong haunch is required, but esthetics are also important. Particularly useful in furniture making because the joint is hidden, it is often chosen in place of a standard haunched tenon (see pp.96–97) for joints such as the front rail-to-leg joints of a chair or the door tops of a low cabinet.

TOOLS AND MATERIALS

Mortise gauge
Mortise chisel or hand drill
Bevel-edged chisel
Tenon saw or band saw
Pencil
Square
Masking tape
Wood glue and brush
Clamps
Block plane

PARTS OF THE JOINT

This joint differs from the standard haunched tenon (see pp.96–97) in that the haunch is sloped (or "tapered"), which strengthens the joint. The mortise is usually blind.

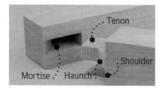

☼ MAKING THE MORTISE

1 Mark out a mortise of the desired width and length onto the mortise piece with a mortise gauge (see pp.91–92), and then mark the length of the haunch (A) across the width.

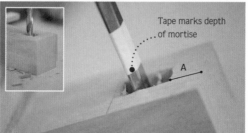

Tape marks depth of mortise

2 Chop out the full-depth section of the mortise with a mortise chisel or a hand drill (inset), finishing off the edges with a bevel-edged chisel.

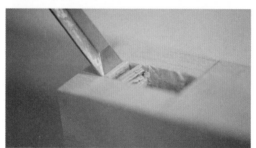

3 Starting at the inside edge, chisel the haunch at an angle of about 45 degrees from the outer edge of the mortise.

MAKING THE TENON

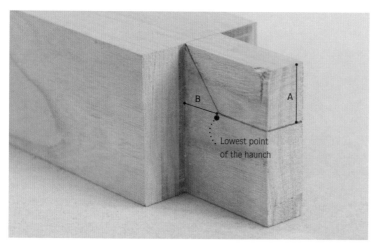

1 Cut the tenon to the full length and depth of the mortise (see pp.93–94), using a tenon saw or band saw. Mark the length of the haunch (A) with a pencil line on the end grain of the tenon, extending the line around both faces of the tenon with a square. Measure the depth of the haunch (B)—the full depth of the mortise less the depth from the base to the lowest point of the haunch—and mark this position on the line indicating the haunch length. Draw a diagonal line from this point to the shoulder.

B

A

Lowest point
of the haunch

2 Cut the bulk of the haunch in a square section with a tenon saw (inset). Remove the remaining waste with a bevel-edged chisel, taking care to chisel down to the marks.

3 Test-fit the joint by interlocking the mortise and tenon, and adjust by paring with a bevel-edged chisel if necessary. Glue, clamp, and leave to dry. Plane the edges of the joint flush to finish.

THE FINISHED JOINT

WEDGED THROUGH MORTISE-AND-TENON JOINT

The wedged through mortise-and-tenon joint is a very strong joint that cannot be withdrawn, making it excellent for use in chairs (particularly the back legs), chests of drawers, or any carcase piece that needs extra support. It can form a decorative feature if contrasting wedges are used, as in the bookcase project (see pp.205–215). Its strength comes from the snug fit of the tenon within the mortise when the wedges are inserted.

TOOLS AND MATERIALS

Pencil
Square
Mortise gauge
Marking knife
Drill and bits
Masking tape
Mortise chisel
Dovetail saw
Bevel-edged chisel
Band saw (optional)
Hammer
Flush-cut saw

PARTS OF THE JOINT

In this strong and often decorative joint, the tenon extends through the mortise piece. The ends of the mortise are shaped to allow the tenon to spread to fit securely when tapered wedges are inserted into slots that have been cut in the end grain of the tenon.

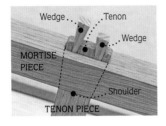

MARKING OUT THE MORTISE

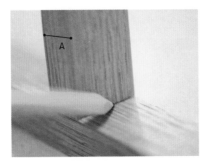

1 Using the thickness of the tenon piece (A) as a guide, use a pencil to mark the length of the mortise on the face of the mortise piece.

2 Square the length marks around all four sides of the mortise piece, using a square and pencil.

3 Set a mortise gauge to the thickness of the tenon required (B) and set the fence of the gauge to the desired position of the mortise. Scribe between the lines marking the length of the mortise on both faces of the mortise piece.

4 Score across the grain at the shoulders with a marking knife to link the marks (B) at both ends of the mortise.

⚞ MARKING OUT THE TENON

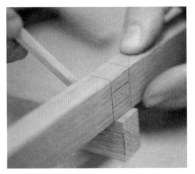

1 Mark the position of the tenon shoulder on the tenon piece, using the thickness of the mortise piece as a guide. Allow an extra ⅛ in (3mm) in addition to the thickness of the mortise piece.

2 Scribe the tenon shoulder line around all four sides of the tenon piece, using a marking knife and square.

3 Use the mortise gauge as previously set to scribe the tenon thickness (B) onto the tenon piece. Scribe across the end grain and down both faces of the tenon to the shoulder line.

⚞ CUTTING THE MORTISE

Tape marks maximum drilling depth

1 Use a drill fitted with a bit a little smaller than the width of the mortise to drill halfway through the mortise piece. Make more than one drill hole, if required.

2 When drilling, be careful to stay clear of the marked edges of the mortise. Drill from the other side to cut through the thickness of the mortise piece.

3 Use a mortise chisel of the same width as the mortise to remove the remainder of the waste and to clean up the edges on both sides of the mortise.

⚞ FLARING THE MORTISE

1 Working on the outside face of the mortise, mark the maximum desired thickness of the wedges (D) at both ends of the mortise with a marking knife.

2 Chisel into the mortise at an angle to almost the full depth of the mortise to create sloping sides. Leave the lower inside edges of the mortise square (inset).

CUTTING THE TENON

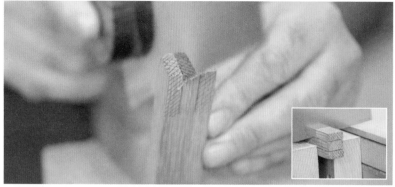

1 Using a dovetail saw, cut the cheeks of the tenon diagonally from each side and then vertically to the shoulder (see pp.93–94). Turn the piece in the vise and cross-cut along each shoulder to release the waste (inset).

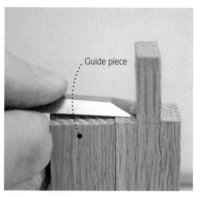

2 Clean up the shoulders with a bevel-edged chisel, using a guide piece clamped alongside the tenon piece.

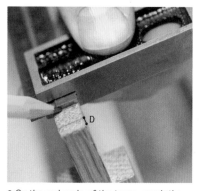

3 On the end grain of the tenon, mark the position of the slots for the wedges the same distance from the edge of the tenon as the width of the wedges (D).

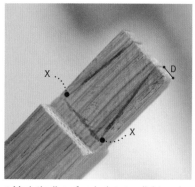

4 Mark the line of each slot at a slight angle from the marks on the end grain of the tenon made in step 3 to a point (X) about ⅛ in (3mm) from the shoulder.

5 Saw from each mark on the end grain at an angle to the marked position near the bottom of the tenon to create two diagonal slots (inset).

MAKING THE WEDGES

1 Cut the wedges from wood of the same thickness as the mortise width (B). Check the fit of the chosen wood by inserting it in the mortise.

2 Using the tenon as a guide, mark the length of the wedges. (This should be a little longer than the length of the tenon.)

3 Extend the mark that indicates the length of the wedges across the face of the wedge piece using a square.

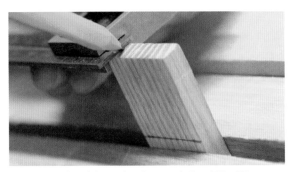

4 From the edge of the wedge piece, mark the width of the wedges (D) on the end grain.

5 Saw from this point toward the length mark, at an angle. Stop just before you reach the mark.

6 To cut the second wedge, saw vertically down from the same point in the end grain to a point level with the previous cut. Repeat steps 4–6 to cut as many wedges as you require.

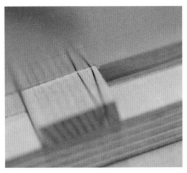

7 Using a dovetail saw (pictured) or a band saw, cut along the base of the wedges to separate them.

ASSEMBLING THE JOINT

Insert the tenon into the mortise so that the tenon end protrudes from the flared end of the mortise. Then use a hammer to tap the wedges into the slots (inset). Use a flush-cut saw to trim the tenon and wedges as closely as possible to the face of the mortise piece (pictured). Use a bench plane to finish, smoothing the exposed end of the joint flush with the face of the mortise piece. This joint does not need to be glued, although glue may contribute to its long-term strength.

THE FINISHED JOINT

KNOCK-DOWN TENON JOINT

A member of the mortise-and-tenon family, the knock-down tenon is commonly used in Asian furniture, as well as in the furniture of the Arts and Crafts Movement. The peg that is inserted through the tenon is removable, which allows the joint to be disassembled easily. This means that pieces can be completely "knocked down" for transport, making the joint particularly useful for large items, such as bookcases and beds.

TOOLS AND MATERIALS

Pencil
Square
Mortise gauge
Drill and bits
Mortise chisel
Tenon saw
Block plane
Bevel-edged chisel
Flush-cut saw (optional)

PARTS OF THE JOINT

This joint is formed by a tenon that protrudes from the mortise sufficiently to accommodate a mortise for a peg. When inserted, the peg acts as a stop against tension. The peg/mortise width should be no more than one third of the tenon width.

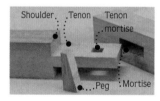

Shoulder Tenon Tenon mortise
Peg Mortise

🔆 MAKING THE MORTISE AND TENON

1 Mark up and cut a mortise through the thickness of the wood, as described for a basic mortise-and-tenon joint (see pp.91–95).

2 Cut the tenon to the required length (see Parts of the joint, left, and pp.93–94). Mark the thickness of the mortise piece on the face of the tenon.

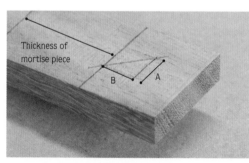

Thickness of mortise piece

B A

3 Mark the size and position of the tenon mortise on the tenon face. Scribe the mortise width (A) with a mortise gauge, then square the required length of the tenon mortise (B) between these marks.

4 Drill out the waste from the tenon mortise with a bit a little smaller than the size of the mortise (inset), then square off the sides of the hole with a chisel.

🪚 MAKING AND FITTING THE PEG

1 Cut the peg longer than required, using stock slightly larger than the tenon mortise. Plane the peg to fit the mortise (inset). Cut a taper along one edge so that the narrow end fits loosely in the mortise.

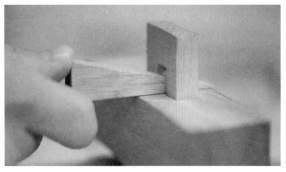

2 With the joint assembled, place the nontapered edge flush to the face of the mortise piece and push the peg into the tenon mortise until it fits tightly.

3 Cut the ends of the peg flush to the edges of the mortise piece, using a flush-cut saw or a tenon saw. No glue is required for this joint.

THE FINISHED JOINT

DRAWBORE TENON JOINT

One of the oldest forms of mortise-and-tenon joint, the drawbore tenon was commonly used in buildings and furniture from the 16th century onward. Devised before the introduction of reliable glues, the joint is assembled dry and then secured by a doweling peg that draws the shoulders tight against the bore.

TOOLS AND MATERIALS

Combination square
Pencil
Bradawl
Marking gauge
Dividers
Drill and lip-and-spur bit
Bevel-edged chisel
Hammer
Flush-cut saw

PARTS OF THE JOINT

The peg hole ("bore") is drilled through both sides of the mortise, and the hole in the tenon is slightly offset so that the joint is pulled tight when the peg is knocked into the hole. The size of the peg is determined by the joint size. The bore should be located at least ½in (12mm) from the end of the tenon.

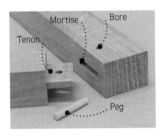

MARKING OUT THE BORE

1 Mark out and cut a basic mortise and tenon joint (see p.91–95). Using a combination square and pencil, mark the ends of the mortise and the tenon shoulder, and extend the marks across the adjacent face of the mortise piece.

2 Mark a line on the face of the mortise piece centered between the lines indicating the mortise length.

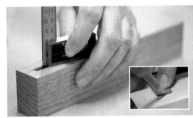

3 Using a combination square set flush to the edge, measure the depth of the mortise (pictured). Using a pencil, transfer the measurement to the mortise face on each of the lines indicating the mortise length (inset). Square the mark across the face.

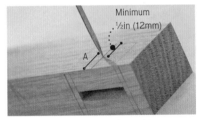

4 Use a bradawl to mark the position of the bore on the center line, at least ½in (12mm) from the line marked in step 2. (Measurement A is the distance of the bore from the edge.)

5 Repeat steps 1 and 2 on the opposite face of the mortise. Use a marking gauge set to measurement A to scribe the position of the bore onto the other face.

DRILLING THE BORE

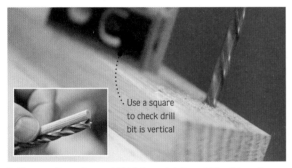

Use a square to check drill bit is vertical

Mark with drill

1 Choose a lip-and-spur drill bit to match the width of doweling (inset) you have selected for the peg (see Parts of the joint, opposite). Drill vertically into the positions marked for the bores through the mortise piece. (Be sure to drill from both sides to avoid break out.)

2 Assemble the mortise and tenon and use a short burst of the drill to mark the position of the bore on the tenon (inset). Be careful not to drill all the way through.

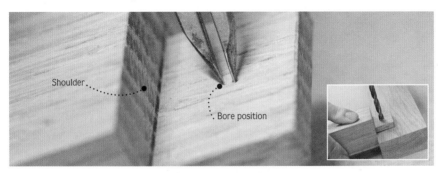

Shoulder

Bore position

3 Remove the tenon and use dividers to mark the position of the bore $1/16$ in (2 mm) closer to the shoulder than the point marked by the drill (pictured). Using the same drill bit, drill a hole in the newly marked position (inset), all the way through the tenon. Use an off-cut to support the tenon during drilling.

INSTALLING THE PEG

Cut the doweling for the peg a little longer than the full thickness of the stock, and chamfer one end with a bevel-edged chisel (inset). With the mortise and tenon assembled, tap the peg through the hole in the top of the mortise piece and through the tenon (pictured). Cut the peg flush with the joint, using a flush-cut saw. Pare any excess length with a chisel. As an alternative to the fluted dowel, a nonfluted dowel made from matching wood can be used.

THE FINISHED JOINT

T-BRIDLE JOINT

Bridle joints are part of the large family of joints related to the mortise-and-tenon joint (see pp.91–95); they are essentially open mortises with a tenon. Although most types of bridle joint have no mechanical hold at all, the larger-than-normal gluing surface area means that, when joined with modern glues, they can be as strong as joints with a closed mortise. The exception to the rule is the T-bridle (also known as an open-slot mortise), which, even without glue, has great inherent strength.

TOOLS AND MATERIALS
Pencil
Square
Mortise gauge
Bevel-edged chisel
Marking knife
Tenon saw
Coping saw
Mortise chisel
Wood glue and brush
Clamps
Bench plane

PARTS OF THE JOINT

In a T-bridle joint, the mortise part is simply an open mortise, which forms a U-shape in the end of the mortise piece. The "bridle," which is enclosed within the mortise, is formed by the tenon. It is similar to a double-sided half-lap and has a housing in both sides. The shoulders on the housings enable it to resist sideways racking very well.

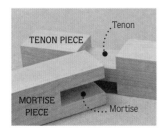

TENON PIECE ···· Tenon

MORTISE PIECE ···· Mortise

⚙ MARKING OUT THE MORTISE AND TENON

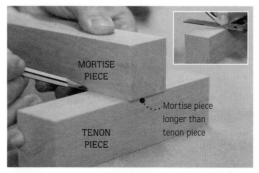

MORTISE PIECE

TENON PIECE

···· Mortise piece longer than tenon piece

1 Set the mortise piece at a right angle to the tenon piece so that it protrudes slightly, and mark the position of the shoulder in pencil on the mortise piece (pictured). Use a square and pencil to extend the shoulder line onto all four sides of the mortise piece (inset).

A

2 Set the mortise gauge to just over one third of the thickness of the mortise piece (A). Scribe the mortise width centrally along the end grain and down both faces to the shoulder mark.

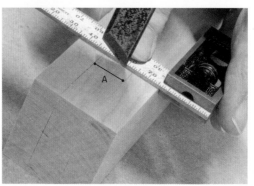

A

3 Scribe the shoulder marks between the scored width on both edges with a marking knife. Then mark the waste of the mortise for removal.

4 Place the mortise piece in position over the tenon piece and mark the position and dimensions of the joint.

5 Extend the marks around all four sides of the tenon piece, using a square and pencil.

TENON PIECE

6 With the mortise gauge still set at the width of the mortise (A), scribe the thickness of the tenon centrally between the marks on both edges of the tenon piece.

7 Mark the waste for removal. Then score the shoulder marks on both faces of the tenon piece, using a square and marking knife.

CUTTING THE MORTISE

1 Secure the piece in a vise and use a tenon saw to cut the mortise diagonally from the end grain to the shoulder mark.

2 Turn the piece in the vise and cut from the other side, being careful to stay within the marks.

3 Turn the piece in the vise for a final time and cut vertically through the cuts to the shoulder mark.

4 Make a relief cut through the center of the mortise to enable you to remove the waste.

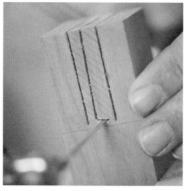

5 Release the waste by cutting from the relief cut to both edges of the mortise with a coping saw.

6 Using a mortise chisel, clean up the base of the mortise to the shoulder, removing any rough edges.

CUTTING THE TENON

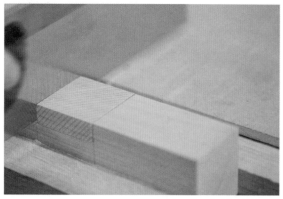

1 Place the tenon piece in a vise and cut the tenon shoulders with a tenon saw. Be sure to cut to the waste side of the lines.

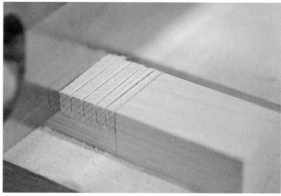

2 Make relief cuts through the waste. Turn the tenon piece upside down and repeat, cutting the shoulders and relief cuts.

3 Chop away the waste with a bevel-edged chisel, then repeat on the reverse face of the tenon piece.

4 Clean up the tenon on both sides by paring the base and edges of both sides with a mortise chisel.

5 Test-fit the joint and, if necessary, use a chisel to adjust the mortise and tenon in order to achieve a good fit.

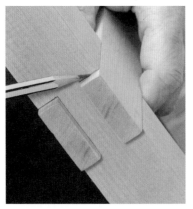

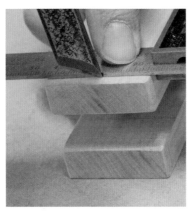

1 Assemble the joint and, using a pencil, mark the excess on the ends of the mortise piece.

2 Disassemble the joint and square the pencil lines on the end grains of the mortise onto both faces with a marking knife.

3 Glue the joint (inset) and assemble. Clamp and leave it to dry.

4 Once the glue has dried, cut along the scored lines with a tenon saw to remove most of the excess from the mortise ends.

5 Prepare the remaining mortise ends for planing by chiseling the edges. This will prevent the grain from breaking out when the ends are planed.

6 Use a bench plane to remove the remainder of the ends, planing them flush to the tenon piece.

THE FINISHED JOINT

CORNER-BRIDLE JOINT

The corner-bridle joint is essentially an open mortise and tenon. The exposed end grain makes it a very attractive joint, but it has no resistance to racking and relies on glue for its strength. A good example of the use of a corner-bridle joint is in chair making, where a leg can be securely attached to a solid seat with a triple corner bridle. The secret is that the gluing area is three times the size of the normal joint.

TOOLS AND MATERIALS

Pencil
Square
Mortise gauge
Marking knife
Tenon saw
Coping saw
Bevel-edged chisel
Wood glue and brush
Block plane

PARTS OF THE JOINT

This joint is used for two pieces of wood of the same dimensions. The tenon piece fits into a U-shaped open mortise. The end grains of both the mortise and the tenon are exposed, giving the joint its distinctive appearance.

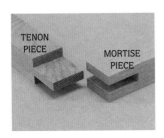

TENON PIECE

MORTISE PIECE

🌑 MARKING THE JOINT

1 Place the first piece of wood on top of the second at a right angle so that the edge of the first is just short of the end grain of the second. Mark around both edges. Square the marks around all four sides (inset). Reverse the pieces and mark up the second piece in the same way.

2 Set a mortise gauge to one third of the thickness of the wood. Scribe centrally around the end grain and down the edges to the marks on both pieces.

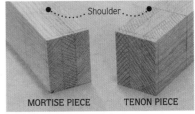

········ Shoulder ········

MORTISE PIECE   TENON PIECE

3 Mark the waste on both pieces—the central area of the mortise piece and the sides (cheeks) of the tenon. Score the cutting line at both shoulders with a marking knife.

🌑 CUTTING AND FINISHING THE JOINT

Set the mortise piece in a vise and remove the waste with a tenon saw and a coping saw, as described for a T-bridle joint, steps 1–6 (see pp.108–109). Set the tenon piece in a vise and cut as described for a basic mortise-and-tenon joint (see pp.91–95) (pictured). Clean up the sides, base, and shoulders of both parts with a chisel. Test-fit the joint (inset) and make any necessary adjustments. Glue the joint, assemble it, and when the glue is dry, plane the ends flush with a block plane.

THE FINISHED JOINT

COMB JOINT

The comb joint (also called a finger joint) is a simplified form of the through-dovetail joint (see pp.116–121). Although it has little mechanical strength, its large gluing surface area means that, once glued, it is very strong. The comb joint requires careful marking out but is quicker to make than a set of dovetails. It is useful for boxes and carcase pieces, and contrasting woods can be used for a decorative effect.

TOOLS AND MATERIALS

Square
Block plane
Marking gauge
Pencil
Dovetail saw
Coping saw
Bevel-edged chisel
Wood glue and brush
Clamps
Marking knife

PARTS OF THE JOINT

This joint consists of two matched sets of interlocking "fingers" (or pins). The pins of one part lodge in the sockets of the other. The joint is strongest when the two sets of pins are of equal size.

Pin
Socket

⚙ MARKING AND CUTTING THE FIRST PIECE

1 Check that both pieces of wood are square, which is essential to achieve an accurate joint. Make any necessary adjustments by planing.

2 Set a marking gauge to slightly more than the thickness of the wood (A). This will create slightly oversized pins that can be trimmed flush when the joint is complete.

3 Use the marking gauge to scribe measurement (A) on both faces and one edge of each of the two pieces being joined, to indicate the position of the shoulders.

4 Decide on the number and size of pins required, and mark the pins square across the end grain of the first piece.

5 Extend the pin marks with a square and pencil from the end grain down each face as far as the shoulder.

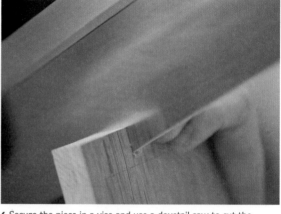

6 Secure the piece in a vise and use a dovetail saw to cut the pins vertically to the shoulder.

7 Remove the bulk of the waste with a coping saw, making a J-shaped cut into the adjacent vertical cut.

8 Turn the piece in the vise and cut the waste from the half pin with the dovetail saw.

9 Remove the remaining waste with a bevel-edged chisel, paring any excess material clean to the shoulder.

◗ MARKING THE SECOND PIECE

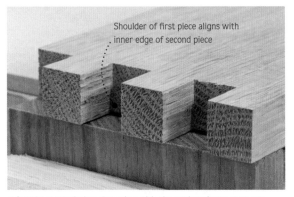

1 Set the second piece in a vise with the end grain uppermost. Place the pins of the first piece over the end grain of the second piece, aligned at the shoulder. The ends of the pins will slightly overhang the outer edge.

Shoulder of first piece aligns with inner edge of second piece

2 Use a marking knife to scribe the position of the pins on the end grain of the second piece.

3 Using a square and marking knife, reinforce the marks indicating the positions of the pins on the end grain of the second piece, then extend them down to the shoulder on both faces (inset).

◗ ASSEMBLING THE JOINT

1 Cut the pins as for the first piece. Test-fit the joint and adjust by paring with a chisel if necessary.

2 Glue and assemble the joint. Clamp the pieces. When the glue is dry, use a block plane to remove the excess from the ends of the pins.

THE FINISHED JOINT

THROUGH-DOVETAIL JOINT

In use since the time of the ancient Egyptians, the through-dovetail is the most well known of all dovetail joints. It is commonly used on boxes and carcases of all sizes because of its strength and decorative look.

Not only is it one of the most attractive joints in woodworking, it is also one of the best mechanically due to its strength in tension, so it is very sound in terms of its construction.

TOOLS AND MATERIALS

Dividers
Pencil
Square
Marking gauge
Marking knife
Dovetail marker
Dovetail saw
Coping saw
Band saw (optional)
Mortise chisel
Clamp
Bevel-edged chisel
Wood glue and brush
Hammer
Block plane

PARTS OF THE JOINT

The interlocking pattern of tails and pins is one of the strongest of all the woodworking joints. The through-dovetail is particularly strong when used in the construction of all four corners of a piece, such as a box, because it has great strength in tension. The spacing of the pins and tails is largely a matter of taste, although using small pins will avoid a machine-made look.

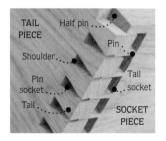

MARKING OUT THE TAILS AND PIN SOCKETS

1 Mark the chosen half-pin length on one end of the end grain of the tail piece. Set a pair of dividers to this length and transfer the measurement to the opposite end of the end grain.

2 Choose the number of pins and tail sockets required. Set the dividers to the estimated combined length of one tail and pin socket (A).

3 Walk the dividers from the first half-pin mark to the other. Because the dividers cross the second half-pin mark, the distance between the half-pin mark and the point of the dividers will be your full pin width. Adjust dividers and repeat the process as required to provide your desired pin width.

Mark each point of contact...

A

4 With the dividers set to the combined length of one tail and pin socket (A) selected in step 3, walk them from the first half-pin mark to the second, marking every point of contact. With the dividers still set to length (A), walk them from the second half-pin mark to the first half-pin mark, marking the new points of contact.

A C
  B

5 Using a pencil and square, extend all the marks that are between the half-pin marks across the end grain. The longer lengths (B) are those of the tails, and the shorter lengths (C) are those of the pin sockets.

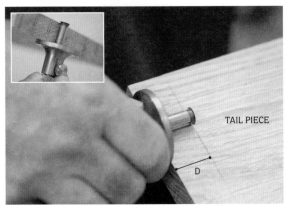

TAIL PIECE

D

6 Mark the shoulder (D) on the tail piece by setting a marking gauge to a fraction more than the thickness of the tail piece (inset), then scribing from the end grain across both faces.

D

7 Extend the shoulder line onto both edges by scribing with a marking knife, guided by a square.

B

8 Use a dovetail marker as a guide for marking the desired angle for the tails. Draw the angles of the tails and pin sockets to the shoulder on both faces in pencil.

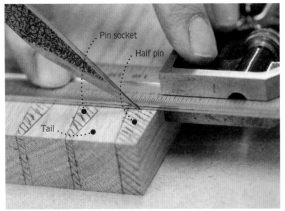

Pin socket
Half pin
Tail

9 Score the shoulders along the base of the half pins and pin sockets on both faces with a marking knife, avoiding the base of the tails.

1 Using a dovetail saw, cut down through the end grain along the marks. Set the wood at an angle in the vise so you can cut vertically down each mark.

2 Complete all the saw cuts down the parallel socket edges. Then adjust the position of the wood in the vise and saw through the other side of the tails.

3 Keep checking that you do not cut past the shoulder line on the side of the wood facing away from you.

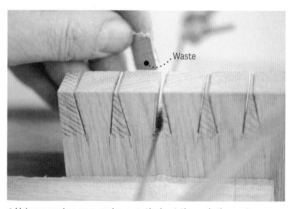

4 Using a coping saw, make a vertical cut through the center of each pin socket, then angle the cut to remove the waste.

5 Use a dovetail saw to remove the half pins at both ends of the joint, cutting to the waste side of the shoulder mark.

6 Secure the wood in a vise and use a mortise chisel to cut and square off the socket bases and edges.

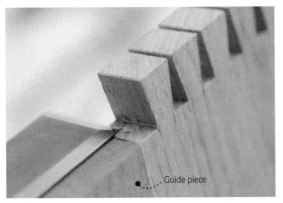

Guide piece

7 Clamp the tail piece against a squared guide piece. Use a bevel-edged chisel to pare the shoulders of the half-pin sockets so that they are clean and square to the marks.

8 Check that the socket bases are square at the shoulders by placing a square through each socket, against the face.

CUTTING TAILS ON A BAND SAW

If your piece requires lots of dovetails, using a band saw is a good way to cut them quickly and accurately. You can even cut more than one set at a time—when making drawers, for example, tape pairs of drawer sides together to cut both in one go. As well as cutting the tails themselves, you can also use the band saw to remove the waste in between them.

1 Make a cut with the band saw straight through the pin socket to the shoulder, and then make angled cuts along the tail marks.

2 Use the band saw to cut the shoulder of each of the half-pin sockets. Then remove the waste from each socket with a chisel, as described in step 6 (see opposite).

🪚 MARKING OUT THE PINS

SOCKET PIECE

D

1 Use the marking gauge, set to measurement D (slightly more than the thickness of the tail piece), to scribe the shoulder (the length of the pins) from the end grain across both faces of the socket piece.

Ends of tails slightly longer than thickness of socket piece

2 Secure the socket piece in a vise, and set the tail piece at right angles over the end grain, making sure the tail piece is precisely aligned at the edges and at the shoulder. Support and weight it to prevent any movement during marking up.

3 Use a marking knife to transfer the position of the tails and pin sockets from the tail piece to the end grain of the socket piece.

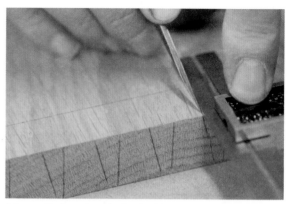

4 Square the lines down to the shoulder mark on both faces of the wood, using a marking knife and square.

CUTTING THE PINS

1 Using a dovetail saw, cut down to the shoulder mark on each side of the pins, taking care not to exceed the lines.

2 Use a coping saw to remove the waste from the tail sockets, ensuring that you follow the lines carefully.

3 Use a marking knife to scribe along the shoulder of the sockets, avoiding the base of the pins. Repeat on the other side.

GUIDE PIECE

4 Align a guide piece to the socket piece shoulder and use a chisel to clean up the sides and bases. Check that the bases are square (see step 8, Cutting the tails, p.119).

CUTTING PINS ON A BAND SAW

Although too delicate to be fully cut with a band saw, the pins can be roughly machined and the waste from the tail sockets removed.

1 Cut into the tail sockets at right angles with the band saw. Be sure to cut well clear of the marks.

2 Remove the waste by hand, using a coping saw to cut to the shoulder in each of the sockets.

ASSEMBLING THE JOINT

1 Assemble the joint. The fit should be snug. Make any necessary adjustments and then apply glue to the joint.

2 Tap the glued pieces into place using a hammer, protecting the wood with a block. Clamp if necessary.

3 When the glue is dry, place the joint in a vise and block-plane the ends of the pins and tails flush to both faces.

THE FINISHED JOINT

JOINTS USING COMMERCIAL CONNECTORS

A range of commercially produced connectors, most of which act like a loose tongue, can be used to add strength to joints. Dowels—a short length of doweling glued into a drilled hole—were the first type to be developed and have been used in the furniture industry for many years (see pp.126–130).

Biscuits (shown here) and dominos—pieces of compressed beech glued into a slot (see pp.124–125)—improve on the dowel by being stronger and because the specialist tools used to cut the slots are easy to use.

TOOLS AND MATERIALS

Square
Pencil
Biscuit joiner
Biscuits
Wood glue and brush
Ruler

PARTS OF THE JOINT

The biscuit fits into matching elliptical slots in the two joining faces, each of which houses exactly half of the biscuit. The biscuit acts in the same way as a tenon in a standard mortise-and-tenon joint (see p.91). Biscuits can be used either singly or as a double joint if there is sufficient thickness in the material. Using more biscuits and arranging them in a double setup increases the gluing surface area and makes the joint stronger.

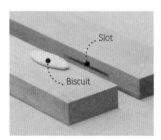

Slot

Biscuit

BISCUIT JOINTS

The biscuit is a very easy and effective means of quickly assembling a joint. The joiner is easy to set up and use, and the biscuit itself has a major advantage over the dowel—it is long grain and so forms a much stronger joint. The biscuit joint can be used in almost any configuration; it is especially good on carcase work with manufactured board material, and it can also be used in both corner joints and T-joints, as well as in divisions and miters.

MAKING AN EDGE-TO-EDGE BISCUIT JOINT

1 Place the two pieces of wood to be joined side-by-side and square a pencil mark across both pieces to indicate where the center of each slot will be. When marking out slots at the ends of each piece, ensure that you leave sufficient space for the length of the biscuit on either side of the center line.

2 Set the height of the biscuit joiner's cutting blade so that the slot will be cut in the middle of each piece of wood. You may need to raise either the base of the biscuit joiner or the piece of wood.

3 Adjust the controls of the blade to the correct setting for the size of biscuit that you plan to use. It should be marked with the different depths for standard biscuits.

4 Align the machine mark on the blade with the first pencil line on the first piece of wood, then machine the slot. Repeat at the other marked lines, then cut the slots in the other piece of wood.

5 Insert a biscuit into each of the slots along the edge of one of the pieces of wood.

6 Push the protruding biscuits into the slots in the other piece of wood to test the fit of the joints.

7 Once you are happy with the fit of the biscuits in the slots, apply glue inside and around the slots, then fit the joint together.

THE FINISHED JOINT

TOOLS AND MATERIALS

Square
Pencil
Domino joiner and cutters
Wood glue and brush
Dominos

PARTS OF THE JOINT

Each component of the domino joint contains a mortise, and the "tenon" is the domino itself—a rectangular-shaped lozenge with rounded, fluted sides that fits into the mortises and connects the pieces. When inserted in its mortise, the domino naturally creates "shoulders," just like a standard mortise-and-tenon (see p.91). Extra strength can be given to the joint by using two dominos alongside each other in a twin "tenon" setup.

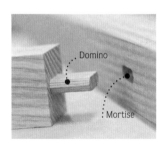

Domino

Mortise

DOMINO JOINTS

Similar in concept to the biscuit (see p.47 and p.122), the domino is even more effective and versatile, although it does not replace it. Essentially a floating tenon made of beech, the domino connector comes in different sizes and lengths for use in joints of different orientations and in components of different thicknesses. It is strong, partly due to its long-grain construction, and can be used in any setting in place of a standard mortise-and-tenon joint, including chairs, doors, and butt-jointed edges to frame-and-panel constructions. The only situation in which it cannot be employed is when a thin carcase material is used, such as manufactured board.

MAKING A DOMINO JOINT

1 Mark the position of the domino mortise in one edge of the first piece by drawing a line on the adjacent face.

2 Mark the position of the domino mortise in the second piece by drawing a line on the adjacent face.

3 Adjust the domino joiner to set the position of the mortise on the first piece, then adjust it to set the height (inset).

4 Adjust the fence to set the position of the cut, then align the joiner with the edge of the first piece of wood.

5 Set the depth of the mortise to be cut and fit a cutter to match the size of domino that you intend to use.

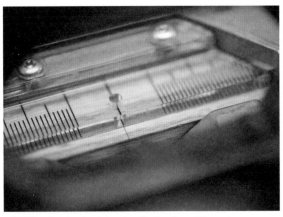

6 Position the domino joiner by aligning the guide mark on the machine with the line on the wood.

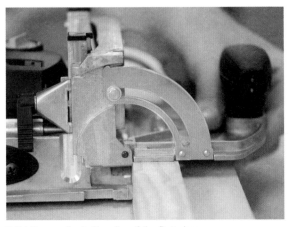

7 Cut the mortise in the edge of the first piece.

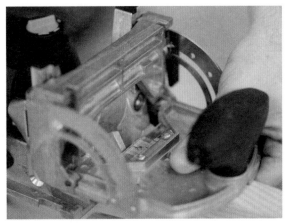

8 Reset the joiner for the second piece and cut the mortise in the marked position.

9 Insert the domino into one of the mortises (pictured), then join the pieces together to check the fit (inset). Once you are satisfied with the fit, apply glue to the mortises and fit the joint together.

THE FINISHED JOINT

TOOLS AND MATERIALS

Marking gauge
Pencil
Square
Drill and bits
Doweling
Center points
Mallet
Wood glue and brush

PARTS OF THE JOINT

Dowels consist of round pieces of wood that act, in constructional terms, like a series of mini-tenons inserted into holes—the equivalent of mortises—in each component. Commercially made dowels feature a series of flutes on them to relieve air pressure as they are inserted. Without this release of pressure, you may not be able to close the joint, especially once wet glue has been applied to the holes.

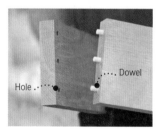

Hole ⋯⋯ Dowel

🔺 DOWEL JOINT USING CENTER POINTS

The main advantage of dowels is that they are quick to produce (see p.130) and can reinforce a simple butt joint very easily. They can be used on just about any section of wood and in any configuration and can offer a solution that wouldn't be possible with a conventional joint. They can be used to align butt-jointed edge joints, as in a corner joint, edge-to-face as in a T-joint, or as a mortise-and-tenon in a frame. In order to be effective, they must be marked out accurately, using center points or a jig. The disadvantage of dowels is the lack of long-grain contact, since they are normally inserted into the end grain. More than one dowel—arranged in a row if possible—can be used, which increases gluing area and strength.

MAKING A DOWEL JOINT

1 Use a marking gauge to scribe along the center of the end grain of the first piece, then place the piece in a vise.

2 Mark the position of each of the holes you require by squaring a pencil mark across the end grain.

3 Select a drill bit to match the diameter of the dowel.

4 Decide on the depth of the holes—usually up to half the thickness of the piece to be joined. Mark the drill bit to this depth and drill a hole at each marked position. Use a square to ensure that you drill vertically.

5 Insert a center point (selected to match the diameter of the dowel) into each of the holes in the end grain.

6 Position the piece to be joined over the end grain of the first piece, using a square to ensure it is centered. Use a mallet to tap the second piece so that the drilling positions are imprinted in it by the center points. Lift the second piece off and remove the center points from the first piece.

7 Support the piece in a vise and drill a hole in each of the marked positions to the same depth as in the first piece.

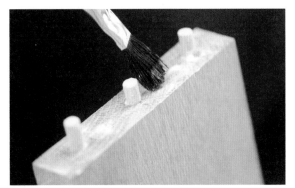

8 Glue the end-grain holes and insert the dowels. Apply glue to the surface of the end grain and fit the joint together.

THE FINISHED JOINT

DOWEL JOINT USING A COMMERCIAL JIG

Doweling jigs save the time spent marking out precise locations for the dowels and ensure a greater level of accuracy than can be achieved by other methods. However, jigs are only capable of jointing a range of thicknesses—this should be considered when designing a project. (The jigs assist in positioning the dowel in the center of a specified thickness.) Cheap versions do not provide the same degree of accuracy as high-quality jigs with metal guide bushes. Adjoining pieces (the sides of a drawer, for example) are clamped in alignment together face-to-face and worked on simultaneously.

SETTING UP THE JIG

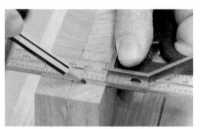

1 Place both pieces side-by-side in a vise and use a pencil and square to mark the position of each hole in their end grains.

2 Select a drill bit and bush of the same diameter as that of your chosen piece of doweling (inset).

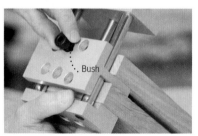

3 Place the pieces in the jig, then insert the first bush into the vertical hole that is centered over the thickness of the end grain.

4 Choose a horizontal hole for the second bush so that it lines up with the first bush.

5 Place the E-clamp in position to keep the pieces equally spaced. When working with long lengths of wood, use an additional spacer piece of the same width as the E-clamp. Secure the whole setup in position in the vise.

6 Loosen the main part of the jig and position it so that the bush is centered over the mark for the first hole. Tighten the jig in position.

SETTING UP THE DRILL BITS

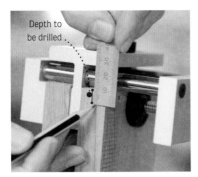

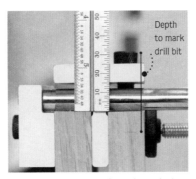

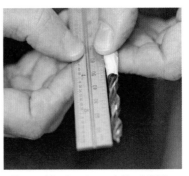

1 Determine the depth to be drilled—a maximum of half the thickness of the stock. Mark the edge of the piece that will be drilled through the end grain to the required depth.

2 Measure the distance from the end grain to the top of the bush and add this distance to the depth to be drilled.

3 Use masking tape to mark the drill bit to the combined length of the drilling depth and the distance from the end grain to the top of the bush.

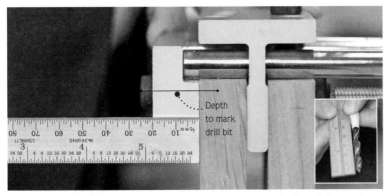

4 For the horizontal drilling position, measure the distance from the face of the wood to the top of the bush and add it to the depth to be drilled (pictured). Mark a second drill bit to the combined measurement (inset). Mark the tape on the bits to indicate which jig position—vertical or horizontal—each bit should be used for.

5 Insert the correct bit and drill into the vertical position in the first piece, being careful not to drill past the marked depth.

6 Use the second bit (marked for the horizontal position) to drill into the face of the second piece.

7 Move the jig to align with the next marked dowel position, then drill vertically and horizontally as before. Drill the remaining marked positions in the same way.

PREPARING THE DOWELS AND GLUING THE JOINT

1 Use a chisel to cut a V-groove along the length of the doweling to hold the glue.

2 Calculate the length of each dowel—the combined depth of each pair of holes, minus $\frac{1}{16}$ in (2 mm) for glue. Cut the doweling into the number of lengths required to join each pair of holes.

3 Smooth the ends of each dowel with sandpaper to remove any rough edges and ease the fit in the holes.

4 Check the fit of the dowels in the end-grain holes, then connect to the second piece to test the fit of the joint.

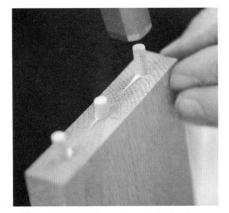

5 Disassemble the joint and apply glue to the holes and the end grain. Tap the dowels into the holes and assemble the joint.

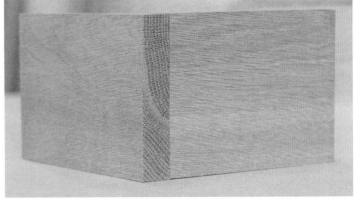

THE FINISHED JOINT

GLUING AND CLAMPING

Gluing and clamping are important stages in any woodworking project. Glue has long been used to join wood and is often the strongest part of a joint. You should keep more than one type of glue in your workshop because different glues have different properties and therefore different advantages for the woodworker.

GLUES AND GLUING

Because most glues are water based, evaporation plays a key role in the curing process. Three types of glue are most useful: polyvinyl acetate (PVA), polyurethane, and powdered-resin wood glue.

APPLYING GLUE

Applying glue straight from a bottle
For some jobs—such as running a line of glue along the edge of a board (above)—you can apply glue directly from the bottle.

Applying glue with a brush Use a brush to apply glue to joint areas, such as mortises and tenons, and for accessing hard-to-reach places, such as dovetail sockets.

Applying glue with a roller A roller is useful for applying glue to large surfaces, since it can help spread the glue evenly and quickly.

CLAMPING

An essential part of the "gluing up" process, clamps (see p.29) are used to hold a carcase together until the glue has had time to fully cure. Clamps are also used to check for squareness. This is a vital consideration—if just one section of a piece is not square, it can affect the whole work.

Clamping miter joints
There are several ways to clamp miter joints. However, if they are being used to form a frame, one of the best methods is to use a band clamp. This fits around the frame and forces the joints together as the clamp is tightened (see right). Always remember to check for squareness.

Clamping mortise-and-tenon joints
Mortise-and-tenon joints must be properly clamped to ensure that the shoulders are closed up and to prevent any air trapped in the mortise from opening up the joint before the glue has cured. It is usually best to use a sash clamp for this type of joint.

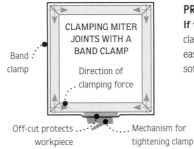

CLAMPING MITER JOINTS WITH A BAND CLAMP

Band clamp

Direction of clamping force

Off-cut protects workpiece

Mechanism for tightening clamp

Direction of clamping force

Sash clamp

Tommy bar for tightening clamp

CLAMPING MORTISE-AND-TENON JOINTS WITH A SASH CLAMP

Off-cut protects workpiece

PROTECTING THE WOOD
If the piece being clamped is not protected, clamping may cause considerable damage. The easiest form of protection is to place a piece of softwood between the jaws and the workpiece.

JIGS AND TEMPLATES

A jig is a device designed to hold a workpiece or guide a tool in a specific way. They are frequently used in combination with machines, improving both accuracy and safety and having the added benefit of speeding up a process. Templates share many of the attributes of a jig, but they are generally flat design patterns of the outline of a component. MDF is an excellent choice of material for jigs and templates because it does not expand or shrink as solid wood does, thereby maintaining accuracy. In general, it is better to use screws rather than glue on a jig, as screws will enable it to be adjusted or dismantled.

JIG FOR DRILLING HOLES

Drilling a number of accurately placed holes can be very time-consuming without a jig. The jig shown here is one for drilling a repeat pattern of holes in the sides of a cabinet with adjustable shelves. The holes will receive metal shelf pegs. The sheet of MDF should be of the same size as the component or designed to line up with an edge or corner. Use an off-cut underneath the MDF for drilling into. Similar jigs can be made with an additional fence for drilling into edges.

1 Mark out the positions of the holes onto a piece of MDF, then drill the holes through it. Use a square as a guide when drilling to ensure that the hole is perpendicular.

2 Locate the jig over the workpiece and secure it with a clamp. Drill through the holes in the jig to the required depth.

JIG FOR TAPERING WIDTH

This simple jig, which is for use on a table saw, is quick to make and effective. It can be used to cut the same taper on a variety of widths (by adjusting the side fence), but it is normally used for cutting identically shaped workpieces. After sawing, the edge will need planing. Alternatively, use a rectangular base, an angled or adjustable fence, an end stop, and toggle clamps to hold the workpiece in position. This kind of jig acts as a sled that is passed through the saw. For further information on how to use a table saw safely, see p.15.

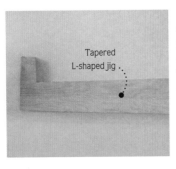

Tapered L-shaped jig

1 Mark out and cut the desired angle from a piece of wood, leaving an L-shape at the end to act as a stop during sawing.

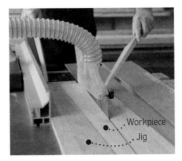

Workpiece
Jig

2 Position the workpiece on the table saw, located in the jig with the end butted up to the L-shape. Adjust the side fence to the required dimension. Feed the work through the saw using push sticks as shown.

⊞ TEMPLATE FOR CUTTING A CURVE

This method produces smooth outlines that need only light sanding. It also provides a means of reproducing identical workpieces. The bulk of the waste is removed with a jigsaw and the finishing cut is made with a bearing-guided cutter. The bearing of the cutter traces the shape of the template. The same method can be used for routing intricate shapes.

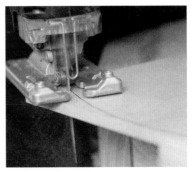

1 Mark both ends and the center of the curve on the top edge of the template. Hammer pins into the marked positions. Place the ruler behind the center pin and in front of the side pins to create a curve. Draw along the back of the ruler to transcribe the curve onto the template (inset).

2 Remove the ruler and the pins and cut to the waste side of the line with a jigsaw (pictured) or band saw.

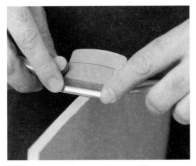
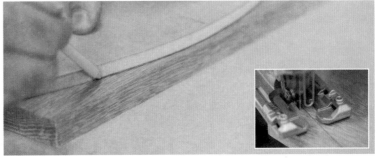

3 Use a flat spokeshave to smooth out the curve to the line. Finish with sandpaper.

4 Draw around the template onto the workpiece (pictured). Remove the template and cut along the line drawn with a jigsaw. Stay $\frac{1}{16}$in (2mm) to the waste side of the line (inset).

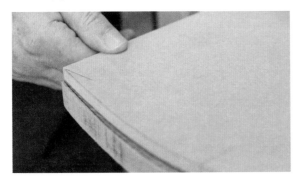

5 Position the template over the workpiece, with the curved edge of the template aligned precisely with the pencil line, and clamp in position for routing.

6 Fit a bearing-guided cutter in the router, adjust the router so that the bearing of the cutter aligns with the edge of the template, and trim off the waste.

VENEERING

Veneering was invented in ancient Egypt and probably had its heyday in the 17th century. More recently, it has made a comeback for ecological reasons; because of the way veneers are cut (see p.164), their thinness makes much better use of the tree and, therefore, the world's wood resources in general.

TOOLS AND MATERIALS

Grease pencil and lead pencil
Metal ruler
Scalpel
Shooting board
Bench plane
Veneer tape
Square (optional)
Paper
Off-cut blocks (for cauls)
PVA glue and roller
Off-cut boards (for clamping)
C-clamps
Sash clamps
Cabinet scraper
Fine-grade sandpaper

ELEMENTS OF A VENEERED PIECE

The core (also called "groundwork" or "substrate") is the structural component (made from MDF or solid wood) beneath the veneer. MDF is the ideal core because it is dimensionally stable, so the glue bond remains intact. As well as a face veneer, a balancing or "backing" veneer must be glued to the reverse side. If a balancing veneer is not used, the board will always warp, no matter how thick it is.

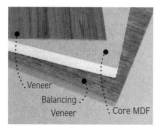

Veneer
Balancing Veneer
Core MDF

⚙ VENEERING A SURFACE

Traditionally, veneers were stuck to a solid wood core using hot animal glue (see p.142). Hot glue is applied to the wood core and the veneer is laid in the direction of the grain, then rubbed down with a veneer hammer until the veneer is flat and the glue has cooled. The veneer can be laid on a flat or curved surface without clamping, but solid wood is inherently unstable, so the glue bond weakens over time. Contact adhesive can be used in place of hot animal glue. In the veneering technique described below, PVA glue can be substituted by powder resin or specialized glues.

CUTTING THE VENEER

1 Lay the core MDF over the face veneer. (When veneering MDF, the grain direction usually runs along the length of the core.) Mark the length with $\frac{1}{16}$ in (2 mm) extra at each end. For large areas, it is likely you will have to join two or more sheets together side-by-side. Mark extra sheets as required.

2 Cut the veneer along the marks using a scalpel (inset). Mark the order of the pieces of veneer. If you are using more than one piece of veneer, butt the pieces together loosely and check that they are larger than your core material on all sides (pictured). Where there is excess veneer, mark and trim, leaving at least $\frac{3}{16}$ in (5 mm) extra width.

BALANCING THE VENEER

1 Mark the balancing veneer for the reverse side of the core in the same way as the face veneer and cut it to length (inset). A less expensive or less attractive veneer may be used, but the grain must run in the same direction as the face veneer. Mark extra sheets as required.

2 Check the fit of the core material over the balancing veneer, ensuring there is at least ³⁄₁₆ in (5 mm) extra on all sides.

SHOOTING THE VENEER

1 For veneers that are to be joined side-by-side, use a shooting board (see p.51) to trim the inside edge of each of the pieces, clamping them firmly in place (inset). Use a no.7 bench plane to shoot the edge, being sure to cut in the direction of the grain to avoid tearing.

2 Check that the inside edge of the veneer is square along a straight edge, such as the side of a plane.

JOINING AND TRIMMING THE PIECES

1 Where veneers require joining, arrange them side-by-side on a flat surface in the order already marked. Push the pieces together tightly so that there is no gap, then place 1¹⁵⁄₁₆ in (50 mm) long strips of veneer tape at 5⅞ in (150 mm) intervals along the joint.

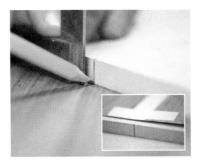

2 If the joint in the face veneers must be centered on the core, mark center lines on the edge of the core as required. Mark center lines on the tape on the face veneer to correspond with the marks on the core (inset).

3 Align the center marks, then mark the excess veneer around the edge of the core, allowing for a ¹⁄₁₆ in (2 mm) overhang (inset). Trim the excess with a scalpel (pictured), using a metal ruler as a guide.

PREPARING TO GLUE THE VENEER

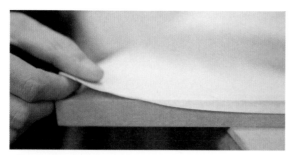

1 Prepare for gluing by taping paper to one surface of a board that is 3¹⁵/₁₆ in (100 mm) longer and wider than the core. Prepare two boards in this way.

2 Make sufficient specially shaped blocks, known as cauls, to clamp at 5⅞ in (150 mm) intervals around the piece. Use a plane to taper the cauls slightly—about ¹/₁₆ in (2 mm)—on one side at each end. This ensures that when clamped at either end, pressure is also exerted in the middle of the piece. Untapered cauls will also be needed.

GLUING THE VENEER

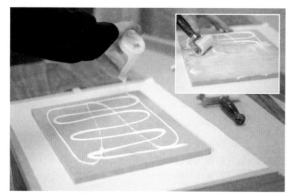

1 Spread PVA adhesive onto the face of the core material. Use a roller to spread the glue evenly (inset).

2 Place the face veneer face down on a surface and place the glued core over it, aligning the center seam of the veneer to the center marks on the edge of the core (inset).

3 Apply PVA adhesive to the other face of the core and spread it in the same way as in step 1.

4 Place the balancing veneer face down. Turn the core over and place the second glued surface on top of the balancing veneer. Tape all three elements together at the edges (inset).

5 Place the veneered piece between the two paper-covered clamping boards prepared earlier (see step 1, Preparing to glue the veneer, opposite). Keep the face veneer uppermost when clamping.

6 Clamp with the cauls on top and the untapered blocks beneath (inset). Tighten the clamps until no gap is visible between the boards and the tapered ends of the cauls.

FINISHING THE VENEER

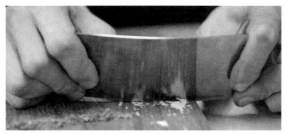

1 Trim the edges of both the face and balancing veneers. Use a knife or scalpel to score the excess (inset). Remove the excess by planing on a shooting board. Do not exert too much force; let the weight of the plane do the work. The edge of veneers with twisted grain may be sanded flush rather than planed.

2 Remove the tape from the face of the veneer using a cabinet scraper. After removing the tape, continue scraping to remove marks on the veneer. A pad sander may be used instead of a scraper for large areas, but take care not to oversand. Lightly sand the face of the veneer with fine-grade sandpaper to finish.

STRIP-EDGING VENEER

Covering the edge of a veneered board with a strip of the same face veneer has the advantage of a perfect color match. The veneer is applied in much the same way as for the face and must overlap the stock all around.

CUTTING THE VENEER

1 Cut the veneer for the edges. First, cut one straight edge with a scalpel, using a metal ruler as a guide.

2 Using the edge to be veneered as a guide, mark the width of the edging piece of veneer, making it just a little bit wider than the stock.

3 Cut the veneer with a scalpel, using a metal ruler as a guide. Then, cut the edging pieces to length across the grain.

GLUING AND CLAMPING THE VENEER STRIP

1 Prepare the blocks for the clamps by sticking packing tape along the side that will be in contact with the veneer. This prevents any glue that seeps out from sticking the block to the veneer.

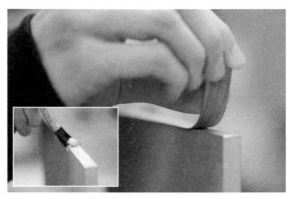

2 Put the core piece in a vise, then apply PVA adhesive to the edge of the core piece with a brush (inset). Place the veneer in position along the glued edge (pictured), being careful to avoid spreading glue on the face of the veneer.

3 Press the veneer firmly onto the edge. It is a good idea to use a clean roller to do this, if possible.

4 Secure the veneer in place using veneer tape.

5 Remove the core from the vise and use off-cuts to raise it above the surface of the workbench.

6 Set the taped block prepared in step 1 alongside the glued edge. If you wish to, you can apply veneer to two opposing edges and clamp them simultaneously.

7 Clamp using sash clamps above and below the piece. Wipe away excess glue with a clean, damp cloth. (Turn the core over to clean the other side.) When the glue has dried, remove the clamps and trim the excess veneer with a knife or block plane and sand flush. Take great care not to sand more than is necessary to avoid damaging the veneers.

FINISHING TECHNIQUES

Finishing describes the process of creating a final finish that is both protective and decorative. Depending on the nature of the workpiece and various functional and esthetic requirements, the timber may need to be sanded; the grain and knots filled; the surface resanded; the wood primed; and the surface painted, varnished, oiled, waxed, or distressed. The exact procedure will depend on the character of the project, the type of timber, any functional requirements, and personal likes and dislikes.

PREPARING SURFACES

The level of preparation required will depend on the nature of the timber, but the surface may need to be sanded, planed, scraped, filled, bleached, stained, or otherwise modified. This work must be carried out before a final finish is applied.

REPAIRING HOLES

If you have clearly visible holes in your workpiece, you may wish to fill them before applying a final finish. To do this, use wood filler or plug the hole with a peg of similar-looking wood. After you have applied a finish, you can fill small holes using colored wax filler. If, for example, you are presented with a hole in an oak workpiece that is going to be varnished or oiled, the hole must first be drilled out, then plugged with a plug cut from the same cut of wood and from the same face, edge, or end grain within the wood. This procedure is best carried out with a drill and plug set.

Spreading filler
Using a flexible filling knife, press the filler firmly into the hole. For small holes (inset), smear wax filler into the area with your thumb.

USING SCRAPERS

A scraper is a thin, flexible sheet of super-hard steel with a sharp, burred edge. It is used for smoothing flat or curved surfaces prior to sanding.

Using a scraper plane
Secure the workpiece to the bench and work in the same direction as the grain. Be sure to remove shavings and not dust—removing dust is a sign that the blade needs to be sharpened.

Using a cabinet scraper
Hold the scraper at each end to create a curve, lean it forward at 45 degrees, and work in the direction of the grain. When all tears in the grain have been removed, the wood is ready for sanding.

USING A RANDOM ORBITAL SANDER

Orbital sanders (see p.44) with large rectangular bases are ideal for material removal and coarse sanding but can also be used for fine sanding.

Random sanding
Work up and down the surface of the workpiece. Do not exert pressure because the weight of the sander is sufficient to do the work. The random action of the machine helps prevent ring marks.

SANDING BY HAND

Hand sanding is sometimes favored over power sanding because it is quieter and tends to produce less dust. For very fine work, it is also far better to sand by hand to avoid ring marks; for some shaped and fretted workpieces, sanding by hand is the only option.

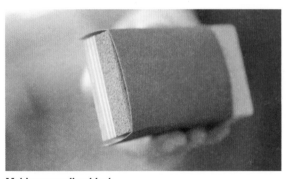

Making a sanding block
Glue cork to an off-cut to make a block approximately 4¼ x 2⅜ x 1³⁄₁₆ in (110 x 60 x 30 mm).

Sanding a flat surface
Sand back and forth in the direction of the grain until you have covered the whole surface. Change to a finer grit of paper and repeat the process, using progressively finer paper from 120–240 grit.

Removing arrises
Use a cork sanding block and work in the direction of the grain. The flexibility of the cork produces a rounded edge. For a sharper, beveled effect, use a wooden sanding block.

Supporting the workpiece
Small components can be held in a vise, leaving both hands free to work the sanding block. This is highly efficient and allows greater control.

SANDING AN AWKWARD SHAPE

Wrap, hold, and support the sandpaper in your hands and work the surface with a gentle yet firm stroking action. Constantly reshape your hands and modify the pressure, allowing your hands to be guided by your sense of touch.

SANDING A SMALL OBJECT

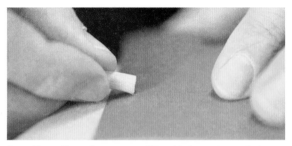

Sometimes the only way you will be able to sand a small piece is to rub it across sandpaper stuck down to a flat surface.

SEALING, STAINING, AND FINISHING

Once the workpiece has been sanded to the required finish (this is a judgment that will vary hugely from workpiece to workpiece and woodworker to woodworker), the timber may need to be stained to add texture and color; sealed to stabilize the surface of the wood; and finished with wax, paint, or varnish to give it texture and esthetic appeal.

FINISHING OPTIONS

FINISH	ADVANTAGES	DISADVANTAGES	APPLICATION METHODS
Danish oil (Low sheen; interior/exterior use)	• Easy to apply and restore • Suitable for all types of timber • Does not chip, crack, or peel • Oils with stain added are available	• Substantially darkens wood • Time-consuming to apply • Less protective than lacquer/varnish	Apply with a brush or cloth and wipe excess from surface. Allow 6 hours to dry. De-nib after first coat. Apply two more coats. Use wax to improve the luster (interior wood).
Tung oil (Low sheen; interior/exterior use)	• Easy to apply and restore • Suitable for all types of timber • Does not chip, crack, or peel	• Has a long drying time • Time-consuming to apply • Less protective than lacquer/varnish	Apply with a brush or cloth and wipe excess from surface. Allow 24 hours to dry. De-nib after first coat. Apply two more coats. Use wax to improve the luster (interior wood).
Wax polish (Medium sheen; interior use)	• Easy to restore • Suitable for all types of timber • Does not chip, crack, or peel • Dark stain polishes are available	• Requires reapplying/rebuffing • Time-consuming to apply • Less protective than lacquer/varnish	Apply with a cloth or 000-grade steel wool and allow to dry for 15 minutes before buffing to a sheen using a cloth or burnishing brush.
Hard wax oil (Low sheen; interior use)	• Easy to apply and renovate • Suitable for all types of timber • Wear-resistant; does not peel or flake • Does not darken wood significantly	• Less protective than lacquer/varnish	Apply undiluted using a synthetic brush; follow direction of grain. Wipe off excess; allow 4–6 hours to dry. Apply second coat. Buff with a soft cloth to increase the shine.
French polish (High sheen; interior use)	• Quick to repair • Color can be fine-tuned/matched • White polish available for white woods • Highly resistant to cracking	• Less protective than lacquer/varnish	Apply several coats using cotton wool inside cotton cloth. Leave 30 minutes between coats; allow to dry overnight. Apply 6+ additional coats. Remove streaking with methylated spirits.
Polyurethane varnish (Matte–high sheen; interior/exterior use)	• Easy to apply • Suitable for all types of timber • Durable • More protective than polish or lacquer	• Shows brush marks and dust • High build can detract from the wood • Darkens wood substantially • Can delaminate or yellow	Apply with a synthetic brush. Brush in direction of grain. First application can be diluted. Allow to dry before de-nibbing. Reapply a second no-diluted coat. Can also be sprayed (see lacquer).
Acrylic varnish (Matte–high sheen; interior/exterior use)	• Easy to apply • Suitable for all types of timber • Low odor, water based, and fast drying • Does not darken wood significantly	• High build can detract from wood • Prolonged exposure to skin oils/sweat can soften finish • Can delaminate or yellow	Apply with a synthetic brush in the same way as polyurethane varnish.
Wax finish varnish (Low sheen; interior/exterior)	• Easy to apply • Has appearance and feeling of wax but gives greater protection • Low odor, water based, and fast drying • Almost no darkening of wood	• Prolonged exposure to skin oils/sweat can soften finish • Can delaminate and yellow	Apply with a synthetic brush in the same way as polyurethane varnish.
Cellulose lacquer (Matte–high sheen; interior)	• Quick to apply; high build; self-leveling • Suitable for all types of timber • High level of protection • Almost no darkening of wood	• Spray room setup required; high odor; hazardous and wasteful • Can crack, delaminate, or yellow • Not possible to restore • Disallows patina	Requires ventilated spraying area and equipment. Thin first coat and allow to dry for 30 minutes. After de-nibbing, apply a second undiluted coat. Apply further coats for greater protection.
Acid catalyst (cold cure) lacquer (Matte–high sheen; interior)	• Fast application, high build, and self leveling • Suitable for all types of timber • Very high level of protection • Almost no darkening	• Spray room setup required; high odor; hazardous and wasteful • Chipping, cold-checking (cracking), and delaminating • Disallows patina and may yellow	Apply in the same way as cellulose lacquer, but mix in an acid catalyst hardener before spraying. Precatalyst lacquer has the hardener already mixed in.

RESTORING FURNITURE

Your main aim when restoring a piece of antique furniture should always be to return it to its original condition—both in terms of functionality and appearance—in a sympathetic and inconspicuous way.

PRINCIPLES OF RESTORATION

The first principle of furniture restoration says that every repair that is made should be reversible. This prevents the piece from being permanently altered and means that any repairs can themselves be revisited at a future date without the integrity of the original piece being compromised. While this principle applies to all restoration techniques, it is most relevant to the choice of glue (see Using animal glue, right). The second principle states that original surfaces should be preserved wherever possible. (This applies to contemporary as well as antique furniture.) All wooden surfaces change color over time, so any careless work with a plane or chisel will remove the oxidized surface to reveal the original color of the wood, causing difficulties when repolishing. If you are unsure as to how to proceed with a project—especially if the furniture is valuable—consult a trained restorer before you start. To restore a piece of furniture, it is sometimes necessary to dismantle its parts.

USING ANIMAL GLUE

Animal glue, which is usually made from the hooves and hides of animals such as cows and horses, was commonly used in the construction of antique furniture. Although it has an unpleasant smell, animal glue is as strong as most modern glues and, because it is water soluble and melts when heated, it has the advantage of being reversible. For these reasons—compatibility with the original glue, strength, and reversibility—animal glue should be the adhesive of choice when repairing and restoring antique furniture.

REPAIRING VENEERS

Veneers (see pp.134–135 and pp.164–165) are thin, decorative sheets of wood fitted onto a solid core. Any veneer covering of an antique will have been attached using animal glue (see above), so a loose veneer can often be secured by reactivating the old glue using heat. A technique called "hot blocking" can be successful. This involves heating a block of MDF or plywood and placing it on top of a sheet of brown paper over the loose veneer. Pressure is then applied to the block with a clamp or weights. The heat from the hot block should soften the glue and the clamp or weights on the block will hold the veneer in contact with the glue while it cools and sets again. If this is not successful, warm animal glue will need to be introduced under the veneer, using a syringe.

FRENCH POLISHING

French polish is made from a natural product called shellac—a secretion from the lac insect that is dissolved in alcohol. French polishing involves applying numerous coats of shellac with a brush or a pad. Each successive coat slightly softens the previous one, resulting in a homogenous buildup of polish. These layers are again slightly softened and evenly distributed around the piece of furniture using a pad, alcohol, and applied pressure. This technique burnishes the polish, ultimately achieving the high, blemish-free shine.

REMOVING WATER MARKS AND STAINS

Marks and stains on an antique surface can usually be categorized as either "white" or "black." If the mark is white or light-colored, it is usually located on the surface film of the polish. If the mark is black or dark-colored, it is usually located on the wood itself, underneath the polish. The white, ring-shaped marks can be dealt with using a very fine abrasive to "cut" the marks out of the polish. A traditional way of doing this is to use a paste made of cigar ash mixed with a small amount of vegetable oil. Alternatively, use burnishing cream or fine steel wool (0000 grade) with a little paste wax.

WORK SAFELY

Although oxalic acid is found naturally in many edible plants—like parsley, spinach, and chard—in its purified form, it is extremely toxic and corrosive. Wear the correct personal protective gear, including gloves and goggles to protect your hands and eyes from splashes, and a dust mask to protect your respiratory tract from noxious fumes. (Always work in a well-ventilated area.) Keep a supply of water at hand so that you can wash yourself if splashed. If swallowed, drink plenty of milk or water. Store oxalic acid safely and out of reach of children.

REMOVING MARKS AND STAINS

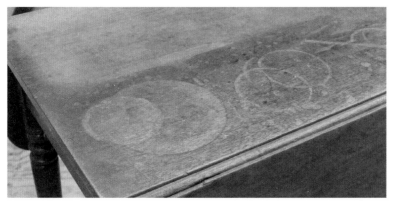

1 To remove marks and stains from a damaged surface, first use fine steel wool (0000 grade) and paste wax to remove the surface polish. This will remove any "white" marks and allow you to access any "black" stains ingrained in the wood itself.

2 Apply a coating of oxalic acid to the wood. This will reduce the staining. Take great care when using oxalic acid.

3 Wash off any oxalic acid residue with water. Using a pad, apply layers of shellac. Carefully distribute it to produce an even finish.

4 Apply more layers of shellac as required and continue to work the polish around the surface until you achieve a high finish.

5 You may wish to soften the shine of the shellac by applying a layer of wax. This will also help protect the polished surface from water.

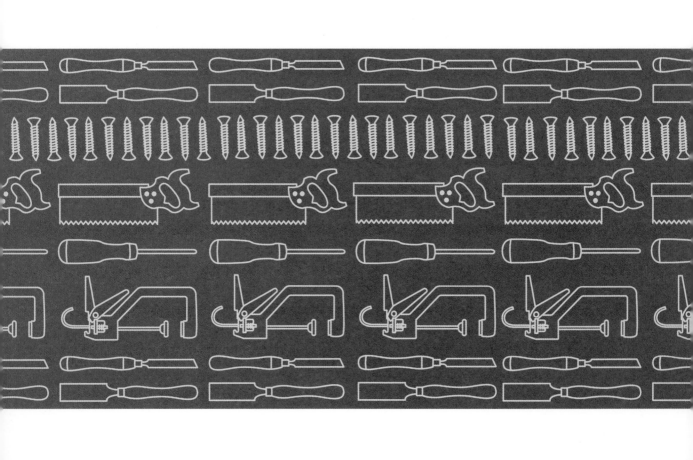

WOODS

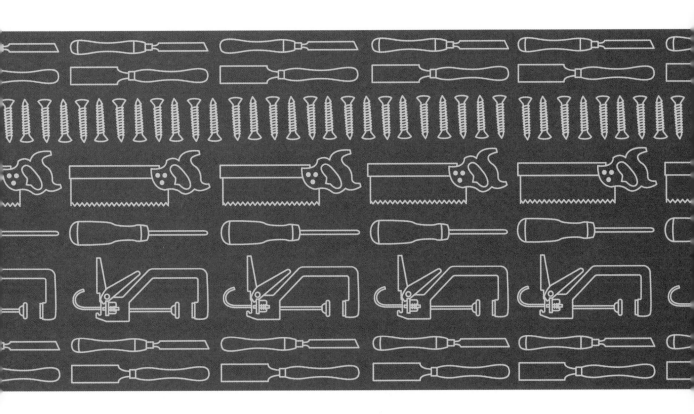

INTRODUCTION

Wood is a sustainable commodity if managed responsibly. Each species of tree produces timber with different qualities, meaning that there is a vast array of woods available for a wide range of functions.

TYPES OF WOOD

Timbers are classed as softwoods or hardwoods. This is based not on the actual hardness of the wood, but on the botanical classification of the species. The trunk of a tree consists of several distinct layers (see p.148 and p.153). Trees growing in seasonal environments commence growth each spring, producing the earlywood. Later in the season, the latewood is produced, which is denser, has smaller cells, and is usually darker. This results in well-defined annual rings, while tropical trees growing in areas without distinct seasons do not have clear rings. The outer, youngest parts of the trunk form the sapwood and the inner, older parts comprise the heartwood. Appearance and physical properties dictate a timber's end uses. The appearance is a combination of the wood's grain, texture, and figure (see opposite). The way in which wood is converted (sawn) can accentuate special kinds of figuring and will also determine its stability (see below). A timber's physical and working qualities are described in many ways and vary from species to species.

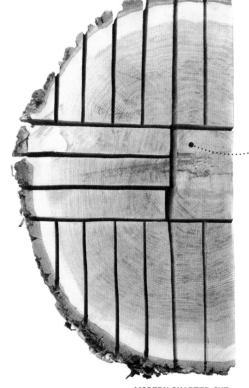

MODERN QUARTER-CUT

Converting a log
If a log is sawed "through-and-through," wastage is minimal, but the boards may warp. Commercial quarter-cutting of a log produces boards that are more stable and less likely to warp.

Heart of trunk is cut square and discarded

Log is sliced straight through in line with the grain

THROUGH-AND-THROUGH

WOOD TERMS

Density	Density is a measure of the weight of a given volume of wood dried to a standard moisture content. Density is often linked with hardness, strength, and ease of working.
Durability	A timber's durability—its resistance to fungal decay—is important in deciding whether it is suitable for outdoor use. Some woods are also notably susceptible (while others are resistant) to insect attack.
Figure	Figure is the wood's surface pattern and can be the result of contrasting streaks of color, conspicuous growth rings, grain pattern, knots, defects, or other natural features.
Grain	Grain describes the orientation of the wood's fibers within the tree. Straight grain is where the fibers lie parallel along the trunk. Interlocked grain occurs when the fibers alternate every few years between growing in a left-handed spiral and a right-handed spiral. Spiral grain is where the direction of the spiral is constant. Wavy-grained wood has fibers in regular short waves. Wood can also have irregular grain.
Heartwood	Nonfunctioning xylem tissue at the center of the trunk is called heartwood. It is darker than sapwood, more durable, and more resistant to insect attack.
Medullary rays	These are bands of cells that grow at 90 degrees to the growth rings. They are distinctive in some woods, such as oak (see Hardwood trunk p.153), while barely visible in others (see Softwood trunk, p.148).
Sapwood	The comparatively soft and perishable wood from the outer part of the trunk is called sapwood. While the tree is still alive, this xylem tissue transports water and minerals and stores food. Sapwood thickness varies between species.
Species name	Timber can have many common and commercial names, which can vary from place to place. For example, the wood known as American sycamore in the US is called American plane in the UK. So for positive identification, the species' scientific name must be used—in this case, *Platanus occidentalis*.
Stability	Even after seasoning (drying), wood reacts to seasonal changes in atmospheric humidity by expanding and contracting. The degree to which this occurs is described as the wood's stability.
Texture	Texture describes the size of the pores and rays in wood. Wood with a coarse texture has large pores, which may need to be filled before a finish is applied.

WORK SAFELY

Wood dust can be a hazard in the workshop because it can irritate the eyes, skin, and respiratory tract. Depending on the species of wood, inhaled dust may lead to shortness of breath or cause allergic bronchial asthma, rhinitis, nosebleeds, headaches, or nausea. In the worst cases, the dust of a particular species, such as the blackbean, can be carcinogenic. It is therefore important to wear protective equipment, such as a face mask, goggles, and gloves (see p.53), when the woodwork technique produces a large amount of dust, and use a dust extractor if possible.

ENDANGERED SPECIES

Illegal logging and overexploitation have led to a shortage of some timbers. When buying timber, therefore, it is important to ensure that it has come from responsible sources—look for the stamp of a recognized body, such as that of the Forest Stewardship Council™. Recycled timber should also be considered.

SOFTWOODS

Softwoods are the timbers of a group of trees that are classified as gymnosperms, which means that their seeds are "naked." Many of the softwood species are conifers. (They bear their seeds in cones.) The trees have needlelike or scalelike leaves, and most are evergreens.

🪚 DISTINGUISHING FEATURES

Timber from softwoods is characterized by the contrasting shades of the earlywood and latewood tissues, giving many softwoods a strong growth-ring figure. Although many softwoods are softer than many hardwoods, there is a large amount of overlap between the two groups. Softwood timber often contains resin ducts, but it has none of the vessels found in hardwoods (see p.153), only the much smaller tracheids (elongated cells that transport water). In reaction to mechanical stress, softwood trees produce compression wood (on the underside of a branch, for example), which is unstable and rarely used. Most are less expensive than hardwoods, meaning they are widely used in the construction industry.

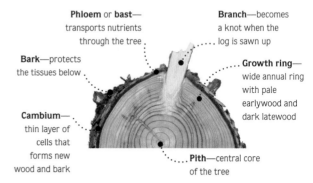

Phloem or **bast**—transports nutrients through the tree

Branch—becomes a knot when the log is sawn up

Bark—protects the tissues below

Growth ring—wide annual ring with pale earlywood and dark latewood

Cambium—thin layer of cells that forms new wood and bark

Pith—central core of the tree

Softwood trunk
In light-colored woods, such as this pine tree, the difference between the outer sapwood and inner heartwood is hard to see. The distinct, wide annual rings reveal that this pine is a fast-growing species.

YELLOW CEDAR *Xanthocyparis nootkatensis* (synonyms *Callitropsis nootkatensis*, *Chamaecyparis nootkatensis*, *Cupressus nootkatensis*)
Other names Alaska or Pacific Coast yellow cedar; Alaska, Nootka, Sitka, or yellow cypress; Nootka false cypress. **Tree characteristics** Native to North American Pacific coastal forest belt, from Alaska to California. Height: 120 ft (37 m). **Wood** Pale yellow heartwood, whitish sapwood; straight grain; fine texture. **Working qualities** Medium density; medium strength but low stiffness; stable; durable; acid-resistant. Easy to work. **Finishing** Good. **Uses** High-class joinery; boat building; external joinery; battery separators.

BALTIC WHITEWOOD *Picea abies*
Other names European whitewood; Norway or European spruce; spruce; white deal. **Tree characteristics** Native to Northern and Central Europe; also grown in UK. Height: 120 ft (37 m). Note: Whitewood shipments may also contain silver fir (see p.150). **Wood** Creamy white to pale brown with distinct growth rings; straight grain; fine texture; good natural luster. **Working qualities** Medium density; weak; medium stability; nondurable; susceptible to insect attack. Easy to work. Hard knots can quickly blunt tools. **Finishing** Good. **Uses** Interior joinery; flooring; plywood. Swiss pine (selected quarter-cut material): soundboards for stringed instruments; violin bellies (front plates).

NORTHERN WHITE CEDAR *Thuja occidentalis*
Other names Eastern white, white, or swamp cedar; American arborvitae. **Tree characteristics** Native to southeastern Canada and northeastern US, especially favoring swampy sites (also grows on cliff faces). Height: 50 ft (15 m). **Wood** Light brown heartwood, white sapwood; straight grain; fine texture; strongly aromatic. **Working qualities** Light; weak and soft; stable; very durable. Easy to work. **Finishing** Good. **Uses** Fencing and fence posts; cabins; roof shingles; telephone poles; boat building, including canoes.

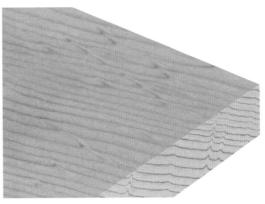

SITKA SPRUCE *Picea sitchensis*
Other names Coast, Menzies, silver, or tideland spruce. **Tree characteristics** Native to North American Pacific coastal forest belt, from Alaska to California; also grown in Europe. Height: 175 ft (53 m). **Wood** Pinkish-yellow to pale brown heartwood, creamy white sapwood; straight (sometimes spiral) grain; medium texture; nonresinous; good natural luster. **Working qualities** Light; medium strength; medium stability; nondurable; susceptible to insect attack. Easy to work. Good steam-bending timber. **Finishing** Very good. **Uses** Plywood; joinery; boat building; musical-instrument soundboards.

CEDAR OF LEBANON *Cedrus libani*
Other names True cedar. **Tree characteristics** Native to mountains of Asia Minor, chiefly Lebanon; also grown in Europe (including UK, where it is planted as a parkland specimen tree) and US. Height: 82 ft (25 m). **Wood** Yellowish-brown to pale brown heartwood with contrasting growth rings, yellowish-white sapwood; straight grain; medium–fine texture; strongly aromatic. Can have ingrown pockets of bark. **Working qualities** Medium density; soft and brittle; medium stability; durable; susceptible to insect attack. Easy to work, but large knots may cause problems. Unsuitable for steam bending. **Finishing** Good. **Uses** Drawer linings; linen chests; fences and gates; decorative veneers (see p.165).

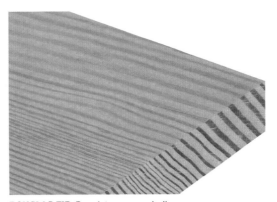

DOUGLAS FIR *Pseudotsuga menziesii*
Other names Douglas spruce; British Columbian or Oregon pine. **Tree characteristics** Native to western North America; also grown in Europe and New Zealand. Height: 200 ft (60 m). Not a true fir. **Wood** Light red- or orange-brown heartwood with wide, darker growth rings, pale yellow sapwood; straight (but can be spiral or wavy) grain; medium texture. **Working qualities** Medium density; strong and stiff; stable; moderate durability. Blunts tools quickly. Nail or screw holes must be prebored. **Finishing** Good, but material with high resin content is best varnished or painted. **Uses** Plywood; heavy and light construction work; joinery; ship building; mining timber.

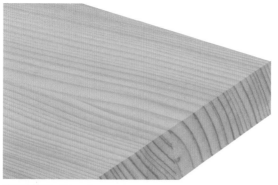

SILVER FIR *Abies alba*
Other names Whitewood; white fir. **Tree characteristics** Native to mountains of Europe, including Pyrenees, Carpathians, and Alps; also grown in UK. Height 148 ft (45 m). Note: shipments of whitewood may also contain Baltic whitewood (see p.148). **Wood** White to pale yellowish brown; straight grain; fine texture; good natural luster. **Working qualities** Medium density; relatively weak; medium stability; nondurable; susceptible to insect attack. Easy to work. **Finishing** Good **Uses** Construction; joinery; flooring; plywood. Central and Eastern European-grown timber: musical-instrument soundboards and violin bellies (front plates).

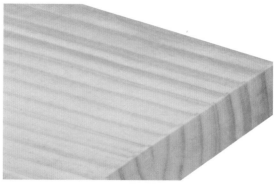

BALTIC REDWOOD *Pinus sylvestris*
Other names Scots pine (UK-grown timber only); red or yellow deal; Archangel, European, Scandinavian, or Russian redwood; Norway or Scots fir. **Tree characteristics** Native to Europe and northwestern Asia; also grown in North America. Height: 66 ft (20 m). **Wood** Pale reddish-brown heartwood with distinct growth rings, creamy white to pale yellow sapwood; usually straight grain; often knotty; variable texture, depending on origin. **Working qualities** Medium density; variable strength; medium stability; nondurable. Easy to work. Gluing is hard if high in resin. Unsuitable for steam bending. **Finishing** Satisfactory. **Uses** Furniture; joinery, including turnery; construction; railroad ties; telephone poles; plywood.

YELLOW PINE *Pinus strobus*
Other names Quebec yellow, white, eastern, northern, northern white, Weymouth, soft, or spruce pine. **Tree characteristics** Native to cool, humid forests of southeastern Canada and northeastern US. Height: 100 ft (30 m). **Wood** Pale yellow to light reddish-brown heartwood with fine brown resin canals, creamy white to pale yellow sapwood; straight grain; medium texture. **Working qualities** Light; soft and weak; very stable; nondurable; susceptible to insect attack. Easy to work. Unsuitable for steam bending. Good carving timber. **Finishing** Good. **Uses** Pattern making; shooting boards (for planing edges of timber); joinery; furniture; musical instruments.

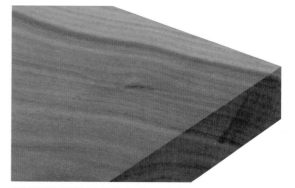

CALLITRIS PINE (a) *Callitris glaucophylla.* (b) *Callitris intratropica* (synonym *C. columellaris* var. *intratropica*)
Other names Cypress; Murray pine. (a) White or western cypress pine. (b) Cypress pine; blue or northern cypress; northern Christmas tree; laguni; karntirrikani. **Tree characteristics** (a) Native to forests in Australia. Height: 82 ft (25 m). (b) Native to sandy soils in northern Australia. Height: 100 ft (30 m). Not true pines. **Wood** Light to dark yellow-brown heartwood, creamy white sapwood; straight grain; fine texture; knotty; aromatic. Termite resistant. **Working qualities** Dense; hard and brittle; very stable; very durable. Nail or screw holes near ends of boards must be prebored. **Finishing** Good. **Uses** Joinery; furniture; turnery; carving; flooring; beehives.

COMMON LARCH *Larix decidua*
Other names European larch. **Tree characteristics** Native to mountains of Central Europe; also grown in UK, western Russia, and New Zealand. Height: 66 ft (20 m). **Wood** Pale reddish-brown to brick-red heartwood with distinct growth rings; may be knotty; straight or spiral grain; fine texture. **Working qualities** Medium density; medium strength (50 percent harder than Baltic redwood); stable; moderate durability; susceptible to insect attack. Satisfactory to work. Knotty material quickly blunts tools. Nail or screw holes must be prebored. Dead or loose knots may cause problems during machining. **Finishing** Good. **Uses** Boat building; joinery; fencing; shingles; telephone poles.

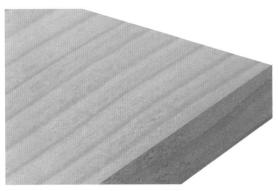

WESTERN HEMLOCK *Tsuga heterophylla*
Other names British Columbia or Pacific hemlock; Alaskan pine; hemlock spruce. **Tree characteristics** Native to Pacific coastal rain forest and the northern Rocky Mountains in North America; also grown in UK, China, and Japan. Height: 148 ft (45 m). **Wood** Pale yellowish-brown heartwood with distinct growth rings that have a purplish tinge; straight grain; fine texture; nonresinous; good natural luster. **Working qualities** Medium density; medium–low strength; stable; nondurable; susceptible to insect attack. Easy to work. Hard, brittle knots. Nail or screw holes near edges must be prebored. **Finishing** Good. **Uses** Construction; joinery; railroad ties; pallets; turnery; plywood; veneers.

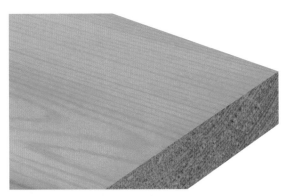

WESTERN RED CEDAR *Thuja plicata*
Other names Pacific red or red cedar; giant or western arborvitae. **Tree characteristics** Native to Pacific coastal forests of North America and to Idaho and Montana; also grown in Europe and New Zealand. Height: 175 ft (53 m). **Wood** Pink-to reddish-brown heartwood (weathers to silvery gray), creamy white sapwood; straight grain; medium–coarse texture.
Working qualities Light; weak; stable; durable. Easy to work. Blue-black staining may occur around iron fittings under moist conditions. Unsuitable for steam bending. **Finishing** Satisfactory. **Uses** Outdoor construction, such as greenhouses, weatherboards, shingles, and fencing; beehives.

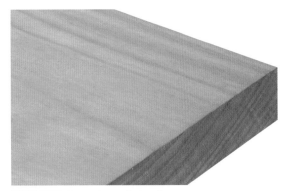

HOOP PINE *Araucaria cunninghamii*
Other names Colonial, Dorrigo, Moreton Bay, Norfolk Island, Queensland, or Richmond River pine; Australian Araucaria; Arakaria. **Tree characteristics** Native to drier rain forests of coastal eastern Australia and mountains of Papua New Guinea. Height: 165 ft (50 m). Not a true pine. **Wood** Pale brown heartwood, whitish sapwood; straight (sometimes spiral) grain; fine texture. **Working qualities** Medium density; soft; stable; nondurable; susceptible to insect attack. Easy to work. Tear-out may occur around knots during planing. Unsuitable for steam bending. **Finishing** Good. **Uses** Furniture; joinery; turnery; boat building.

YEW *Taxus baccata*
Other names Common or European yew. **Tree characteristics** Native to Europe, Asia Minor, Algeria; also grown in Myanmar (Burma) and the Himalayas. Height: 50 ft (15 m). **Wood** Orange-brown heartwood with black or purple streaks, creamy yellow sapwood; tiny knots and ingrown bark often present; straight, curly, or irregular grain; medium texture. **Working qualities** Dense; medium strength; stable; durable; susceptible to insect attack. Hard to work. Curly or irregular-grained samples may tear out during planing. Nail or screw holes must be prebored. Hard to glue. Excellent steam-bending and turning timber. **Finishing** Excellent. **Uses** Turnery; veneers; bent chair parts; longbows.

VIRGINIAN PENCIL CEDAR *Juniperus virginiana*
Other names Pencil, eastern red, or red cedar; juniper; eastern or red juniper. **Tree characteristics** Native to a wide range of habitats (rocky outcrops to moist swampy soils) in southeastern Canada and eastern US. Height: 60 ft (18 m). Not a true cedar. **Wood** Reddish-brown heartwood with darker growth rings, creamy white sapwood; straight grain; fine texture; strongly aromatic. **Working qualities** Medium density; soft; stable; durable. Easy to work. May tear around knots during planing. Nail or screw holes must be prebored. Unsuitable for steam bending. **Finishing** Very good. **Uses** Pencils; cigar boxes; coffins; decorative veneers.

OTHER SOFTWOODS TO CONSIDER
American pitch pine (a) *Pinus palustris*. (b) *P. elliottii*
  Other names (a and b) Southern pine; Gulf Coast pitch pine. (a) Longleaf, yellow, pitch, or turpentine pine. (b) Slash or longleaf pitch pine. **Uses** Heavy construction work; ship building; joinery; flooring; plywood; pallets.
Sugar pine *Pinus lambertiana*
  Other names Big, California sugar, gigantic, great sugar, or shade pine. **Uses** Joinery; pattern making; organ pipes and piano keys; food containers; flooring; plywood.
Western white pine *Pinus monticola*
  Other names Idaho white, mountain, silver, or white pine. **Uses** Joinery; furniture; packing cases; boat building; plywood.
Thuya burr *Tetraclinis articulata*
  Other names Arar; alerce; citron burl; thyine wood. **Uses** Mostly used for decorative veneers, as size availability is limited.

RECYCLING WOOD
When planning a project, consider whether you can use old wood for part or all of it. Timber, and particularly structural timber (such as beams or joists, for example), is usually suitable for reuse as long as it is sound. Check for damage when buying old wood from a reclamation yard or other sources of recycled timber. As well as having the advantage of being thoroughly seasoned, reclaimed wood may look better than new timber.

PREPARING RECYCLED WOOD
Old timbers often have areas of woodworm or rot, but once the worst areas are removed, the remaining wood is usually structurally sound. Old nails and other fittings should also be removed.

1 Rusted nails may snap off if you try to pry them out of a piece of timber with a claw hammer or pry bar. If this happens, use a hammer and punch to knock the broken shaft of the nail below the wood's surface.

2 With large timbers that are affected with woodworm or rot, use an ax or hatchet to cut away the affected wood. Once the worst bits have been cut away, brush the wood down and treat it to kill any woodworm and protect it from further attack by insects or rot.

HARDWOODS

Hardwoods are the timbers from a wide range of broadleaved trees that belong to the flowering plant group, the angiosperms, which produce "covered" seeds.

DISTINGUISHING FEATURES

A significant feature of hardwoods is that the many different species contain a larger range of colors, textures, and kinds of figure than softwoods. Hardwoods are often slower-growing and more durable than softwoods and are usually more expensive. As their name suggests, hardwoods are harder than most softwoods, but exceptions include balsa (see p.159), which is actually the softest of all commercial timbers. Hardwood timber contains several kinds of cells, including small tracheids and large tubes, called vessels, that transport water. In some species (for example, oaks), the vessels are large enough to be seen with the naked eye. Pores on the surface of a piece of timber are actually the severed ends of these vessels. The relative sizes and arrangements of the vessels dictate the timber's texture, with larger vessels giving a coarser texture.

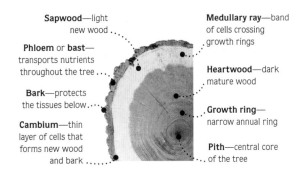

Sapwood—light new wood

Phloem or bast—transports nutrients throughout the tree

Bark—protects the tissues below

Cambium—thin layer of cells that forms new wood and bark

Medullary ray—band of cells crossing growth rings

Heartwood—dark mature wood

Growth ring—narrow annual ring

Pith—central core of the tree

Hardwood trunk
This cross-section of an oak trunk shows the heartwood and the sapwood, numerous thin annual rings (which, when counted, give the age of the tree), and the distinctive medullary rays radiating from the center.

AMERICAN ASH (a) *Fraxinus americana*. (b) *F. pennsylvanica*. (c) *F. nigra*
Other names (a) Canadian or white ash. (b) Green or red ash. (c) Black or brown ash. **Tree characteristics** Native to North America. Height: 131 ft (40 m). **Wood** Grayish-brown heartwood sometimes with pink tinge; straight grain; coarse texture.
Working qualities Medium density; strong and elastic, with excellent shock resistance; stable; nondurable; susceptible to insect attack. Easy to work. Nail or screw holes must be prebored in harder grades of the timber. Very good steam-bending timber provided knots are absent. **Finishing** Very good. **Uses** Sporting goods; tool handles; boat building; furniture.

SOFT MAPLE (a) *Acer rubrum*. (b) *A. saccharinum*. (c) *A. macrophyllum*
Other names (a) Red maple. (b) Silver maple. (c) Big-leaf or Oregon maple. **Tree characteristics** (a) and (b) Native to eastern North America. (c) Native to Pacific coastal forest of North America. Height: 100 ft (30 m). **Wood** Creamy white or pale reddish-brown heartwood, grayish-white sapwood; usually little figure; straight grain; fine texture. **Working qualities** Medium density; medium strength; stable; nondurable; susceptible to insect attack. Satisfactory to work. Can be hard to glue. Nail or screw holes must be prebored. **Finishing** Excellent. **Uses** Furniture; joinery; flooring; turnery; musical instruments.

HOLLY (a) *Ilex aquifolium.* (b) *I. opaca*
Other names (a) European holly. (b) American or white holly.
Tree characteristics (a) Native to Europe and western Asia.
(b) Native to southeastern US. Height: 66 ft (20 m). **Wood** Pale
creamy white, sometimes with greenish tinge; little or no figure;
irregular grain; fine texture. **Working qualities** Very dense; hard
and tough; not stable; perishable; susceptible to insect attack.
Hard to work. Reduced cutting angle required for planing or
molding. Excellent turning timber. Only available in comparatively
small sizes. **Finishing** Excellent. Sometimes dyed black to imitate
ebony. **Uses** Decorative inlay lines and marquetry motifs
(substitute for boxwood); musical-instrument parts; turnery.

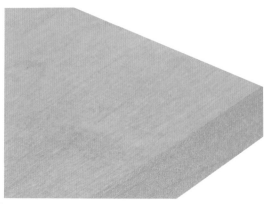

YELLOW BIRCH *Betula alleghaniensis*
Other names American, Canadian yellow, gray, hard, Quebec,
or swamp birch; betula wood. **Tree characteristics** Native to
southeastern Canada and northeastern US, especially in uplands
and mountain ravines. Height: 66 ft (20 m). **Wood** Reddish-brown
heartwood, white or pale brown sapwood; straight grain; fine
texture; good natural luster. **Working qualities** Dense; strong;
not stable; perishable; susceptible to insect attack. Easy to work.
Reduced cutting angle required for planing areas with curly grain.
Nail or screw holes must be prebored. Very good steam-bending
timber. **Finishing** Excellent. **Uses** High-quality furniture; flooring;
turnery; upholstery frames; high-quality plywood.

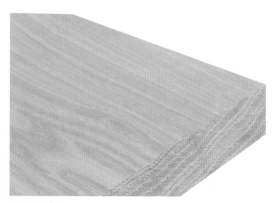

HICKORY *Carya* spp.
Other names Pignut, mockernut, red, shagbark, shellbark, and
white hickory. **Tree characteristics** Native to deciduous forests
of eastern North America. Height: 100 ft (30 m). **Wood** Brown
to reddish-brown heartwood, pale brown sapwood; straight
(sometimes wavy or irregular) grain; coarse texture. **Working
qualities** Very dense; strong and flexible; stable; nondurable;
sapwood susceptible to insect attack. Hard to work. Reduced
cutting angle required for planing or molding. Nail or screw
holes must be prebored. Can be hard to glue. Excellent steam-
bending timber. **Finishing** Good. **Uses** Ax handles; sporting
goods; furniture.

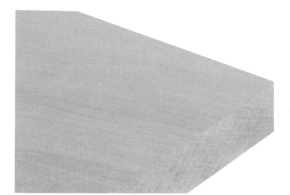

HARD MAPLE (a) *Acer saccharum.* (b) *A. nigrum*
Other names Rock maple. (a) Sugar maple. (b) Black maple.
Tree characteristics Native to Canada and eastern US; (b) grows
farther west than (a). Height: (a) 131 ft (40 m), (b) 82 ft (25 m).
Wood Pale brown heartwood with reddish tinge and sometimes
dark brown heart, white sapwood with reddish tinge; straight, curly,
or wavy grain; fine texture; good natural luster. **Working qualities**
Dense; strong; medium stability; nondurable; sapwood susceptible
to insect attack; abrasion-resistant. Hard to work. Reduced cutting
angle required for planing or molding. Nail or screw holes must be
prebored. **Finishing** Excellent. **Uses** Heavy-duty flooring; butcher
blocks; turnery; furniture; decorative veneers.

MOUNTAIN ASH *Eucalyptus regnans*
Other names Australian or Tasmanian mountain oak;
Victoria or white ash; stringy or swamp gum. **Tree
characteristics** Native to southeastern Australia. Height:
120 ft (37 m). **Wood** Pale to light brown with a pinkish tinge
and distinct gum veins; can have fiddleback figure; straight,
interlocked, or wavy grain; coarse texture. **Working qualities**
Medium density, strength, and stability; moderate durability;
susceptible to insect attack. Satisfactory to work. Nail or screw
holes must be prebored. Unsuitable for steam bending.
Finishing Good. **Uses** Furniture; flooring; weatherboards;
plywood; decorative veneers from selected logs.

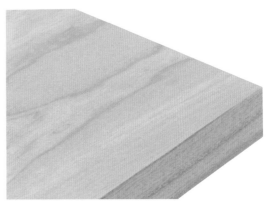

EUROPEAN ASH *Fraxinus excelsior*
Other names Common ash. **Tree characteristics** Native
to Europe and southwestern Asia. Height: 120 ft (37 m).
Wood Cream to pale brown heartwood; can have fiddleback
figure; straight grain; coarse texture; good natural luster.
Olive ash has dark brown heartwood, sometimes with black
streaks, resembling olivewood. **Working qualities** Dense;
tough and strong; medium stability; nondurable; susceptible
to insect attack. Easy to work. Nail or screw holes must
be prebored. Excellent steam-bending timber. **Finishing**
Excellent. **Uses** Tool handles; sporting goods; boat building;
furniture; turnery; decorative veneers (see p.165).

LIME *Tilia × europea* (synonym *T. × vulgaris*)
Other names Common or European lime. **Tree characteristics**
Native to Northern, Central, and Southern Europe. Height: 100 ft
(30 m). **Wood** Creamy yellow to pale brown; no figure; straight
grain; fine texture. **Working qualities** Medium density; medium
strength; medium stability; perishable; susceptible to insect
attack; resistant to splitting. Easy to work. Can be woolly.
Reduced cutting angle required for planing. **Finishing** Good.
Uses Toys; musical-instrument parts; architectural models;
the preferred timber choice for carving.

HORNBEAM *Carpinus betulus*
Other names Hardbeam. **Tree characteristics** Native to
Europe, eastward to Iran. Height: 82 ft (25 m). **Wood** Grayish-
white heartwood with greenish streaks; has fleck figure on
quarter-cut material, can also have mottle figure; irregular
grain; fine texture. **Working qualities** Dense; strong; not
stable; perishable; susceptible to insect attack; split-resistant;
abrasion-resistant. Satisfactory to work. Nail or screw holes
must be prebored. Good turning and steam-bending timber.
Finishing Very good. **Uses** Musical-instrument parts; flooring;
drumsticks; decorative veneers.

SWEET CHESTNUT *Castanea sativa*
Other names European or Spanish chestnut. **Tree characteristics** Native to southeastern Europe. Height: 115 ft (35 m). **Wood** Pale brown heartwood similar to European oak, but without oak's flake figure (see p.158), creamy white sapwood; straight or spiral grain; coarse texture. **Working qualities** Medium density; medium strength; stable; durable; sapwood susceptible to insect attack. Easy to work. Blue or black staining may occur around iron fittings under moist conditions, and fittings may corrode. Good steam-bending timber.
Finishing Excellent. **Uses** Furniture; coffins; fencing and posts.

BOXWOOD *Buxus sempervirens*
Other names Common, European, Iranian, Persian, or Turkish boxwood. **Tree characteristics** Native to Europe and eastern Asia. Height: 30 ft (9 m). **Wood** Pale yellow sometimes with grayish-brown areas; little figure; straight or irregular grain; fine texture. **Working qualities** Dense; strong; stable; durable; susceptible to insect attack. Hard to work. Edges of veneers can be splintery. Nail or screw holes must be prebored.
Finishing Very good. **Uses** Turnery, such as chessmen; carving; engraving blocks; tool handles; musical-instrument parts; inlay lines, stringings, and marquetry inlay motifs.

EUROPEAN BIRCH (a) *Betula pendula*. (b) *B. pubescens*
Other names (a and b) Common birch. (a) Silver birch. (b) Downy, hairy, or brown birch. **Tree characteristics** Native to Europe as far north as Lapland. Height: 66 ft (20 m). **Wood** Creamy white to pale brown; straight grain; fine texture; good natural luster; many decorative figures.
Working qualities Medium density and strength; stable; perishable. Easy to work. Reduced cutting angle required for planing areas with curly grain. Can be woolly. Good steam-bending timber if knots are absent. **Finishing** Very good.
Uses High-quality joinery and plywood; turnery, such as bobbins and domestic ware; decorative veneers (see p.165).

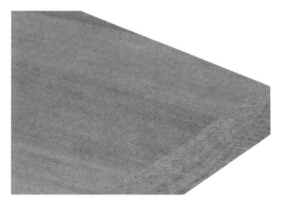

AMERICAN WHITEWOOD *Liriodendron tulipifera*
Other names Tulipwood; canoe wood; saddletree; tuliptree; tulip, white, or yellow poplar; whitewood. **Tree characteristics** Native to southeastern US; also grown in Europe. Height: 120 ft (37 m). **Wood** Pale greenish-brown heartwood with greenish-gray streaks, creamy sapwood; can have blister figure; straight grain; fine texture. **Working qualities** Medium density, strength, and stability; nondurable; sapwood susceptible to insect attack. Easy to work. Does not sand well. **Finishing** Satisfactory. Often chosen for surfaces that will be painted. (Timber does not polish well.) **Uses** Pattern making; furniture; turnery; joinery; carving; plywood; veneers.

AMERICAN WHITE OAK *Quercus alba*
Other names Arizona, Appalachian, Quebec, stave, or white oak.
Tree characteristics Native to eastern US and southeastern Canada. Height: 100 ft (30 m). **Wood** Pale yellowish- to pinkish-brown heartwood, creamy white to pale brown sapwood; has flake figure on quarter-cut material; straight grain; medium–coarse texture. **Working qualities** Dense; strong; medium stability; durable; susceptible to insect attack; abrasion-resistant. Northern-grown wood is easier to work than southern-grown. Excellent steam-bending timber. Can be hard to glue. Nail or screw holes must be prebored. **Finishing** Good. Does not fume well. **Uses** Furniture; boat building; flooring; barrels.

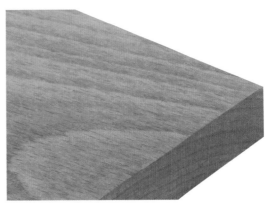

EUROPEAN BEECH *Fagus sylvatica*
Other names Common Beech. **Tree characteristics** Native to Europe, as far east as the Caucasus. Height: 100 ft (30 m). **Wood** Pale pinkish brown sometimes with dark veining or heart (steamed beech is reddish brown); has fleck figure on quarter-cut material; straight grain; fine texture. **Working qualities** Dense; medium strength; medium stability; perishable; susceptible to insect attack. Easy to work. Nail or screw holes must be prebored. Good turning and steam-bending timber. **Finishing** Excellent. **Uses** Furniture; high-class joinery; turnery; domestic ware; tools and tool handles; plywood; decorative veneers. Warning: Do not use spalted beech (formed when logs are attacked by fungus) for food utensils.

RED OAK *Quercus rubra*
Other names American, Northern, or Southern red oak. **Tree characteristics** Native to eastern US and southeastern Canada; also grown in Europe. Height: 90 ft (27 m). **Wood** Pale brown heartwood with reddish tinge; less figure than other oaks; straight grain; coarse texture. **Working qualities** Dense (less so than European oak); hard; medium stability; nondurable; sapwood susceptible to insect attack. Northern-grown wood is easier to work than southern-grown. Excellent steam-bending timber. Can be hard to glue. Nail or screw holes must be prebored. **Finishing** Good. **Uses** Furniture; joinery; boat building; flooring; plywood.

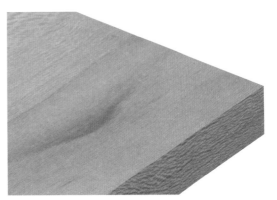

LONDON PLANE *Platanus* × *hispanica* 'Acerifolia' (synonym *P. acerifolia*)
Other names Common or European plane. **Tree characteristics** A manufactured hybrid, unknown in the wild, planted in Europe and the Americas. Height: 100 ft (30 m). **Wood** Light reddish-brown heartwood; highly decorative figure on quarter-cut material; straight grain; fine–medium texture. **Working qualities** Medium density; medium strength; stable; perishable; sapwood susceptible to insect attack. Satisfactory to work. Can bind during sawing. Medullary rays can tear out during planing. Good steam-bending timber. **Finishing** Excellent. **Uses** Furniture; joinery; decorative veneers; turnery.

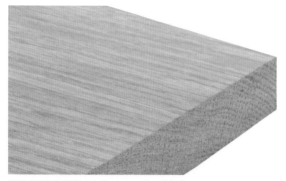

EUROPEAN OAK (a) *Quercus robur.* (b) *Q. petraea*
Other names English, French, Polish, or Slavonian oak.
(a) Pedunculate oak. (b) Sessile oak. **Tree characteristics** Native to Europe, the Mediterranean, and western Asia. Height: 100 ft (30 m). **Wood** Pale brown to brown heartwood, creamy white to pale brown sapwood; has flake figure on quarter-cut material; straight grain; coarse texture. **Working qualities** Dense; strong; medium stability; durable; sapwood susceptible to insect attack. Ease of working varies. Good steam-bending timber. Blue or black staining may occur around iron fittings under moist conditions, and fittings may corrode. **Finishing** Excellent. **Uses** Furniture; heavy construction; boat building; barrels.

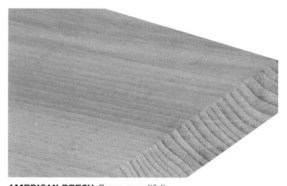

AMERICAN BEECH *Fagus grandifolia*
Other names Beech. **Tree characteristics** Native to hardwood forests of eastern North America. Height: 148 ft (45 m). **Wood** Reddish-brown heartwood, creamy white sapwood; has fleck figure on quarter-cut material; straight grain; fine texture (but slightly coarser than European beech). **Working qualities** Dense (slightly more so than European Beech); medium strength; medium stability; perishable; susceptible to insect attack. Easy to work. Can burn when cross-cutting or drilling. Good turning and steam-bending timber. **Finishing** Good. **Uses** Furniture; high-class joinery; turnery; tools and tool handles; plywood; decorative veneers; food containers.

AMERICAN CHESTNUT *Castanea dentata*
Other names None. **Tree characteristics** Native to hardwood forests of eastern North America. Height: 20 ft (6 m), due to effects of chestnut blight. **Wood** Pale brown heartwood similar to European oak (but without oak's flake figure), creamy white sapwood; straight or spiral grain; coarse texture. **Working qualities** Medium density; medium strength; stable; durable; sapwood susceptible to insect attack. Easy to work. Nail or screw holes must be prebored. Blue or black staining may occur around iron fittings under moist conditions, and fittings may corrode. **Finishing** Very good. **Uses** Furniture; coffins; stakes and posts.

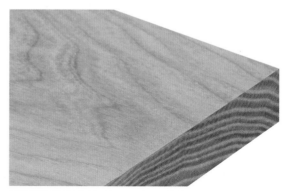

EUROPEAN ELM (a) *Ulmus glabra.* (b) *Ulmus × hollandica.*
(c) *U. procera* and other species
Other names (a) Mountain, Scots, Scottish, white, or wych elm; Irish leamhan. (b) Cork bark or Dutch elm. (c) English or nave elm. **Tree characteristics** Native to (a) and (b) Northern Europe; (c) England and Wales. Height: 148 ft (45 m). **Wood** Pinkish-brown or dull brown heartwood sometimes with olive-green streaks; has fleck figure on quarter-cut material; straight or irregular grain; coarse texture. **Working qualities** Medium density, strength, and stability; nondurable in air but very durable underwater; susceptible to insect attack; split-resistant. Satisfactory to work. Can be woolly. (c) is unsuitable for steam bending. **Finishing** Very good. **Uses** Boat building; furniture; flooring; veneers (see p.164).

BALSA *Ochroma pyrimidale* (synonym *O. lagopus*)
Other names Catillo; guano; lanero; polak; tami; topa. **Tree characteristics** Native to West Indies and Central and South America; also grown in India and Indonesia. Height: 82 ft (25 m). **Wood** Commercial timber is chiefly the white to pinkish-oatmeal sapwood; straight grain; fine texture; good natural luster. **Working qualities** Extremely light; very soft, but strong in relation to its weight; stable; perishable; susceptible to insect attack. Easy to work. Nails and screws do not hold, but the timber glues well. Unsuitable for steam bending. **Finishing** Satisfactory. Highly absorbent, so needs large quantities of finishing material. **Uses** Model making; insulating and buoyancy material; corestock for metal-faced sheets in aircraft and wind turbines.

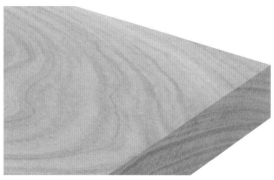

EUROPEAN CHERRY *Prunus avium*
Other names Sweet or wild cherry; gean; mazzard. **Tree characteristics** Native to Europe and western Asia. Height: 82 ft (25 m). **Wood** Pale pinkish-brown heartwood, pale creamy brown sapwood; can have mottle or fiddleback figure; straight grain; fine texture; good natural luster. **Working qualities** Medium density, strength, stability, and durability; sapwood susceptible to insect attack. Easy to work. Reduced cutting angle required for planing or molding cross-grained material. Good steam-bending timber. **Finishing** Excellent. For best results, degrease before applying stains. **Uses** Furniture; turnery; carving; musical instruments; veneers.

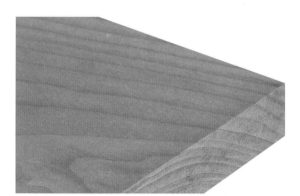

AMERICAN CHERRY *Prunus serotina*
Other names Black, cabinet, choke, Edwards Plateau, rum, wild, or whiskey cherry; capulin; New England mahogany. **Tree characteristics** Native to eastern North America; also grown in Central and Eastern Europe. Height: 82 ft (25 m). **Wood** Reddish-brown heartwood, creamy to pinkish-white sapwood; straight grain; fine texture; good luster. **Working qualities** Medium density; medium strength; medium stability; medium durability; sapwood susceptible to insect attack. Easy to work. Good steam-bending timber. **Finishing** Excellent. Can be stained to imitate mahogany. **Uses** Furniture; high-quality joinery; turnery; carving; musical-instrument parts; decorative veneers.

RED ALDER *Alnus rubra*
Other names Oregon, Pacific Coast, or Western alder. **Tree characteristics** Native to lowland areas of the Pacific coastal forests of North America. Height: 120 ft (37 m). **Wood** Pale yellow to reddish brown; usually little figure; straight grain; fine texture. **Working qualities** Medium density; soft and weak; stable; perishable (but durable underwater); susceptible to insect attack. Easy to work. Reduced cutting angle required for planing. Good steam-bending timber. **Finishing** Good. **Uses** Turnery; carving; kitchen cabinets; plywood; veneers.

PEAR (a) *Pyrus communis*. (b) *Sorbus torminalis*
Other names (a) Common pear; pearwood. (b) Swiss pear; wild service tree. **Tree characteristics** Native to Europe and western Asia. Height: (a) 40 ft (12 m); (b) 82 ft (25 m). **Wood** Pinkish-brown heartwood (steamed pear is slightly darker); usually little figure, but can have mottling on quarter-cut material; straight grain; fine texture. **Working qualities** Dense; hard but brittle; stable; perishable; susceptible to insect attack. Satisfactory to work. Excellent for turning. Unsuitable for steam bending.
Finishing Excellent. Can be stained black as an ebony substitute.
Uses Decorative turnery; musical instruments.

JARRAH *Eucalyptus marginata*
Other names Swan or Western Australian mahogany. **Tree characteristics** Native to coastal belt of southwestern Western Australia. Height: 148 ft (45 m). **Wood** Dark brownish-red heartwood, pale yellow sapwood; boat-shaped marks caused by beefsteak fungus give attractive figure on flat-sawn material; straight, interlocked, or wavy grain; coarse texture. **Working qualities** Very dense; hard and strong; medium stability; very durable. Hard to work. Reduced cutting angle required for planing or molding. Nail or screw holes must be prebored.
Finishing Very good. **Uses** Marine construction; ship building; railroad ties; weatherboards; furniture; decorative veneers.

TEAK *Tectona grandis*
Other names Djati; gia thi; kyun; jati sak; mai sak; pahi; sagon; sagwan; tegina; tedi; tekku. **Tree characteristics** Native to rain forests in Asia; also grown in Africa, the Caribbean, and Central America. Height: 148 ft (45 m). **Wood** Golden brown to brown heartwood; can have mottled figure; straight or wavy grain; coarse texture; feels greasy. **Working qualities** Medium density; strong, hard, but somewhat brittle; very stable; very durable; susceptible to insect attack; fire- and acid-resistant. Satisfactory to work. Nail or screw holes must be prebored. Glues best on freshly sanded surfaces. **Finishing** Satisfactory. **Uses** Ship and boat building; furniture; garden furniture; flooring; joinery.

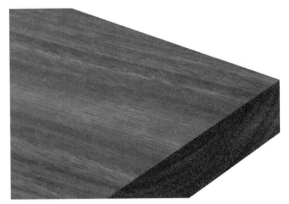

SPOTTED GUM (a) *Corymbia maculata* (synonym *Eucalyptus maculata*). (b) *E. citriodora*
Other names (a) Spotted iron gum. (b) Lemon eucalyptus, lemon-scented gum. **Tree characteristics** Native to eastern Australia. Height: 130 ft (40 m). **Wood** Light brown to dark reddish-brown heartwood, white sapwood; can have fiddleback figure; straight or wavy grain; coarse texture; feels greasy.
Working qualities Very dense; hard and strong; moderate stability; durable; sapwood susceptible to insect attack. Satisfactory to work. Reduced cutting angle required for planing or molding. Nail or screw holes must be prebored.
(a) Good steam-bending timber. **Finishing** Very good.
Uses Tool handles; boat building; flooring; joinery.

CAMPHORWOOD *Cinnamomum camphora* (synonym *Laurus camphora*)
Other names Camphor tree; camphor laurel; ho wood. **Tree characteristics** Native to mountainous areas of China, Japan, and Taiwan. Height: 100 ft (30 m). **Wood** Yellowish brown with dark brown streaks; growth-ring figure; wavy, straight, or interlocked grain; good natural luster; strongly aromatic. **Working qualities** Medium density; relatively soft and weak; moderately stable; durable. Easy to work. Metal fittings in contact with the timber may corrode. **Finishing** Good. **Uses** Furniture, especially wardrobes and linen chests; decorative veneers.

ANDAMAN PADAUK *Pterocarpus dalbergioides*
Other names Andaman redwood; Andaman padouk; vermillion wood. **Tree characteristics** Grows from India to New Guinea. Height: 120 ft (37 m). **Wood** Brick-red to brownish-red heartwood, light-colored sapwood; can have striped or curly figure on quarter-cut material; interlocked grain; medium–coarse texture; good natural luster. **Working qualities** Dense; hard; stable; very durable. Satisfactory to work. Unsuitable for steam bending. Nail or screw holes must be prebored. Reduced cutting angle required for planing quarter-cut material. **Finishing** High-quality furniture and joinery; boat building; flooring; decorative veneers. **Uses** Very good, provided grain is filled.

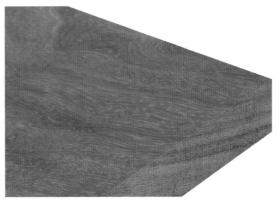

TASMANIAN BLUE GUM *Eucalyptus globulus*
Other names Blue or southern blue gum; bluegum eucalyptus; fever tree. **Tree characteristics** Native to southern Australia and Tasmania; also grown in US, Chile, and the Mediterranean region. Height: 150 ft (45 m). **Wood** Pale brown heartwood with pinkish tinge; interlocked grain; medium texture. **Working qualities** Very dense; very hard and strong; not stable; moderately durable; susceptible to insect attack. Easy to work. **Finishing** Good. **Uses** Construction; joinery; flooring; furniture.

AFRICAN PADAUK *Pterocarpus soyauxii*
Other names Barwood; bosulu; camwood; corail; mbe; mututi; ngula; West African padouk. **Tree characteristics** Grows in tropical West and Central Africa. Height: 131 ft (40 m). **Wood** Red- to dark purple-brown heartwood with red streaks, dull white sapwood; straight or interlocked grain; fine–medium texture. **Working qualities** Dense; strong; extremely stable; very durable; abrasion resistant. Easy to work. Nail or screw holes must be prebored in small stock. **Finishing** Excellent. **Uses** High-quality furniture and joinery; parquet flooring (especially over underfloor heating); decorative veneers.

KINGWOOD *Dalbergia cearensis*
Other names Bois violet; violet wood; violetta. **Tree characteristics** Grows in South America (chiefly Brazil). Height: 30 ft (10 m). **Wood** Purplish-brown heartwood with black or yellow streaks giving highly decorative growth-ring figure, whitish-brown sapwood; straight grain; fine texture; good natural luster; feels waxy. **Working qualities** Extremely dense; very strong; stable; durable. Satisfactory to work. Only available in small sizes or as veneers. **Finishing** Very good, especially with wax finishes. **Uses** Decorative veneers and bandings; antique restoration; turnery.

INDIAN ROSEWOOD *Dalbergia latifolia*
Other names Black, Bombay, East Indian, Indonesian, or Sonokeling rosewood; Indian or Bombay blackwood; biti; eravidi; Indian or Java palisander; kalaruk; malabar; shisham; sissoo. **Tree characteristics** Grows in southern India and Indonesia. Height: 100 ft (30 m). **Wood** Dark purplish-brown heartwood with darker streaks, creamy white sapwood; can have ribbon figure; interlocked grain; moderately coarse texture; strongly aromatic. **Working qualities** Very dense; strong but not stiff; extremely stable; very durable. Hard to work. Unsuitable for nailing. **Finishing** Excellent, provided grain is filled. **Uses** High-quality furniture; musical instruments; veneers.

BLACK WALNUT *Juglans nigra*
Other names (Black) American, Canadian, or Virginia walnut; walnut; canaletto. **Tree characteristics** Native to mixed hardwood forests of eastern US and Canada; also grown in Europe. Height: 66 ft (20 m). **Wood** Dark brown to purplish-black heartwood, pale brown sapwood; highly figured, often burry timber comes from stumpwood; straight or wavy grain; medium–coarse texture. **Working qualities** Medium density; tough and hard; stable; very durable; sapwood susceptible to insect attack. Easy to work. Good steam-bending timber. **Finishing** Excellent. **Uses** High-quality furniture; gun stocks; veneers.

AUSTRALIAN BLACKWOOD *Acacia melanoxylon*
Other names Tasmanian blackwood; black wattle. **Tree characteristics** Native to mountains of southeast Australia; also grown in South Africa, India, Sri Lanka, Chile, and Argentina. Height: 82 ft (25 m). **Wood** Yellow-brown to dark reddish-brown heartwood with darker brown growth rings, creamy to grayish-white sapwood; can have fiddleback figuring; straight, interlocked, or wavy grain; medium texture; good natural luster. **Working qualities** Medium density; hard; stable; very durable; susceptible to insect attack. Satisfactory to work. Reduced cutting angle required for planing or molding. Can be hard to glue. Good steam-bending timber. **Finishing** Excellent. **Uses** High-quality furniture; turnery; boat building; veneers.

PURPLEHEART *Peltogyne* spp.

Other names Amaranth; aramante; guarabu; koroboreli; morado; nazareno; pau roxo; purplewood; saka; sakavalli; tananeo; violetwood. **Tree characteristics** Grows in tropical Central and South America. Height: 148 ft (45 m). **Wood** Vivid purple heartwood matures to dark brown, dull white sapwood; striped or roey figure on quarter-cut timber; straight or interlocked grain; fine to moderate texture; good natural luster. **Working qualities** Very dense; stiff and strong; stable; very durable. Hard to work. Quickly blunts tools. Nail or screw holes must be prebored. Good turning timber. **Finishing** Excellent. **Uses** Heavy construction work, such as bridges or docks; flooring; furniture; turnery; veneers.

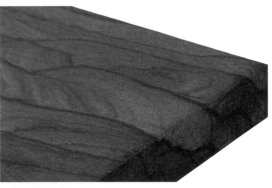

ZIRICOTE *Cordia dodecandra*

Other names Bocote; canalete; laurel; peterebi; sericote; siricote; ziracote. (Note: Other Cordia species may be sold as ziricote.) **Tree characteristics** Grows in Belize, Guatemala, Honduras, and Mexico. Height: 90 ft (27 m). **Wood** Reddish-brown heartwood with irregular dark streaks, yellowish-brown sapwood; straight or interlocked grain; medium texture; good natural luster. **Working qualities** Dense to very dense; hard; stable; moderately durable. Satisfactory to work. **Finishing** Very good. **Uses** High-class furniture; turnery; flooring; boat building; decorative veneers.

QUEENSLAND WALNUT *Endiandra palmerstonii*

Other names Australian (black) walnut; Australian laurel; oriental wood; walnut bean. **Tree characteristics** Native to coastal tableland rain forest in northeast Australia. Height: 140 ft (43 m). Not a true walnut. **Wood** Dark brown heartwood with pink, green, or black streaks, pale brown sapwood; can have attractive checkered figure; irregular grain; medium texture; good natural luster. **Working qualities** Dense; hard but brittle; nondurable; susceptible to insect attack. Hard to work. Quickly blunts tools. Tungsten-carbide tipped (TCT) blades advised for sawing and planing. **Finishing** Very good. **Uses** High-quality furniture; flooring; veneers.

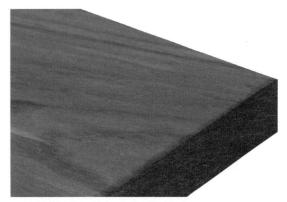

PAU FERRO *Swartzia madagascariensis*

Other names Boto; cimbe; kampanga; kisasamba; msekeseke; mussacuasso; nacuata; oken. **Tree characteristics** Grows in Sudan, Mozambique, and Zimbabwe. Height: 131 ft (40 m). **Wood** Dark reddish-brown heartwood, with yellow or dark brown bands; wavy or interlocked grain; medium texture. **Working qualities** Extremely dense; strong, hard, and stiff; medium stability; durable; susceptible to insect attack. Hard to work. Nail or screw holes must be prebored. **Finishing** Excellent. **Uses** Construction; furniture; flooring; musical-instrument parts; turnery. Note: The pau ferro of Brazil and Bolivia (*Machaerium scleroxylon*) is used as a Brazilian rosewood substitute; also for musical-instrument parts, especially guitars; turnery.

VENEERS

Veneers are thin sheets of wood that are sliced from a log and used for decoration or construction (as plywood). Today, special cutting equipment can produce large decorative "leaves" less than ¹⁄₆₄ in (0.5 mm) thick. Traditionally, however, veneers were produced by carefully sawing logs into thin layers about ⅛ in (3 mm) thick. Such saw-cut veneers are still made today and are largely used for antique restoration.

▲ TYPES OF VENEERS

Veneers are available in a range of natural colors and a variety of figures. The type of figure is determined by the species of wood and where and how it is cut from the tree. This means that each sheet of veneer is unique. Cutting methods include flat-slicing to display flat grain; quarter-slicing to display side grain and medullary rays, if present; and rotary cutting, which peels off a continuous sheet of veneer from the log's circumference. Veneers allow the use of timbers that are fragile due to their irregular grain, such as burrs, and therefore have insufficient strength for most projects, such as furniture or even jewelry boxes, because the grain might crumble under the weight of the finished item. Cutting such timbers into veneers solves this problem, as the solid "ground" onto which the veneer is fitted (see p.134) carries the physical load of the item. Fragile veneers can therefore be used for the same projects as veneers cut from straight-grained timbers, but they must be handled with great care. Burrs (or burls) are abnormal growths on trunks. Veneers cut from them are extremely beautiful, with their masses of dark knots, but they are weak due to their irregular grain, and the leaves come in odd shapes and sizes. Wavy-grained woods give a 3D-effect figure known as "fiddleback," with bands of light and dark grain "rippling" across the veneer leaf. Other veneers with unusual patterns caused by irregular or wavy grains include bird's-eye maple and masur birch.

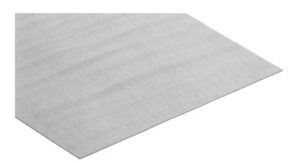

FIDDLEBACK SYCAMORE *Acer pseudoplatanus*
Other names Figured sycamore. **Tree characteristics** Native to Europe and western Asia. Height: 100 ft (30 m). **Wood** Special form of sycamore with creamy white to pale brown heartwood; rippled grain, giving an undulating 3D-effect figure; good natural luster. **Size availability** Large. **Finishing** Excellent. **Uses** Decorative veneering of high-quality furniture, paneling, and musical instruments.

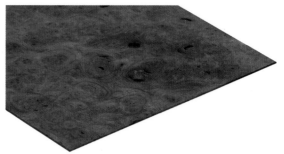

BURR ELM *Ulmus glabra, Ulmus × hollandica, U. procera,* and other species.
Other names Elm burr. **Tree characteristics** Native to Europe. Height 148 ft (45 m). **Wood** Special form of elm (see European Elm, p.158) with dull brown, orange-brown, or pinkish background, crammed with numerous darker brown knots with circular "eyes"; sometimes has olive-green streaks; irregular grain; coarse texture. Cluster elm has small areas of burrs surrounded by normal straight grain. **Size availability** Small sheets, sometimes in irregular shapes. **Finishing** Very good. **Uses** Decorative veneering of small items.

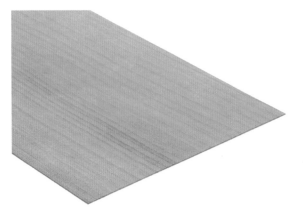

CEDAR OF LEBANON *Cedrus libani*
Other names True cedar. **Tree characteristics** Native to mountains in Asia Minor, chiefly Lebanon; also grown in Europe and US. Height: 82 ft (25 m). **Wood** Yellowish-brown to pale brown heartwood with contrasting growth rings, yellowish-white sapwood; straight grain; medium–fine texture; strongly aromatic. Can have ingrown pockets of bark (see Cedar of Lebanon, p.149). **Size availability** Good. **Finishing** Good. **Uses** Decorative veneering, especially for the insides of boxes and wardrobes; paneling.

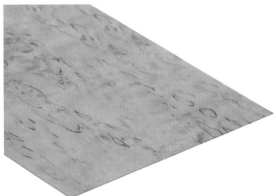

MASUR BIRCH *Betula pendula* and *B. pubescens*
Other names Karelian birch or birch burr (but not a true burr). **Tree characteristics** Native to Europe, as far north as Lapland. Height: 66 ft (20 m). **Wood** Special form of birch (see p.156) that has a creamy white to pale brown background with irregular dark brown markings and streaks, which are often curved; irregular grain; fine texture; good natural luster. **Size availability** Sourced from the base of selected trees. Veneer sheets are wide but not long (less than 6½ ft/2 m). **Finishing** Very good. **Uses** Decorative veneering of high-quality furniture, boxes, and paneling.

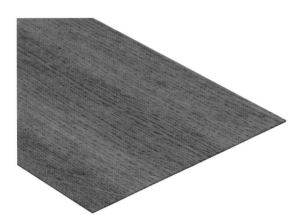

BROWN OAK *Quercus robur* and *Q. petraea*
Other names None. **Tree characteristics** Native to Europe and western Asia. Height: 100 ft (30 m). **Wood** Special form of oak (see European Oak, p.158) with rich chocolate-brown color; flake figure on quarter-cut material; straight grain; coarse texture. Tiger oak has irregular dark brown streaks. Brown oak and tiger oak burrs are sometimes offered for sale. **Size availability** Good. **Finishing** Excellent. **Uses** Decorative veneering of high-quality furniture and paneling.

FIDDLEBACK ASH *Fraxinus excelsior*
Other names Figured ash. **Tree characteristics** Native to Europe (where it favors moist, rich soils) and southwestern Asia. Height: 120 ft (37 m). **Wood** Special form of ash (see European Ash, p.155) with cream to pale brown heartwood; rippled grain, giving an undulating 3D-effect figure; coarse texture; good natural luster. **Size availability** Medium-size widths and lengths. **Finishing** Excellent. **Uses** Decorative veneering of high-quality furniture.

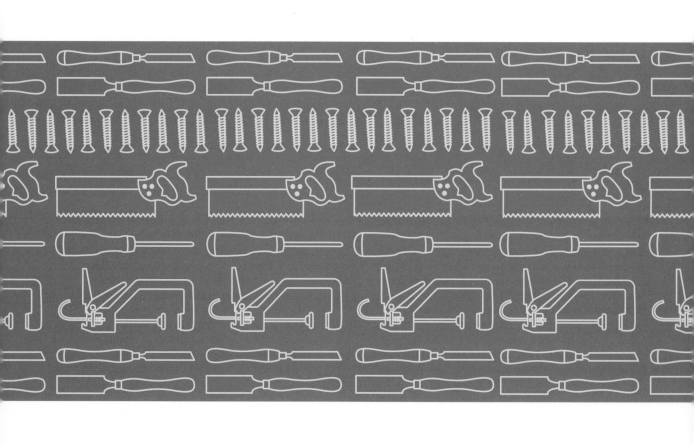

PROJECTS

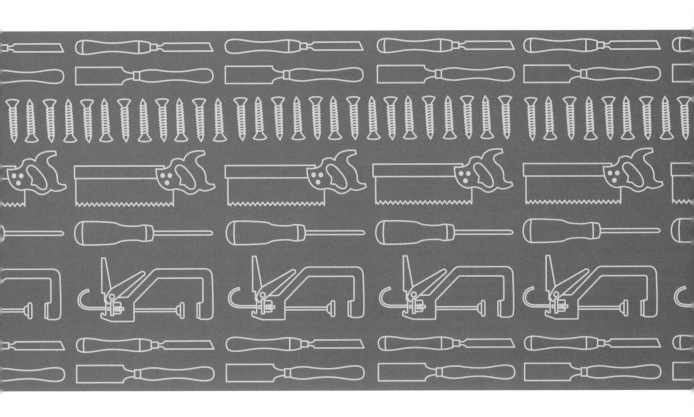

CHOPPING BOARD

Making a chopping board is a great way to familiarize yourself with the technique of joining sections of timber to create a single piece with a larger surface area. Beech is the traditional wood for chopping boards, but you could try tight-grained timbers, such as maple or pear, for an alternative finish.

CUTTING LIST

ITEM	MATERIAL	NO.	LENGTH	WIDTH	THICKNESS
Board piece	Beech	8	23⅝ in* (600 mm)	1⅜ in (350 mm)	1¾ in (450 mm)

*Includes excess to allow for cutting to size

TOOLS AND MATERIALS
Pencil
Ruler
Wood glue and brush
Sash clamps
Square
Bench plane
Panel saw or band saw
Shooting board
Cabinet scraper (optional)
Sandpaper
Food-safe oil

DIMENSIONS
17¹¹⁄₁₆ x 11 x 1¾ in
(450 x 280 x 45 mm)

KEY TECHNIQUE
Butt joint (see pp.68–69)

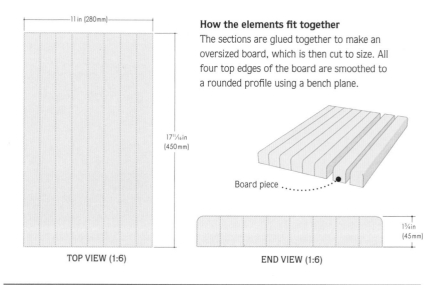

11 in (280 mm)

17¹¹⁄₁₆ in (450 mm)

TOP VIEW (1:6)

How the elements fit together
The sections are glued together to make an oversized board, which is then cut to size. All four top edges of the board are smoothed to a rounded profile using a bench plane.

Board piece

1¾ in (45 mm)

END VIEW (1:6)

🪚 GLUING AND SIZING THE BOARD

1 Arrange the pieces according to appearance and grain direction (see pp.68–69). Check that they fit together. Draw a V-mark across the assembly with a pencil and metal ruler to mark the position of the pieces.

Off-cuts protect the wood during clamping

2 Apply glue to the joining edges and assemble the pieces in the sash clamps, lining up the V-mark. Clamp the assembly tightly in the sash clamps and wipe away any excess glue. Leave to dry overnight.

3 Mark the finished length—17¹¹⁄₁₆ in (450 mm)—and square the lines across the assembled pieces using a square (inset). Cut the end grains to the length lines either by hand, using a panel saw (pictured), or on a band saw.

4 Shoot the end grains smooth and square using a bench plane guided by a shooting board.

FINISHING THE BOARD

1 Secure the board against an end-stop and plane both surfaces flat, working across the grain first (pictured). As you work, use the edge of the plane to check the board for flatness (inset). Smooth both surfaces flat with either a cabinet scraper or a piece of sandpaper.

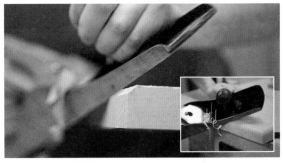

2 Use a bench plane to chamfer the edges of the upper face of the board. Work across the grain (along with short sides) first, then with the grain (along with long sides). Work around all four edges in the same order several more times, progressively taking more off each edge until you have a finished, rounded shape (inset).

3 Sand all four edges smooth. Apply olive oil or a similar food-safe oil for a nontoxic finish.

THE FINISHED PIECE

COAT RACK

This simple coat rack requires minimal materials and a basic range of tools. The length of the backboard and number of pegs can easily be modified to suit the space available and the amount of hanging capacity required. You will need to attach fittings to the backboard, appropriate to the wall surface, to secure the coat rack safely in the chosen position.

TOOLS AND MATERIALS
Pencil
Square
Marking gauge
Drill with bits
Chisel
Bench plane
Marking knife
Tenon saw
Block plane
Sandpaper
File
Wood glue and brush

DIMENSIONS
47¼ x 3⁹⁄₁₆ x 1¾ in
   (1200 x 90 x 45 mm)

KEY TECHNIQUE
Basic mortise-and-tenon joint
   (see pp.91–95)

CUTTING LIST					
ITEM	MATERIAL	NO.	LENGTH	WIDTH	THICKNESS
Backboard	Oak	1	47¼ in (1200 mm)	1³⁄₁₆ in (90 mm)	¹³⁄₁₆ in (20 mm)
Peg	Oak	4	2⁹⁄₁₆ in (65 mm)	1 in (25 mm)	¹³⁄₁₆ in (20 mm)

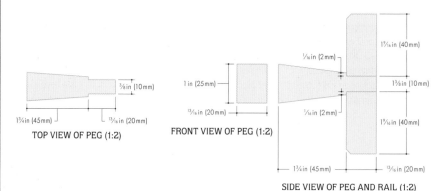

TOP VIEW OF PEG (1:2)

FRONT VIEW OF PEG (1:2)

SIDE VIEW OF PEG AND RAIL (1:2)

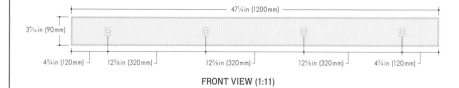

FRONT VIEW (1:11)

How the elements fit together
The pegs are mortised through the full thickness of the backboard for maximum strength and durability. The peg tenons have a shoulder all around, which lends them extra strength for taking the weight of heavy coats or other items.

⛊ MARKING THE MORTISES ON THE BACKBOARD

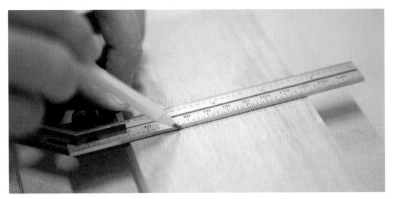

1 With the backboard cut to size, square a line across the width of the board to mark the center-point of each peg mortise (see Front view diagram, opposite, for positions).

2 Mark the mortise width with a pencil ³⁄₁₆ in (5 mm) to either side of the center-point line.

3 Extend the marks across the full width of the backboard with a pencil and square.

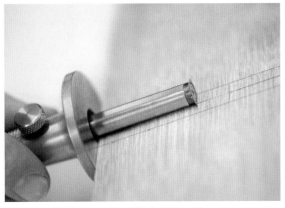

4 Use a marking gauge set to 1¹⁹⁄₁₆ in (40 mm) to scribe a line between the mortise width marks from each edge of the backboard to mark the mortise length.

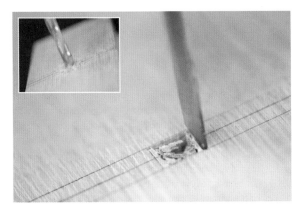

5 Use a drill to remove the bulk of the mortise waste (inset), then clean up the edges with a chisel (pictured). Repeat steps 1–5 for all mortises.

6 Secure the backboard in a vise, then chamfer the front edges of the backboard with a bench plane.

🪚 MARKING OUT THE PEGS

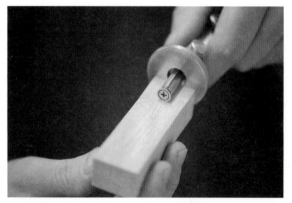

1 Mark the tenon shoulder on each peg piece ¹³⁄₁₆ in (20 mm) from one end grain, then square the mark around all four sides.

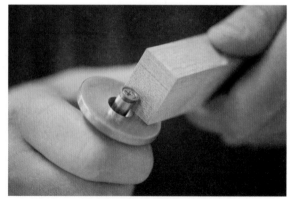

2 Use a marking gauge set to ⁵⁄₁₆ in (7.5 mm) to scribe across the same end grain from the short edges. Extend the marks down both faces to the shoulder.

3 Reset the marking gauge to ³⁄₁₆ in (5 mm) and scribe along the end grain from each face and down the edges to the shoulder.

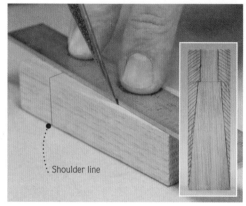

Shoulder line

4 Use a marking knife to make two marks on the shoulder line on each face, ¼ in (6 mm) from each edge. Score a diagonal line from each mark to the untenoned corners (pictured). Mark both faces of all four peg pieces in the same way, and use a pencil to mark the waste for removal (inset).

🪚 CUTTING THE TENONS AND TAPERS

1 Use a tenon saw to cut the tenons down the scribed lines to the shoulder, then cross-cut along the shoulders (inset). Repeat on the remaining three pegs.

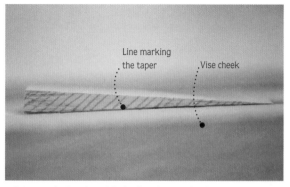

Line marking the taper　　Vise cheek

2 Set a peg in the vise with the line that marks the taper in alignment with the top of the vise cheeks.

3 Plane to the line with a block plane, then repeat on the opposite edge. Taper all of the pegs in the same way.

4 Smooth all of the surfaces and remove any arrises with sandpaper. File the edges at the untenoned ends of the pegs (inset).

ATTACHING THE PEGS

1 After testing the fit, apply glue to all of the peg tenons and insert each firmly into its mortise. Clean up any excess glue.

2 Once the glue has dried, use a block plane to smooth the tenons on the rear of the backboard.

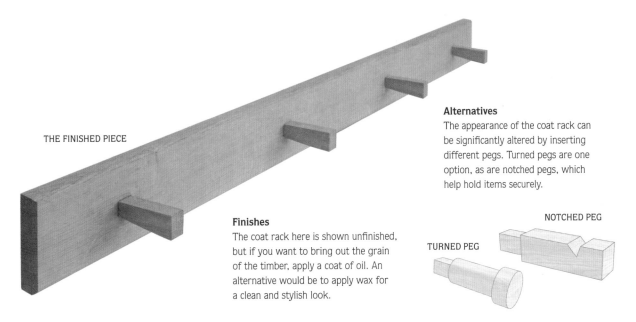

THE FINISHED PIECE

Finishes
The coat rack here is shown unfinished, but if you want to bring out the grain of the timber, apply a coat of oil. An alternative would be to apply wax for a clean and stylish look.

Alternatives
The appearance of the coat rack can be significantly altered by inserting different pegs. Turned pegs are one option, as are notched pegs, which help hold items securely.

NOTCHED PEG

TURNED PEG

MIRROR FRAME

Being able to produce a good miter joint is an invaluable woodworking skill because it can be employed in a range of projects, including picture frames, boxes, plinths, baseboards, and architraves.

This particular frame uses a slightly more advanced keyed miter joint (see pp.88-89), which increases the surface area onto which glue can be applied.

TOOLS AND MATERIALS

Sash clamp
Marking gauge
Shoulder plane or router
Marking knife
Ruler
Bench plane
Combination square
Miter saw or miter block
Bevel-edged chisel
45-degree shooting board
Wood glue and brush
Ratchet strap clamp
Finishing oil
Sandpaper and block
Mirror (16 x 16 in/406 x 406 mm)
Small hammer
Panel pins

DIMENSIONS

17¹⁵⁄₁₆ x 17¹⁵⁄₁₆ x 1³⁄₈ in
   (455 x 455 x 35 mm)

KEY TECHNIQUE

Keyed miter joint (see pp.88–89)

CUTTING LIST

ITEM	MATERIAL	NO.	LENGTH	WIDTH	THICKNESS
Frame piece	Walnut	4	19¹¹⁄₁₆ in* (500 mm)	1³⁄₈ in (35 mm)	1³⁄₁₆ in (30 mm)
Key	Ply	4	³⁄₈ in (10 mm)	³⁄₈ in (10 mm)	¼ in (6 mm)
Backing board	Hardboard	1	16 in (406 mm)	16 in (406 mm)	⅛ in (3 mm)

*Includes excess to allow for cutting to size

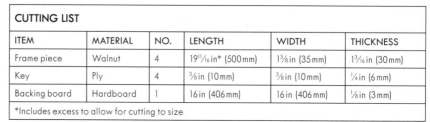

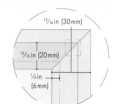

DETAIL OF FRONT
OF MITER (1:3)

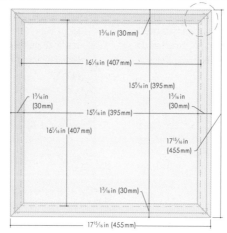

FRONT VIEW (1:7)

CROSS-SECTION VIEW (1:7)

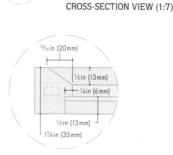

DETAIL OF MITER
SECTION (1:3)

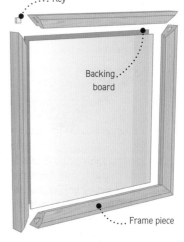

How the elements fit together
The mitered corners are strengthened by the use of plywood "keys," which also help keep the miters flush with one another when being glued. A rebate in the back of the frame accommodates the mirror, which is held in place with pins.

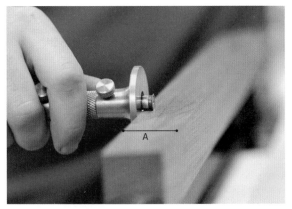

1 Secure each frame piece edge-up and score a line along the edge (A) with a marking gauge set to ¼ in (6 mm). Then score another line along face B (see step 2) with the gauge set to ½ in (13 mm).

2 Cut a rebate to the marked lines with a shoulder plane (pictured) or a router (see below left). Repeat steps 1 and 2 for the remaining three frame pieces.

Machine-cutting the rebate
You can use a router with a straight cutter to cut a rebate ¼ in (6 mm) wide by ½ in (13 mm) deep between the scored lines along the length of each frame piece.

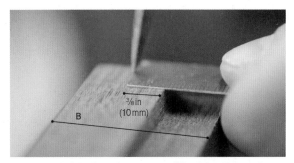

3 At the end of the first piece, measure ⅜ in (10 mm) from the edge of the rebate on the face (B), and extend the line along the length of the face with a marking gauge.

4 On the adjacent side (C), mark ⅜ in (10 mm) from the outside edge of the frame. Scribe the line along the length of the piece.

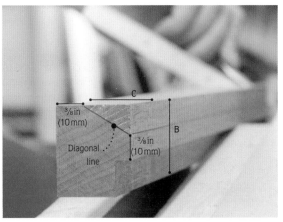

5 Join the marks by scribing a diagonal line across the corner on both end grains. Mark all three remaining frame pieces in the same way.

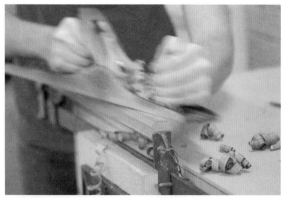

6 Secure the piece in a vise with the corner just marked uppermost. Plane the waste to create the splay. Repeat steps 3–6 for the remaining pieces.

Splay

7 Use a combination square and marking knife to scribe a 45-degree angle (see diagram on p.174 for measurements) on both ends of each piece, the splay uppermost.

8 Cut the miters to the waste side of the marks to allow for finishing with a plane. Use a miter saw (pictured) or a miter block.

9 Place each piece on a 45-degree shooting board (see p.51) and plane each end exactly to size.

◢ MARKING OUT THE MORTISE

1 Mark the mortise position on the mitered surface. Set the marking gauge at ⁹⁄₁₆in (14.5mm) and score a line from edge to edge. Measure and mark a line at ¹³⁄₁₆in (20.5mm) from the other side, leaving a mortise width of ¼in (6mm).

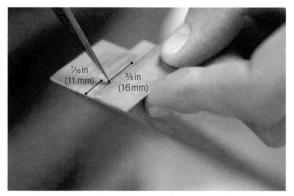

⁷⁄₁₆in (11mm) ⁵⁄₈in (16mm)

2 Mark the mortise length of ⁵⁄₈in (16mm), with the base of the mortise ⁷⁄₁₆in (11mm) from the bottom of the miter.

⚙ CUTTING AND FITTING THE MORTISES AND KEYS

1 Cut the mortise by hand with a bevel-edged chisel (pictured) to a depth of ⅜ in (10mm) from the maximum extent of the miter. Cut four "keys" ⅜ in (10mm) square from ¼ in (6mm) plywood, and insert a key into one mortise of each piece (inset).

2 After checking the fit, glue all the mortises and keys and assemble the frame, carefully inserting each key into its matching mortise.

3 Clamp the assembled frame firmly with a ratchet strap (see p.29) and leave the glue to dry overnight.

⚙ FINISHING THE FRAME

Sand all the surfaces of the frame assembly smooth once the glue is dry (inset). Securing the frame in a vise makes this job easier. Carefully apply one or two coats of finishing oil to all parts of the frame (pictured) and leave it to dry.

THE FINISHED PIECE

⚙ SECURING THE MIRROR

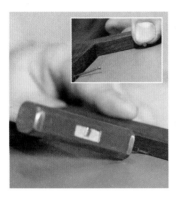

Place the mirror in the frame. Use a small hammer to insert panel pins at an angle at regular intervals into the inside edge of the back of the frame (pictured). Use your thumb to push the pins horizontal to hold the mirror securely within the rebate (inset).

LAUNDRY HAMPER

A simple project for the woodworker, this laundry hamper is a practical item to have in the home. The design utilizes a biscuit-jointed MDF box for its internal structure—a useful technique that can be employed in a range of woodworking projects because it provides a quick, strong corner joint. The tongue-and-groove cladding is pinned and glued to the MDF core—another adaptable technique that can be used for covering surfaces around the home, such as boxes built around pipe work or cladding on the sides of a bathtub.

TOOLS AND MATERIALS
Pencil
Square
Router and bits
Chisel
Band saw or jigsaw
Metal ruler
Biscuit joiner
12 size-10 biscuits
Wood glue and brush
Sash clamps
Tape measure
Sandpaper
Drill with bits
4 screws (8 x 1⅜ in/4 x 30 mm)
Block plane
Bench plane
Nail gun or hammer
Coping saw
Panel pins

DIMENSIONS
24⁷⁄₁₆ x 14⁷⁄₁₆ x 14⁷⁄₁₆ in
   (620 x 366 x 366 mm)

KEY TECHNIQUES
Biscuit joints (see pp.122–123);
Fixed tongue-and-groove joint
   (see pp.72–73);
Butt joint (see pp.68–69)

CUTTING LIST					
ITEM	MATERIAL	NO.	LENGTH	WIDTH	THICKNESS
Wide side	MDF	2	23⅝ in (600 mm)	13¼ in (336 mm)	¹¹⁄₁₆ in (18 mm)
Narrow side	MDF	2	23⅝ in (600 mm)	11⅞ in (300 mm)	¹¹⁄₁₆ in (18 mm)
Tongue-and-groove cladding	Pine	16	23⅝ in (600 mm)	3⁹⁄₁₆ in (90 mm)	⅜ in (10 mm)
Lid	Oak	4	15¾ in* (400 mm)	3¹⁵⁄₁₆ in* (100 mm)	¹³⁄₁₆ in (20 mm)
Batten	Oak	2	11⅞ in (300 mm)	¹³⁄₁₆ in (20 mm)	¹³⁄₁₆ in (20 mm)
Base	MDF	1	12⅝ in (320 mm)	12⅝ in (320 mm)	¹¹⁄₁₆ in (18 mm)

*Includes excess to allow for cutting to size

SIDE VIEW (1:9)

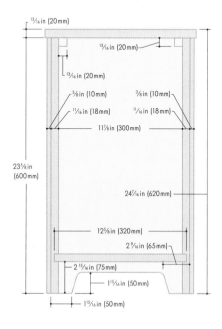

CROSS-SECTION (1:9)

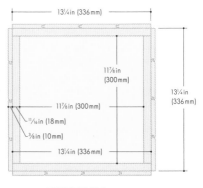

TOP VIEW (1:9)

UNDERSIDE OF LID (1:9)

How the elements fit together
The MDF core is biscuit-jointed and concealed within tongue-and-groove joined pine cladding. The lid is a panel made from oak boards. It is secured over the box by two battens screwed to its underside.

Lid

Batten

Narrow side

Base

Cladding

Wide side

🪚 CUTTING THE HOUSING FOR THE BASE

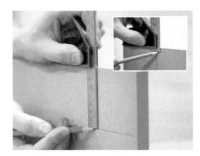

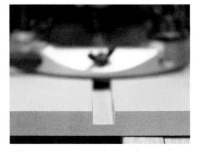

1 Mark the lower edge of the housing 2¹⁵⁄₁₆ in (75 mm) from the bottom of the four side pieces. Mark a stop ⁵⁄₁₆ in (7 mm) from both edges of the two wide sides (inset).

2 Use a router to cut the housing on the two narrow sides above the marked lines to a width of ¹¹⁄₁₆ in (18 mm) and a depth of ⅜ in (10 mm). Extend the housing through the full width of each piece.

3 Cut the housing on the wide sides to the marked stop (inset), then square off the ends with a chisel.

▲ MARKING OUT THE FEET

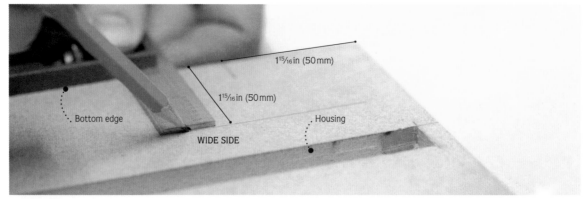

1 Mark a point on the bottom edge of a wide side, on the same face as the housing, 1¹⁵⁄₁₆ in (50 mm) from one side. Repeat from the other side, on the same face. Then draw a line across the width of the side 1¹⁵⁄₁₆ in (50 mm) from the bottom edge. Repeat on the other wide side.

2 Mark a point 2⁹⁄₁₆ in (65 mm) from each edge on the lines just drawn. Draw lines to join those points to the marks made on the bottom edges in step 1 (inset).

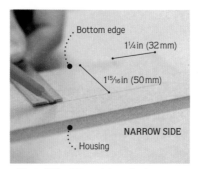

3 Mark 1¼ in (32 mm) from both edges of one narrow side, on the same face as the housing. Then draw a line across the side 1¹⁵⁄₁₆ in (50 mm) from the bottom edge.

4 Mark a point 1⅞ in (47 mm) from both edges along the lines just drawn, then join the points to the marks made in step 3. Repeat steps 3–4 on the other narrow side.

▲ CUTTING OUT THE FEET

1 Cut out the feet of all four sides using a band saw (pictured) or jigsaw. Cut on the waste side of the marked lines.

2 Trim back to the marked lines with a router. Clamp a straight edge of spare wood to the piece to act as a fence (guide) for the router.

▲ JOINTING THE SIDES

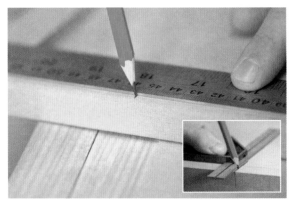

1 Mark the positions for three biscuit joints along both vertical (long) edges of each wide side, spaced approximately equidistantly above the base housing. Extend the marks across the full width of the edges (inset).

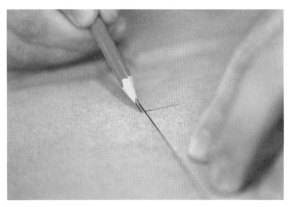

2 Set a narrow side alongside a wide side and transfer the marks onto the inner face of the narrow side.

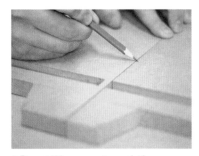

3 Repeat this process to mark the guide positions for the biscuit joiner on the opposite side of the inner face. Repeat steps 2 and 3 for the remaining narrow side.

4 Use a biscuit joiner to cut size-10 slots in both vertical (long) edges of the narrow sides. Center the biscuit joiner on each of the marks on the inner face.

5 Cut the slots in the wide sides in the same way, but in the inner face. This time, center the biscuit joiner on each of the marks on the edges.

▲ ASSEMBLING THE SIDES AND BASE

1 Insert a size-10 biscuit into each of the slots in the edges of the narrow sides, then test-assemble the structure. Insert the base in the housing to check the fit.

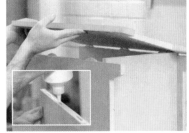

2 Apply glue liberally to the biscuits and the edges of the sides (inset). Assemble three sides, insert the base, and then place the fourth side in position.

3 Clamp the assembly with sash clamps and check for squareness with a tape measure. Clean up any excess glue.

1 Join the lid pieces (see Butt joint, pp.68–69) and cut to the final size (see the diagram on p.178). Sand smooth.

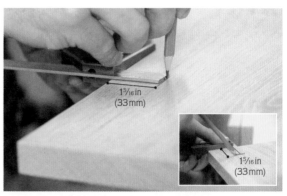

2 Mark a line 1⁵⁄₁₆in (33mm) from each edge on the underside of the lid. Then mark a point 1⁵⁄₁₆in (33mm) from the end grain at each end of both lines (inset). These marks define the positions of the battens.

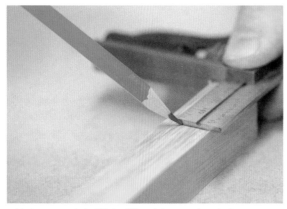

3 Mark a screw hole 1³⁄₁₆in (20mm) from each end of both battens.

4 Drill clearance holes to match the screws, centered within the batten width.

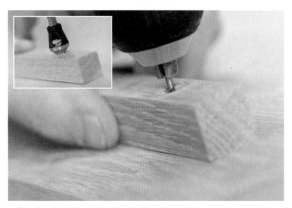

5 Countersink the holes (inset). Place the battens on the underside of the lid in the marked positions, then drill pilot holes partway into the lid through the clearance holes.

6 Screw the battens into position. Use a block plane to chamfer the outside edges of the battens (inset).

▲ FITTING THE TONGUE-AND-GROOVE CLADDING

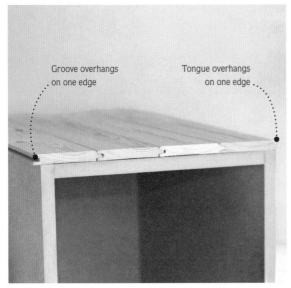

Groove overhangs on one edge

Tongue overhangs on one edge

1 Assemble four pieces of tongue-and-groove cladding and position them against one side of the box. Align them flush to the top edge so that the tongue and the groove of the outside pieces overhang the sides.

Workpiece held in vise

2 Draw a pencil line to mark the position of the overhang on the underside of each of the outer slats (inset). Use a bench plane to trim the outer edges to the line.

3 Apply wood glue to the side of the box, spreading it evenly over the entire surface with a brush (inset). Then set the assembled slats in position on the glued side. Adjust them to align as in step 1 (above).

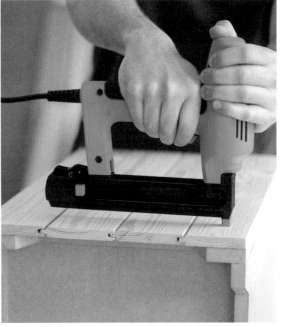

4 Nail the cladding to the box side with panel pins using a nail gun (pictured) or by hand with a hammer. Insert a pin at the top and bottom of each slat approximately 1 in (25 mm) from the end. Allow the glue to dry.

⬤ CUTTING OUT THE LEGS AND FINISHING THE BOX

1 Roughly cut the shape of the legs from the cladding using a coping saw, following the shape of the MDF carcase.

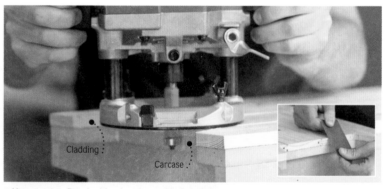

Cladding

Carcase

2 Use a router fitted with a bearing-guided straight cutter to trim the cladding flush to the carcase base. Sand the edges smooth (inset).

3 Repeat steps 1–4, fitting the tongue-and-groove cladding (see p.183), for the remaining three sides. Then repeat steps 1–2 (above) to cut out the remaining legs.

4 Once all the cladding is in place, use a block plane to chamfer the outer edges of the cladding along each corner of the box.

THE FINISHED PIECE

WINE RACK

This straightforward and accessible project is an excellent way for the novice woodworker to gain confidence in the technique of using dowels as a method of jointing. The instructions here are suitable for a six-bottle unit, but you can increase its capacity by either incorporating longer façades or by making the stiles longer and adding an extra row of façades (see Alternatives, p.190).

CUTTING LIST

ITEM	MATERIAL	NO.	LENGTH	WIDTH	THICKNESS
Stile	Maple	4	13¾ in (350 mm)	13/16 in (20 mm)	13/16 in (20 mm)
Rail	Maple	4	3⁹/16 in (90 mm)	13/16 in (20 mm)	13/16 in (20 mm)
Façade	Cherry	4	19⅞ in (505 mm)	2⅜ in (60 mm)	⁹/16 in (15 mm)
Dowel connector	Beech	24	13/16 in (20 mm)	⅜ in (10 mm)	⅜ in (10 mm)

TOOLS AND MATERIALS

Pencil
Ruler
Drill with ⅜ in (10 mm) bit
Masking tape
Wood glue and brush
F-clamps
Tape measure
C-clamps
Combination square
Protractor
Coping saw
Sandpaper

DIMENSIONS

19¹⁵/16 x 13¾ x 5³/16 in
(505 x 350 x 130 mm)

KEY TECHNIQUE

Dowel joints using center points
(see pp.126–127)

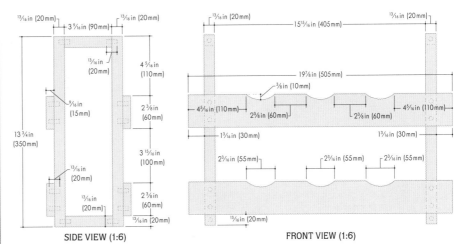

SIDE VIEW (1:6)

FRONT VIEW (1:6)

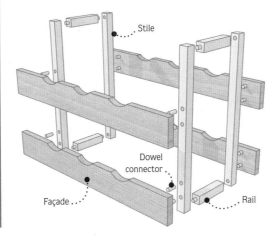

Façade

Dowel connector

Stile

Rail

How the elements fit together

The stiles and rails of the upright frames are joined by dowel connectors, which also attach the façades to the front and back. Three scoops on each rail provide support for six bottles.

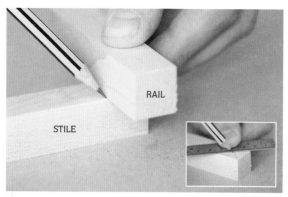

1 Mark the width of a rail at one end of a stile with a pencil line (pictured), aligning the rail against the end grain of the stile. Mark the center point between this mark and the end grain by drawing diagonals from corner to corner (inset). Mark both ends of all four stiles in the same way.

2 Use masking tape to mark a drilling depth of ³⁄₈ in (10 mm) on a ³⁄₈ in (10 mm) drill bit. Drill a hole to this depth in each of the marked positions.

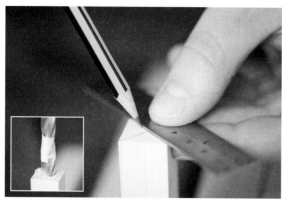

3 Mark the center of the end grain at both ends of all four rails (horizontal pieces), then drill through each mark to a depth of ³⁄₈ in (10 mm) and a width of ³⁄₈ in (10 mm) (inset).

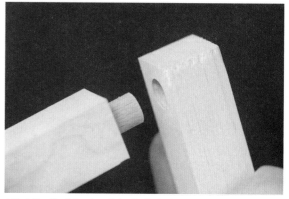

4 Test the fit of the dowels in the holes in the stiles and rails. Adjust if necessary to ease the fit.

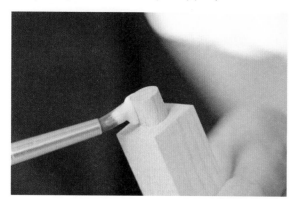

5 Use a brush to apply glue to the holes and dowels of the stiles and rails, then assemble the frames.

6 Clamp the frames and use a tape measure to check for squareness. Wipe off any excess glue and leave to dry.

🪚 MARKING UP THE BOTTLE SUPPORTS IN THE FAÇADES

1 Clamp all four façades together with the top edge and end grains aligned. Mark a line square across the edges of all the pieces at the midpoint of the length.

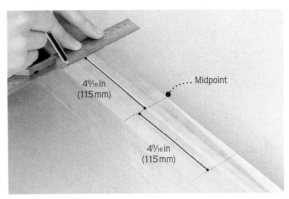

2 Draw a line 4⁹⁄₁₆ in (115 mm) from either side of the midpoint and square the marks across the edges.

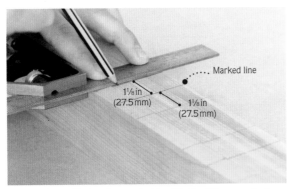

3 Mark 1⅛ in (27.5 mm) on each side of both of these marked lines, then square the marks across the edges.

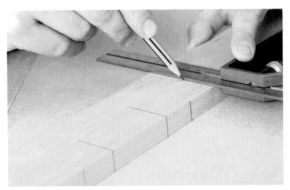

4 Unclamp the pieces, then extend the marks made in step 3 across one face of each piece.

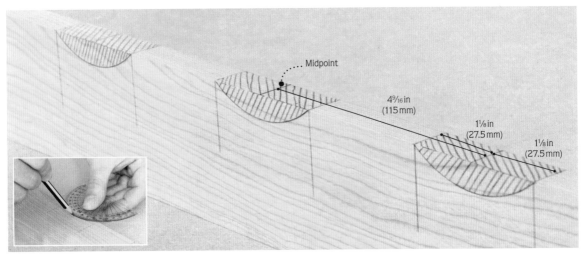

5 Place a protractor between each pair of lines so that the edges intersect at the top edge of the façade (inset). Draw around the protractor to mark a uniform curve for the bottle holders in each position. Mark the waste for removal.

⬛ CUTTING THE BOTTLE SUPPORTS

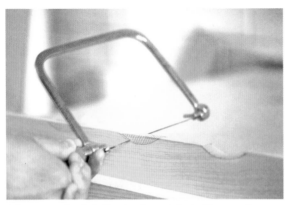

1 Secure one façade in the vise, then cut the bottle supports on the waste side of the marks with a coping saw.

2 Use coarse sandpaper to remove the waste to the marks. Repeat steps 1–2 for the remaining façades.

⬛ ASSEMBLING THE RACK

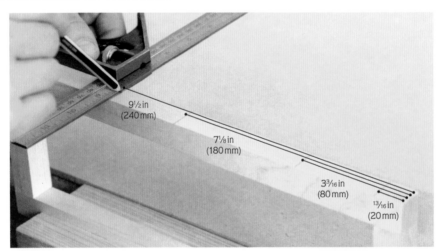

9½ in (240 mm)

7⅛ in (180 mm)

3³⁄₁₆ in (80 mm)

¹³⁄₁₆ in (20 mm)

1 Set one end frame in a vise with the edge of the stile positioned horizontally. Square four lines across the outer edge at the distances shown from the end grain.

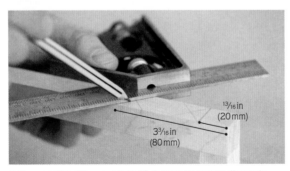

¹³⁄₁₆ in (20 mm)

3³⁄₁₆ in (80 mm)

2 Use a combination square at 45 degrees to project diagonals as shown. The point at which the diagonal lines intersect is the center point for the dowel holes.

3 Drill into the point of each intersection to a depth of ⅜ in (10 mm), using a ⅜ in (10 mm) drill bit.

4 Repeat steps 1–3 for the outer edges of the remaining three stiles. Check that all marks for hole placement are aligned with the marks on the first stile before drilling any holes.

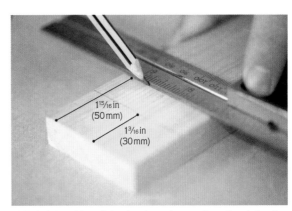

5 Mark the position of the dowels on the rear face of each façade. Square two lines across the face 1³⁄₁₆ in (30 mm) and 1¹⁵⁄₁₆ in (50 mm) from the end grain at both ends of the façade.

6 Set the combination square to 45 degrees and mark four intersecting diagonals from each edge, within the lines.

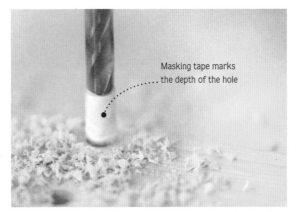

Masking tape marks the depth of the hole

7 Drill a hole into each of the positions marked by the intersecting diagonals to a depth of ³⁄₈ in (10 mm). Repeat steps 5–7 for the other three façades.

8 Insert a dowel connector into every hole in each façade, then insert them into the holes in the end frames to check the fit.

1 Remove the façades from the end frames, then sand all elements to remove any rough edges.

2 Brush glue into the dowel holes in the façades and end-frame stiles, then assemble the wine rack.

3 Securely clamp each façade and end-frame joint, then leave the assembly to dry.

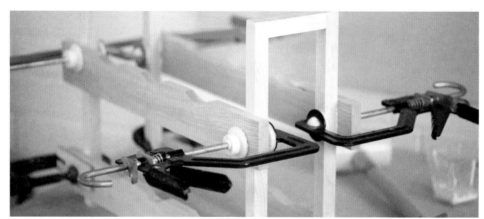

THE FINISHED PIECE

ALTERNATIVES

If you are a more confident woodworker, try adapting the wine rack to your specific needs or to the décor of the room for which it is intended. You could, for example, increase (or decrease) the height of the stiles and add additional façades if applicable. Alternatively, increase the length of the façades themselves to fit the space available. (You may need to incorporate an additional central stile for support.) Esthetic alternatives could involve experimenting with different shapes. (Perhaps you could shape the bottom edge of the façade to complement the curves in the top edge.) Or try using different woods—walnut would be a suitable dark wood.

JEWELRY BOX

Box making is a complete genre of fine woodworking in its own right, and the design of this jewelry box uses several classic approaches and techniques. When working on such a small scale, it is especially important to work accurately—any mistakes or gaps will be obvious, especially when working with lighter timbers, such as maple or sycamore. The outer box is constructed as an enclosed cube before being cut in two to make the box and lid.

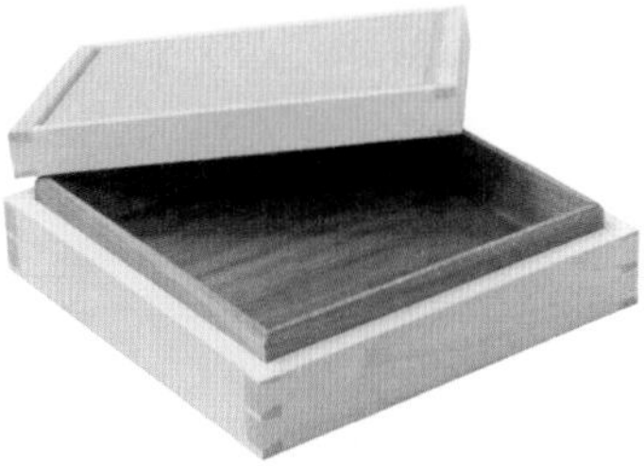

TOOLS AND MATERIALS

Bench plane
Shooting board
Marking gauge
1-in-8 dovetail marker
Marking knife
Pencil
Combination square
Dovetail saw
Coping saw
Narrow-bladed chisel
Table-mounted router
Shoulder or rebate plane
Several grades of sandpaper
Double-sided tape
Masking tape (optional)
Finishing oil (optional)
Wood glue and brush
Clamps
Tape measure or ruler
Block plane
Band saw
45-degree shooting board

DIMENSIONS

5⅞ x 5⅞ x 1 9/16 in
(50 x 150 x 41 mm)

KEY TECHNIQUE

Through-dovetail joint
(see pp.116–121)

CUTTING LIST					
ITEM	MATERIAL	NO.	LENGTH	WIDTH	THICKNESS
Tail side piece	Maple	2	5 15/16 in* (152 mm)	1 11/16 in* (43 mm)	5/16 in (8 mm)
Socket side piece	Maple	2	5 15/16 in* (152 mm)	1 11/16 in* (43 mm)	5/16 in (8 mm)
Lid piece	Maple	1	5 9/16 in (142 mm)	5 9/16 in (142 mm)	5/16 in (7 mm)
Base piece	Walnut	1	5 9/16 in (142 mm)	5 9/16 in (142 mm)	5/16 in (7 mm)
Lining piece	Walnut	4	5 7/16 in* (139 mm)	7/8 in (22 mm)	1/8 in (3 mm)

*Includes excess to allow for cutting to size

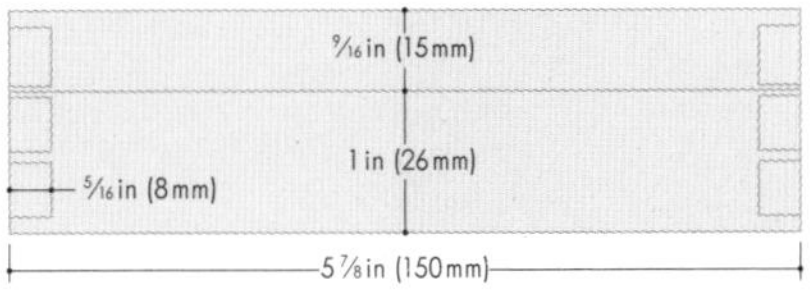
9/16 in (15 mm)
1 in (26 mm)
5/16 in (8 mm)
5 7/8 in (150 mm)

FRONT VIEW (1:2)

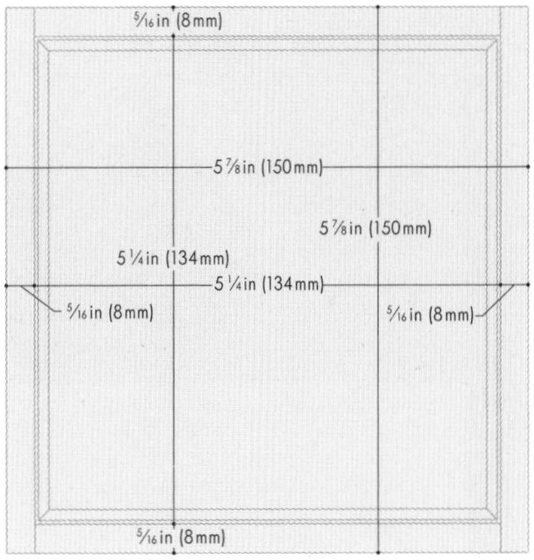
5/16 in (8 mm)
5 7/8 in (150 mm)
5 7/8 in (150 mm)
5 1/4 in (134 mm)
5 1/4 in (134 mm)
5/16 in (8 mm)
5/16 in (8 mm)
5/16 in (8 mm)

TOP VIEW (1:2)

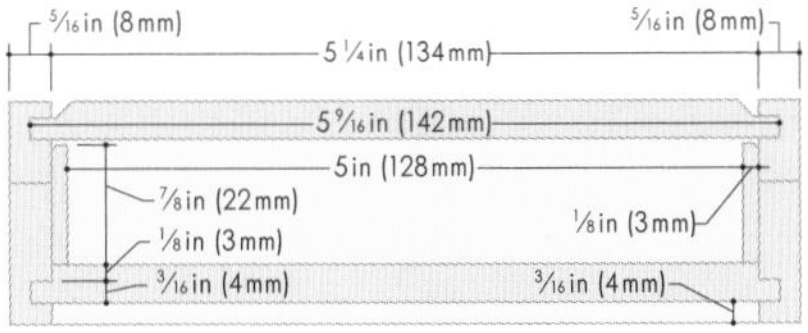
5/16 in (8 mm)
5 1/4 in (134 mm)
5/16 in (8 mm)
5 9/16 in (142 mm)
5 in (128 mm)
7/8 in (22 mm)
1/8 in (3 mm)
1/8 in (3 mm)
3/16 in (4 mm)
3/16 in (4 mm)

CROSS-SECTION (1:2)

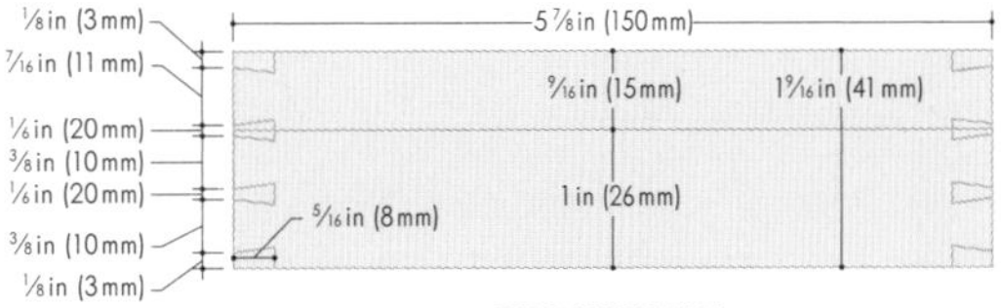
1/8 in (3 mm)
7/16 in (11 mm)
3/4 in (20 mm)
3/8 in (10 mm)
3/4 in (20 mm)
3/8 in (10 mm)
1/8 in (3 mm)
5 7/8 in (150 mm)
9/16 in (15 mm)
1 9/16 in (41 mm)
1 in (26 mm)
5/16 in (8 mm)

SIDE VIEW (1:2)

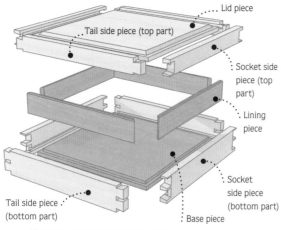

Lid piece

Tail side piece (top part)

Socket side piece (top part)

Lining piece

Socket side piece (bottom part)

Tail side piece (bottom part)

Base piece

How the elements fit together

Two grooves that run along the inside edges of the sides provide a housing for the base and lid panels. The box lining has mitered corners and provides a lipping over which the lid fits.

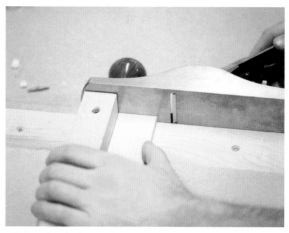

1 Using a bench plane and shooting board, square off the end grains of all four side pieces to approximately 1/16 in (2 mm) oversize.

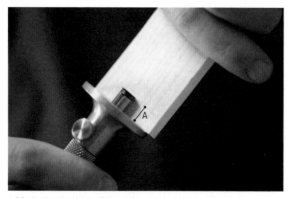

2 Mark the shoulder of the tails and pins (A) on both sides of each end of the four side pieces, using a marking gauge set to 1/32 in (1 mm) more than the thickness of the side pieces. (See also Through-dovetail joint, pp.116–121, for detailed instructions on making dovetail joints.)

3 Use a 1-in-8 dovetail marker to mark tail angles on both faces and ends of the two tail side pieces. Leave a gap between two tails to create a wide pin socket, which should be twice as wide as the other sockets.

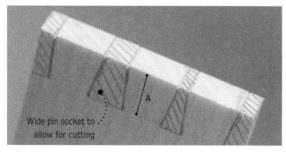

Wide pin socket to allow for cutting

4 Mark the waste with a pencil. The wide pin socket mentioned in step 3 allows the box to be split. (See step 2, Separating the lid from the box, p.196.)

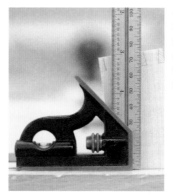

5 Secure one of the tail side pieces in a vise, using a combination square to align it so that one set of tail marks is perpendicular to the bench.

6 Use a dovetail saw to cut along the vertical marks to the shoulder. Then adjust the wood so that the remaining tail marks are vertical. Cut and repeat on the other end.

7 Remove the waste from between the tails by cutting with a coping saw and narrow-bladed chisel. Repeat steps 4–7 for the other tail side piece.

☀ MAKING THE PINS

Wide pin socket

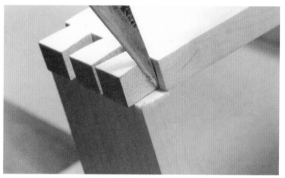

1 Secure one of the remaining two side pieces (the socket side pieces) in a vise. Rest a tail side piece on its end grain, touching its shoulder at right angles.

2 Scribe the tail positions onto the end grain of the socket side piece with a marking knife, ensuring that the tail side piece is supported securely.

3 Use a square to extend the marks vertically down both faces to the shoulder. Repeat for both ends of both socket side pieces.

4 Cut the pins to the shoulder with a dovetail saw (as per steps 5–7, Making the tails, opposite), then remove the waste cleanly with a narrow-bladed chisel.

⬛ CUTTING THE GROOVES AND REBATES

Grooves on each socket piece extend into sockets

Grooves on each tail piece are stopped

1 Using a table-mounted router fitted with a ³⁄₁₆ in (4 mm) bit, with the fence and depth set to ³⁄₁₆ in (4 mm), cut a groove along both edges of the inner side of all four pieces. Test the fit of the pins and sockets of all four side pieces.

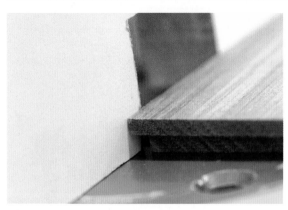

2 Cut a rebate along all four upper edges of the base piece, either with a shoulder plane or with the router. Set the fence to ¹⁄₈ in (3 mm) and the depth to ³⁄₁₆ in (4 mm).

3 Using a shoulder plane, or the router with the same settings, cut a rebate along all four upper edges of the lid piece.

Scored line marks start of chamfer

4 Mark a chamfer around all sides of the top of the lid piece with a marking gauge, ¹⁄₄ in (6 mm) from the edge.

5 Place the lid piece in a vise and cut the chamfer, using a shoulder or rebate plane. Work across the grain first.

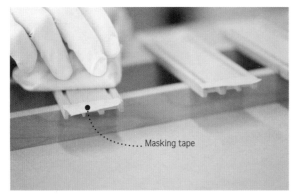

1 Sand the inside surfaces. If an oiled finish is desired, cover the inside faces of the tails and pins with masking tape to prevent them from being oiled, as oil reduces the effectiveness of the glue.

Masking tape

2 Use a clean rag to apply oil to the inside surfaces of the side, base, and lid pieces. For best results, apply three coats, allowing five hours' drying time between each coat.

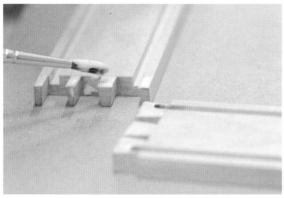

3 When the oil has dried, use a fine brush to apply glue to the tails and pins, then assemble three of the side pieces.

4 Insert the lid piece and base piece into the grooves on the inside faces of the three side pieces without applying glue. Glue the fourth side piece in place.

5 Clamp the assembly and check for squareness with a tape measure or ruler. Make any necessary adjustments, then set aside to allow the glue to dry.

⬤ SEPARATING THE LID FROM THE BOX

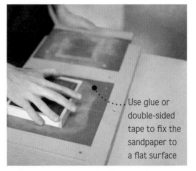

1 Once the glue has dried, use a block plane to remove the excess length of the tails and pins on all four sides of the box.

2 Separate the box into two parts by cutting it in two with a band saw. Line up the blade with the center of the largest pin (see step 3, Making the tails, p.192).

3 Clean any excess glue from the internal corners with a chisel, then sand flat the newly sawn edges of both parts of the box, using progressively finer grades of sandpaper.

Use glue or double-sided tape to fix the sandpaper to a flat surface

⬤ MAKING THE BOX LININGS

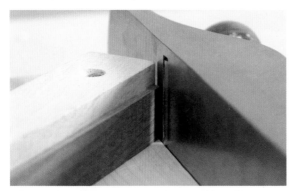

1 Cut the lining pieces to precise lengths by marking off exact dimensions from the inside of the box. Miter the ends with a bench plane guided by a 45-degree shooting board.

2 Chamfer the outer face of the upper edge of each of the lining pieces with a block plane. Fit the lining pieces inside the box (inset) without gluing.

3 Test the fit of the lid. When you are happy with the fit, oil the lining pieces and insert in position unglued.

THE FINISHED PIECE

WALL CABINET

This small wall-mounted cabinet is a practical storage unit for the bathroom or kitchen. Consisting of a jointed carcase, internal shelf, door, and back, it is a good piece for the novice woodworker to make to get comfortable with the basic principles of cabinet design. There are many kinds of wall fittings available; choose one that is suitable for the wall on which you intend to place the cabinet.

TOOLS AND MATERIALS

Marking gauge
Dividers
Marking knife
Square
Pencil
Tenon saw or band saw
Coping saw
Bevel-edged chisel
Ruler
Rubber mallet
Wood glue and brush
Masking tape
Sash clamps
Bench plane
Router and bearing-guided
    rebate cutter
Hammer
8 panel pins
2 brass butt hinges and screws
Bradawl
Drill with bits
Screwdriver
Sandpaper
Liming wax
Door catch

DIMENSIONS

$17^{11}/_{16}$ x $14^{3}/_{16}$ x $6^{9}/_{16}$ in
    (450 x 360 x 168 mm)

KEY TECHNIQUES

Dado joint (see pp.80–81);
    Comb joint (see pp.113–115)

CUTTING LIST

ITEM	MATERIAL	NO.	LENGTH	WIDTH	THICKNESS
Side	Oak	2	$17^{13}/_{16}$ in* (452 mm)	$5^{7}/_{8}$ in (150 mm)	$^{11}/_{16}$ in (18 mm)
End	Oak	2	$13^{7}/_{8}$ in* (352 mm)	$5^{7}/_{8}$ in (150 mm)	$^{11}/_{16}$ in (18 mm)
Shelf	Oak	1	$13^{1}/_{8}$ in (334 mm)	$5^{1}/_{8}$ in (130 mm)	$^{11}/_{16}$ in (18 mm)
Back	Oak-faced MDF	1	$17^{1}/_{16}$ in (434 mm)	$13^{1}/_{8}$ in (334 mm)	$^{3}/_{16}$ in (4 mm)
Door	Oak	1	$17^{11}/_{16}$ in (450 mm)	$14^{3}/_{16}$ in (360 mm)	$^{11}/_{16}$ in (18 mm)

*Includes excess to allow for cutting to size

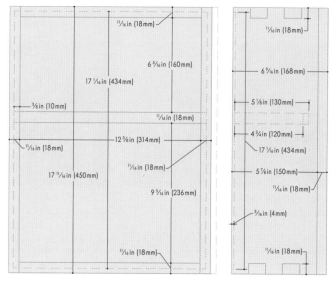

FRONT VIEW (1:6)

SIDE VIEW (1:6)

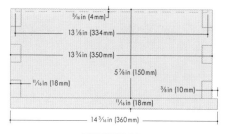

TOP VIEW (1:6)

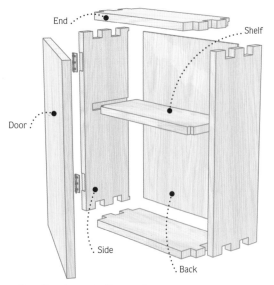

End

Shelf

Door

Side

Back

How the elements fit together
The carcase is comb jointed. The interior shelf is fitted into stopped housings on the inside of each side piece. Pinned into a rebate, the back panel helps keep the carcase square.

🪚 MARKING OUT THE COMB JOINTS ON THE SIDES AND ENDS

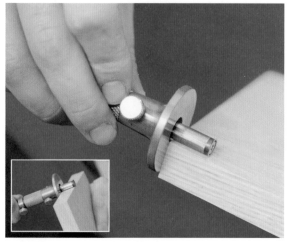

1 Set the marking gauge to $^{13}/_{16}$in (20mm)—the thickness of the timber of the carcase pieces plus $^1/_{16}$in (2mm) (inset). Scribe this measurement around all sides of both ends of the four carcase pieces to indicate the shoulder of the joint.

2 Set a pair of dividers to $1^3/_{16}$in (30mm) and mark holes to divide the end grains of each piece into five equal segments.

3 Mark the divisions with a marking knife and square, scoring across the width of the end grains of each piece.

4 Extend the marks to the shoulder on both faces of all four pieces, using the square and marking knife.

5 Mark the waste to be removed with a pencil. Be sure to mark alternating segments on the side pieces, and the top and bottom pieces (see Comb joint, pp.113–115).

1 With the piece secured in a vise, cut through the end grain with a small tenon saw, keeping to the waste side of the marks.

2 Release the waste with a coping saw. Cut slightly clear of the marks to allow for finishing.

3 Trim the bases and edges of the sockets with a bevel-edged chisel. If necessary, clamp a guide to allow you to chisel accurately.

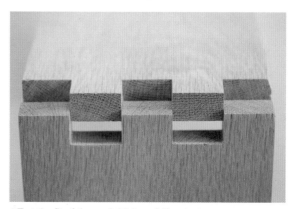

4 Test the fit of the comb joints and, if necessary, chisel away excess material to allow a tight fit.

CUTTING COMBS WITH A BAND SAW

You can use a band saw to cut the comb joints. To remove the central sections, you will need to use a chisel as well.

1 Make a series of relief cuts through the waste with the band saw to ease its removal with a chisel (see right).

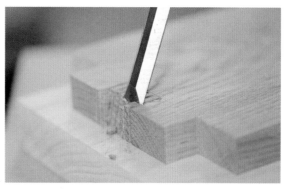

2 Use a bevel-edged chisel to chop away the waste, being careful not to exceed the marking lines.

MARKING AND CUTTING THE STOPPED HOUSING

1 Mark the housing for the shelf on the inside face of each side piece, 6⁵⁄₁₆ in (160 mm) from the shoulder at the top.

2 Mark the thickness of the wood—1¹⁄₁₆ in (18 mm)—at a point 7 in (178 mm) from the shoulder at the base of the comb.

3 Square the marks from both of these positions 4¾ in (120 mm) across the face to define the length of the housing.

4 Extend the marks down the back edge of the piece, and use the marking gauge to scribe the housing depth of ⅜ in (10 mm).

5 Scribe the housing stop ⅞ in (23 mm) from the front edge. Repeat steps 1–5 to mark the housing on the other side piece in the same way.

6 Remove the waste from each housing by hand or machine, as described for dado joints (see pp.80–81). Finish the edges by hand with a bevel-edged chisel.

🪚 MAKING THE SHELF

1 Mark the stop on the front edge of both ends of each shelf piece, ⅜in (10mm) deep (the housing depth) and ³⁄₁₆in (5mm) along the face. Extend the marks onto the end grain and the other face.

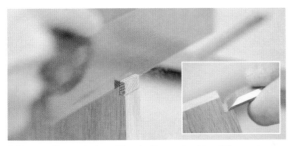

2 Remove the waste by cutting to the waste side of the marks with a small tenon saw (pictured). Finish cutting with a bevel-edged chisel (inset).

Shelf back is not flush with carcase side

3 Check the fit of the shelf in the housings. Note that the back of the shelf should not be flush with the side piece, to allow space for the back piece.

🪚 ASSEMBLING THE CARCASE

1 Do a test assembly of the carcase elements and shelf. Check the joints for squareness and adjust if necessary. Dismantle and apply glue (inset). Protect the wood from the glue with masking tape (to be removed before assembly).

2 Assemble the pieces and then clamp together to ensure that the carcase dries squarely. Once the glue is dry, remove the clamps and plane the joints flush (inset).

FITTING THE CABINET BACK

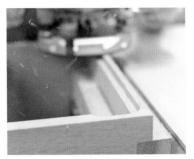

1 Use a router fitted with a bearing-guided rebate cutter set to a depth of ³⁄₁₆ in (4 mm) and width of ³⁄₈ in (10 mm) to cut a rebate along the inner edge of the frame.

2 Square off the corners and clean up the edges around the shelf housing, using a bevel-edged chisel.

3 Test fit the cabinet back and adjust it if necessary. Make a mark ³⁄₁₆ in (5 mm) from the edge of the back piece on all sides, and tap in two panel pins on each side.

FITTING THE HINGES TO THE CARCASE

1 Mark the position of the rebates for the two brass butt hinges on the front edge of one side of the carcase frame. The first is 1¹⁵⁄₁₆ in (50 mm) from the bottom and the second 1¹⁵⁄₁₆ in (50 mm) from the top.

2 Place the hinge in the first position and mark its length. Repeat for the second hinge position.

3 Extend the marks onto the outside face of the carcase side. Repeat for the second rebate.

4 Set a marking gauge to the thickness of the hinge (inset), and scribe between the length marks for each hinge on the outside face of the carcase.

5 Chisel away the waste to the marks for both hinge rebates and clean up, being careful not to exceed the marks.

6 Insert the hinge into the rebate, checking that it is flush with the wood. Mark the screw holes with a bradawl.

7 Drill pilot holes (and clearance holes if using traditional screws). Choose the drill bit and gauge the depth to suit the screws.

8 Insert the screws by hand with a screwdriver. Fit the second hinge, drill the screw holes, and insert the screws.

🪚 FITTING THE HINGES TO THE DOOR

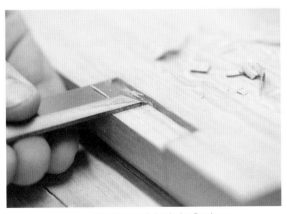

1 Mark the hinge positions on the inside face of the door, using the same measurements as on the carcase.

2 Cut the rebates with a chisel and check the fit, then screw in the other flap of the hinges to fit the door.

⬛ FINISHING THE CABINET

1 Sand the surfaces and edges of every part of the cabinet to achieve a perfectly smooth finish.

2 Finish the outside of the wall cabinet. Remove the door and apply liming wax (pictured), following the manufacturer's guidelines, or a different finish of your choice (see p.141).

3 Screw a ball catch or other catch of your choice into position in the top corner of the cabinet on the opposite side to the door hinges.

4 Hold the door against the carcase and mark the position of the catch on the inside face. Fit the other part of the catch in that position. Refit the door.

THE FINISHED PIECE

BOOKCASE

This bookcase uses wedged through mortise-and-tenon joints (see pp.100–103) for both esthetic effect and structural strength. The wedges, made from a contrasting color of timber, fulfill a visual as well as structural role, forming a key decorative feature of the piece. The shelves are progressively deeper from top to bottom and are spaced at different heights to accommodate a range of book sizes.

TOOLS AND MATERIALS
Wood glue and brush
Sash clamps and C-clamps
Jointer-thickness planer or bench plane
Table saw or panel saw
MDF 39 x 10 x ¼in/
   (1,000 x 250 x 6mm)
Ruler
Pencil
Pair of compasses
Band saw or coping saw
Block plane
Sandpaper
Router and cutters
Square
Bevel-edged chisel
Marking gauge
Drill with bits
Small tenon saw
Router table (optional)
Screwdriver
4 screws (No.8 x 1³⁄₁₆in /4 x 30mm)
Hammer
Flush-cut saw
Finishing oil

DIMENSIONS
37⅜ x 21½ x 8⁷⁄₁₆ in
   (951 x 545 x 215mm)

KEY TECHNIQUES
Butt joint (see pp.68–69); Wedged
   through mortise-and-tenon joint
   (see pp.100–103); Jigs and
   templates (see pp.132–133)

CUTTING LIST

ITEM	MATERIAL	NO.	LENGTH	WIDTH	THICKNESS
Side	Oak	4	39⅜in* (1000mm)	4¾in (120mm)	¹³⁄₁₆in (20mm)
Shelf 1	Oak	1	21⅝in* (550mm)	7⅞in (200mm)	¹³⁄₁₆in (20mm)
Shelf 2	Oak	1	21⅝in* (550mm)	6¹¹⁄₁₆in (170mm)	¹³⁄₁₆in (20mm)
Shelf 3	Oak	1	21⅝in* (550mm)	5¹¹⁄₁₆in (145mm)	¹³⁄₁₆in (20mm)
Shelf 4	Oak	1	21⅝in* (550mm)	5⅛in (130mm)	¹³⁄₁₆in (20mm)
Brace	Oak	1	20⅝in* (525mm)	2⁹⁄₁₆in (65mm)	¹³⁄₁₆in (20mm)
Wedge	Walnut	1	19¹¹⁄₁₆in* (500mm)	1¹⁄₁₆in (27mm)	¹⁄₁₆in (2mm)

*Includes excess to allow for cutting to size

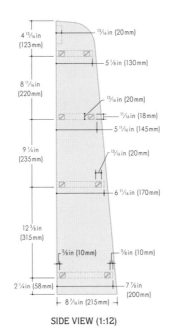

SIDE VIEW (1:12)

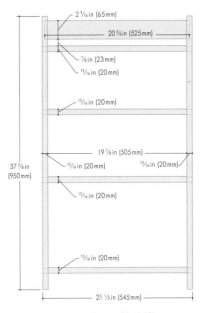

FRONT VIEW (1:12)

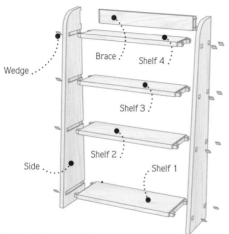

How the elements fit together

The shelves have two through tenons on each end and a stub tenon (short-tenoned section) between the two that locates into a housing. Wedges in the tenons firmly lock the joint in the mortise. A brace is also screwed across the top to provide extra stability.

PREPARING THE SIDE PIECES

1 Join the side pieces with glue (see Butt joint, pp.68–69) and clamp. Wipe off any excess glue and leave to dry.

2 Plane the joined side pieces on a jointer (pictured) or by hand using a bench plane.

3 Cut the pieces to a width of 8⁷⁄₁₆ in (215 mm) and length of 37⅜ in (950 mm) with a table saw or by hand with a panel saw.

MAKING THE TEMPLATE FOR THE SIDES

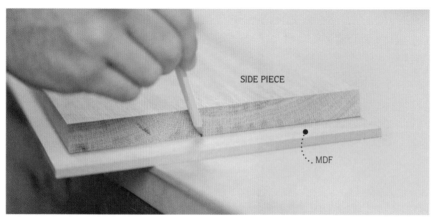

SIDE PIECE

MDF

1 Set a side piece over the MDF, aligned to one corner, and draw around it. On the MDF, working from the same corner, mark 3⁹⁄₁₆ in (90 mm) along the long edge and 5½ in (140 mm) along the short edge. Use a square to extend the marks across the MDF to the point at which they intersect.

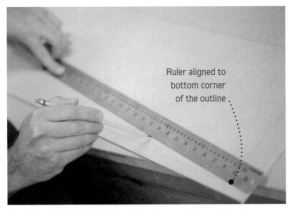

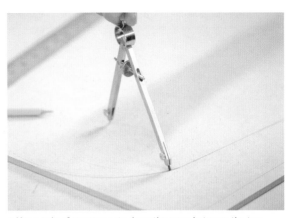

2 On the MDF, mark a diagonal line from the bottom corner of the outline of the side piece to the intersection point marked in the previous step. This will form the start of the curve of the shelf side.

3 Use a pair of compasses to draw the curve between the top of the diagonal line and the top corner of the MDF.

4 Cut out the template from the MDF on a band saw (pictured) or by hand with a coping saw. Cut away the waste in sections.

5 Clean up the template edges. Use a block plane to smooth the straight edges and sandpaper for the curved edge.

CUTTING THE SIDE PIECES

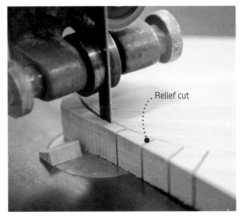

Relief cut

2 Cut each side piece roughly to shape with a band saw, removing the waste in stages using relief cuts (see p.16) and giving the blade room to maneuver. Be sure to cut to the waste side of the marks to allow for finishing (see next step).

1 Place the template onto each of the side pieces in turn, and draw around it to mark the shape.

4 Cut the side to shape, working in the direction of the grain to avoid tearing the wood. Repeat on the second side piece.

Bearing runs along the template

3 Clamp the template under a side piece, then adjust a router and bearing-mounted cutter so that the bearing runs along the template.

MARKING OUT AND CUTTING THE SHELF HOUSINGS

1 Mark the position of the first shelf housing on one side piece (see the diagram on p.205), using a pencil and square.

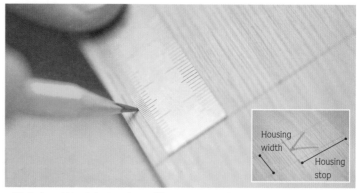

Housing width

Housing stop

2 Mark the width of the housing at ¹¹⁄₁₆ in (18mm)—¹⁄₁₆ in (2mm) less than the thickness of the shelf piece. Mark the length of the housing, which is calculated as the length of the shelf less a ³⁄₈ in (10mm) stop from the front edge (inset).

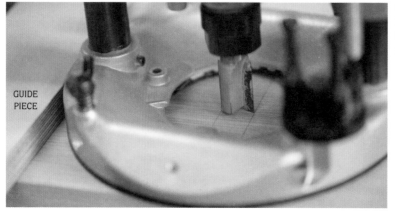

GUIDE PIECE

3 Set the router to a depth of ¹⁄₈ in (3mm), then insert a router cutter no larger than the width of the housing. Using a straight edge as a guide, cut the housing.

4 Use a bevel-edged chisel to square off the housing stop. Repeat steps 1–4 for the remaining housings on both side pieces.

5 Use a pencil and square to mark the width of each housing on the back edge and outside face of the side pieces.

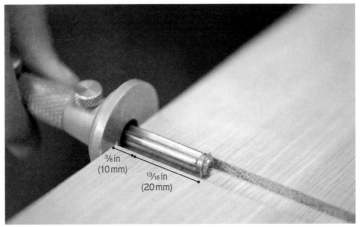

6 Using a marking gauge, mark two mortises $^{13}/_{16}$ in (20 mm) in length within each housing, $^{3}/_{8}$ in (10 mm) from each edge.

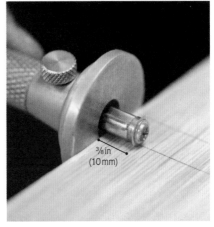

7 Mark the mortise positions on the outside face of the side piece.

8 Clamp the side piece over a piece of spare wood and remove most of the waste from each mortise using a drill fitted with a bit no wider than the housing. Drill completely through the side piece.

9 Square off the sides of the mortises with the chisel. Turn the piece over and complete the edges on the other side. Cut all of the mortises in all of the housings in the same way.

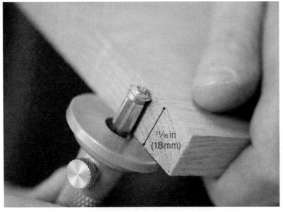

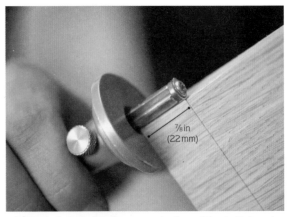

1 Use a marking gauge to scribe the tenon thickness—$^{11}/_{16}$in (18mm)—on the end grain at both ends of Shelf 1.

2 Scribe the length of the tenons on the face of the shelf piece at both ends using the marking gauge set to $^7/_8$in (22mm).

3 Cut a $^1/_{16}$in (2mm) shoulder for the tenons at both ends using a router. Set the fence on the router against the end grain to position the cutter accurately, and set the depth to $^1/_{16}$in (2mm).

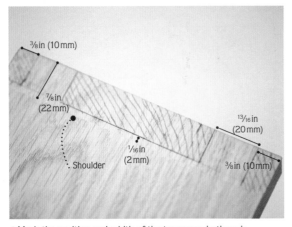

$^3/_8$in (10mm)

$^7/_8$in (22mm)

$^{13}/_{16}$in (20mm)

$^1/_{16}$in (2mm)

$^3/_8$in (10mm)

Shoulder

4 Mark the position and width of the tenons on both ends of Shelf 1. Repeat steps 1–4 for Shelves 2–4.

5 Cut out the tenons with a band saw (pictured) or by hand with a coping saw. Repeat the tenons on Shelves 2–4.

1 Draw a diagonal line from corner to corner on the end grain of each tenon, ensuring that all the diagonals are parallel.

2 Using a small tenon saw, cut a diagonal slot along the marks to the full length of each tenon.

3 Cut the veneer pieces for the wedges to the required length of 1 ¹⁄₁₆ in (27 mm) with a small tenon saw.

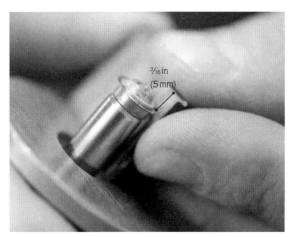

4 Mark the start of the taper ³⁄₁₆ in (5 mm) from the edge of each wedge. Repeat on the other side.

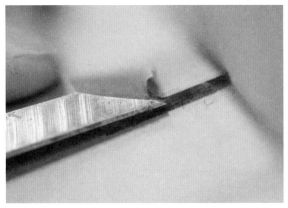

5 With a chisel angled downward, pare the wedges, starting at the mark, to achieve a taper. Repeat on the other side.

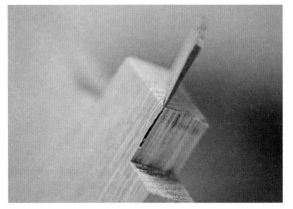

6 The thin end of the wedges should be narrow enough to fit into the diagonal slot in the end grain of the tenon.

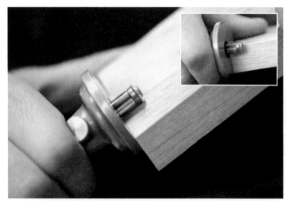

1 Measure and mark the shoulder at ³⁄₈ in (10 mm) from the end grain on the face of the brace. Extend the marks halfway down each of the edges (inset).

2 Reset the marking gauge to half the thickness of the brace, then mark this measurement on the end grain and around the edges of the brace.

3 Cut the shoulder on the brace with a table-mounted router (pictured) or chisel the shoulder by hand. Set the router depth to half the thickness of the brace.

4 Place the brace in the desired position on the side piece and mark it with a pencil.

5 Set the router to the depth of the rebate of the brace (inset). Cut the rebate in the side piece with the router.

6 Square up the edges of the rebate with the chisel. Repeat steps 1–6 to cut the rebate on the second side piece.

ASSEMBLING THE BOOKCASE

1 Assemble and test fit all the parts except for the wedges of the bookcase. Make any necessary adjustments.

2 With the brace in position, mark two screw holes at each end of the back of the brace, centered within the rebate width.

3 Drill pilot holes through the brace and into the rebate, and finish with a countersink bit. Insert the screws (inset).

4 When you are happy with the fit, dismantle the bookcase and sand all the surfaces except the outward-facing surfaces of each side prior to gluing.

1 Apply wood glue to all of the tenons and housings using a brush, then assemble the main elements of the bookcase.

2 Clamp one shelf at a time to prepare it to receive the wedges. Apply glue to the tip of each wedge and hammer each one into its slot. Place a block between the hammer and wedge to prevent splitting.

3 Complete the clamping, using blocks to distribute the pressure on either side of each shelf.

4 Wipe away any excess glue and leave to dry. Pare off any glue that remains when partly dry with a chisel or pointed stick.

⬙ CUTTING THE TENONS FLUSH

1 Use a flush-cut saw to cut each of the wedged tenon ends flush to the sides of the bookcase.

2 Use a block plane to plane the wedged tenon ends smooth to the face of the bookcase sides. Sand and finish with oil.

THE FINISHED PIECE

WEDGED TENON DETAIL

ALTERNATIVES

You can adapt this design by increasing the height of the sides and adding more shelves. You can also increase the length of the shelves, although if you require them to be more than a third longer, you should create an extra vertical support in the center to carry the additional weight of the loaded shelves. In the alternative version pictured here, the wedged tenons have been left proud of the bookcase sides.

GLOSSARY

Aperture
The gap or opening between two parts of the same structure—for example, the distance between two table legs.

Arris
The sharp edge between angled surfaces. (A rectangular section piece of wood has 12 arrises.) It is usually rounded or beveled before finishing.

Assemble
Put together, in the correct formation, the various parts required to construct a particular object or section.

Base
The lowest supporting layer that forms the foundation of any structure.

Bearing-guided cutter
A router cutter with a bearing mounted on the shaft. The bearing rotates freely around the shaft and traces the edge of the workpiece or template, guiding the cutter without the aid of a fence or other jig. It is also called a template profile cutter.

Bench hook
A wooden board with two smaller blocks of wood attached horizontally, at opposite ends and on opposite sides. Latched over a workbench, it acts as a stable barrier against which another piece of wood can be held firmly in place.

Box stay
A metal brace that holds a box lid open in order to stop it from slamming shut or opening beyond a desired point.

Break out
The unsightly damage to a cut or hole that is sometimes made as the blade, cutter, or bit exits the wood, breaking and tearing the fibers from the surface. Using backing material to support the workpiece (an off-cut, for example) or working from both sides reduces or eliminates break out.

Buttons
Small, step-shaped wooden fittings that are used to attach a table top to its frame.

Carcase
The basic structure of any box-shaped piece of furniture, such as a cabinet.

Caul
A strong flat board (sometimes curved)—used when gluing veneer to a core—that distributes the force exerted by cross-bearers and a clamping system.

Chamfer
The flattened-down (or beveled) edge of a piece of wood, typically cut to a 45-degree angle.

Cheek (tenon)
The name given to the sides of a tenon. *See* Tenon.

Countersink
A conical hole bored into a piece of wood—when a screw is fully inserted into the hole, the top of the screw should fit neatly into the countersink and sit flush with the level of the wood.

Cross-cut
A cut that is made at a right angle to the direction of the wood grain.

Cutting line
A line marked with pencil or scored into the surface of the wood that forms a guide along which a saw or similar tool can cut.

De-nib
Remove the nibs by raising the grain and fine sanding or, after a sealing coat, just fine sanding. *See* Nibs.

Depth mark
A marking on the surface of a piece of wood that indicates how deep into the wood a cut (with a saw, or similar) should penetrate.

Dividing rail
A rail that is inserted into a space to create two separate cavities.

Double rebate
Two matching grooves that are cut to leave a thin strip of wood (called a tongue) running between them.

Face
The two flat sides of a piece of wood (as opposed to the edges).

Fence
Usually part of a tool or machine that helps guide the tool or the workpiece. For example, the fence of a band saw is set a particular distance from the blade; the workpiece is passed across the machine and against the fence, producing a piece of wood with parallel sides.

Figure
The surface pattern of a piece of wood, including growth rings, grain patterns, color streaks, and knots.

Floating panel
A panel fitted loosely within a frame. The panel is not glued but instead allowed to swell and shrink within grooves (or rebates and beading). Necessary in solid wood construction. *See also* Frame-and-panel construction.

Flush-cut saw
A flexible hand-held saw with teeth that only cut on the pull stroke. It can cut protruding dowels or tenons flush to the wood's surface without causing extraneous damage.

Frame-and-panel construction
A piece of furniture is defined as "solid wood" when made solely from wood, and neither veneer nor manufactured board. A door cannot be made from a single piece of wood or wood joined edge-to-edge, because it would warp and swell and shrink; it has to be made as a frame (sometimes with divisions) with loose panels set in grooves. As such, it is more flexible and able to expand and contract with fluctuating humidity and temperatures. *See also* Floating panel.

Gluing area
The area of the wood that is to be glued.

Grain
The orientation of a wood's fibers and the texture created as a result.

Groove
A long indentation or gutter cut into a piece of wood to follow the grain.

Hardwood
Hardwood timber is found in a group of broad-leaved, primarily deciduous, trees that are classified as angiosperms. (Their seeds are encased in a shell.) They boast a variety of colors and are more durable than softwoods. They are also usually—but not always—harder (denser) than softwoods.

Housing
The cut-out groove in a piece of wood, into which another piece of wood is snugly fitted (housed).

Housing piece
The piece of wood into which the housing is cut.

Joining edge
The edge of a piece of wood that is joined—either by glue or another mechanism—to the edge of another.

Joint
The point at which two or more pieces of wood are joined together—by gluing, slotting, or screwing—to create a frame or structure.

Kerf
The width of the groove or cut made by a cutting tool, such as a saw. A dovetail saw has a narrow kerf, a band saw has a medium kerf, and a circular saw has a wide kerf. Also a slot for a key.

Key (veneer)
A miter joint can be reinforced after it has been constructed using pieces of veneer set in kerfs that bridge the two parts of the joint. The kerfs can also be set at angles other than 90 degrees for a stronger and more decorative effect.

Knocked down
Disassembled or taken to pieces.

Knot
A defect in the surface of wood where there is variable grain direction, creating a dark knotlike mark on the wood.

Lap
The strip of wood on a socket piece that encases the tails of the lapped dovetail joint.

Lap joint
A joint that is created by the overlapping of two pieces of wood and securing them together.

Mark out
To draw relevant guidelines or shapes on a piece of wood, in preparation for cutting.

MDF
A medium-density fiberboard made from wood fibers and resin fused together under intense heat and pressure. It is a better-quality alternative to chipboard, although it does not have the tensile strength of plywood. It is an ideal substrate for veneering and is dimensionally stable. (It does not warp, swell, or shrink.) Unfortunately, the dust produced when it is machined is a particular health hazard, and you must always wear a face mask when working with it.

Miter block
A cutting aid for hand-held saws, this wood block has deep grooves arranged at different angles, through which a saw can be positioned to ensure that it cuts at the required angle.

Mortise
The hole or recess in a piece of wood, designed to receive the matching tenon of another piece of wood, forming a joint.

Mortise depth/width
The depth or width to which a mortise is cut into a piece of wood.

Mortise piece
The piece of wood into which the mortise is cut.

Nibs
The raised fibers on a surface before it is truly smooth. Also the raised fibers and sealed-in dust after a sealing coat has been applied.

Off-cuts
Surplus material (for example, wood) that remains after the main pieces have been cut.

Oil content
Some woods, such as teak or iroko, have a very high oil content, meaning that they may require no special finish once a piece has been crafted. Oil is a natural defense against rot.

Panel pins
Slim, round nails typically used for attaching beadings and moldings in place.

Pare
To remove or cut away excess material in order to create a specific shape, such as using a chisel to shave wood into a right angle.

Peg
A small, tapered notch of wood that is inserted into a mortise to act as a stop against tension and hold two pieces of wood together.

Pilot hole
A small test hole that is bored into a piece of wood; it acts as a stabilizer into which the drill can be positioned to bore a larger hole over it to the required dimensions. Pilot holes are also used for screws to avoid shearing the screw or splitting the wood.

Pin
The matching, interlocking fingers (pins) carved into the end grain of two pieces of wood. The pins of one piece fit neatly into the sockets of the other, allowing the two pieces to slot together.

Plywood
A manufactured board that is molded into thin sheets and layered on top of one another, with the grains of each sheet running in opposite directions for additional strength.

Quarter-cut
A means of extracting wood from its log—the log is cut into quarters, and each quarter then cut into strips running perpendicular to the wood rings. This provides a consistent grain and gives the wood stability.

Racking
If a structure suffers from racking, it is unable to resist side-to-side movement and requires reinforcement.

Ratio
The relation in value or quantity between two different things.

Rebate
A groove that is cut along one edge of a piece of wood to give a two-tiered, or step, effect.

Relief cut
A preliminary cut made perpendicular to the cutting line when cutting a curve. Relief cuts "relieve" the tension on the saw blades when cutting around a curve.

Ripping
Sawing wood along the grain.

Sand
To rub down a wood surface with a piece of sandpaper (*see below*).

Sandpaper
Abrasive paper that can be rubbed over a rough wood surface to smooth it out.

Sap (bleeding)
A sticky substance that oozes from knots and fissures in softwood and can also sometimes bleed out after the wood has been crafted. (If this is a likelihood, then a preventative knotting solution should be applied.)

Sapwood
The young wood found on the outer edges of a tree trunk or branch. Unlike heartwood, it is living wood that transfers water up from the roots toward the leaves. It is often avoided because it is a different color to the bulk of the wood; does not absorb stain in the same way as the surrounding wood; and is soft, weak, and susceptible to rot.

Scarf joint
This acts as a lengthening device by joining the identically shallow-beveled edges of two pieces of wood and gluing them into one long strip.

Score
Mark a line along a piece of wood by cutting lightly into the surface.

Scribe
To mark a guideline into a piece of wood with a tool, such as a marking gauge.

Seasoning
Drying out wood prior to using it for woodworking (a lengthier process for hardwoods than softwoods because they are more dense). In theory, this ensures that the dimensions of the wood remain constant and do not fluctuate with humidity.

Shake
A crack or split in the wood.

Shank
The shaft or stem of a fastening or tool.

Shoot
The final, accurate planing of an end or edge.

Shrinkage
Occurs in timber as it dries. Seasoned wood in a finished piece is subject to shrinkage as the moisture in the air changes seasonally. All structures must permit shrinkage and expansion.

Socket piece
A piece of wood that has been cut with a slot or socket, into which a tenon or tailpiece can be fitted.

Softwood
The timber from a group of coniferous, primarily evergreen, trees that are classified as gymnosperms. (Their seeds have no protective casing.) They are softer than most but not all hardwoods and have strong growth-ring patterns.

Splay
A widening of a shape or related parts. A wedged tenon is splayed at the end.

Splinters
Thin, spiky shards of wood that protrude or break off from the wood's surface when it is rough.

Squareness
When the distances between the diagonally opposite corners of a square are of equal length.

Stile
The vertical part of a frame.

Stock
The raw, uncrafted piece of wood from which a workpiece is created. Also part of a tool.

Stop
A device in a jig or machine that restricts movement, controlling depth or size, for example. It is usually involved in performing repeat operations.

Stub tenon
A short tenon that is usually square in shape and will not penetrate through a mortise.

Surface
The outermost layer of a material.

Taper
A gradual narrowing in depth or width.

Tearing
When wood is cut roughly, causing the wood fibers to rip and splinter.

Tempering
The process that is applied to steel (especially tools), improving its hardness.

Template
An outline drawing, shape, or pattern that provides a method for accurately transferring a design onto the final material.

Tenon
A protrusion on the end of a piece of wood that is designed to fit into a mortise of matching dimensions, forming a joint.

Tenon face
The wide, flat sides of a tenon.

Tenon piece
The piece of wood into which the tenon has been cut.

Tolerance
The scope of variation of an object's characteristics, including weight, dimensions, and density.

Tongue
A protrusion of wood that is designed to fit exactly into a corresponding groove.

Trammel
A homemade device or beam compass which acts like a pair of compasses for drawing large circles. Also an attachment for routing circles.

V-groove
A V-shaped groove that is cut into the surface of wood with a bevel-edged chisel.

V-mark
A V-shaped pencil mark that is made across pieces of wood when creating a butt joint—the pieces can be accurately aligned by using the pencil marks.

Veneer
A thin sheet of wood that is glued to the surface of a core material to give the impression of solid wood. Burr wood can usually only be used as a veneer in a piece of furniture. Pictures and patterns (marquetry and parquetry) are made from various veneers arranged for decorative effect.

Vise
A screw mechanism with two panels that is tightened to hold a workpiece firmly ready for cutting, planing, shaping, and so on.

Warp
A distortion within the surface of a piece of wood.

Waste side
The side of a workpiece from which waste is removed. When referring to a cutting line, it is the side of the line which is considered to be waste.

Wedge
A tapered piece of wood wedged securely into a slot to fit a joint in place or for another holding purpose.

Workpiece
A piece of wood that is being worked on or has been worked on, using either hand or machine tools.

INDEX

ACKNOWLEDGMENTS

FIRST EDITION

For her excellent research and legwork, thanks go to Nasim Mawji.

For help and advice during the early stages of development, thanks go to Peter Korn, Rod Wales, and Jon Binzen.

For assistance with the book and photography, special thanks go to the staff and students of the Building Crafts College: Len Conway, Dave Pearham, John Wilkie, Cornelius Lynch, Marcus Dadson, Jacob Arch, Joe Beever, John Fishwick, Keturah Hayden, Catherine James, Kelli Knight, Zuber Miah, Jason Muteham, Alfred Newall, Joseph Sivell, and Mark Tindley.

For additional photography of timbers, thanks go to both David Mager Photography and Julie Renouf Photography.

For consultancy work, thanks go to Alan, Gill and Glyn Bridgewater of AG&G Books, Hamish Hill, and Marc Schmidt.

For providing tools and manufacturers' shots, special thanks go to Axminster Tool Centre (www.axminster.co.uk).

For providing additional tools and manufacturers' shots, thanks go to Bagpress; DeWalt/Black & Decker; E. C. Emmerich; Felder UK; Festool; Hegner UK; Jet; Makita; Metabo; TTS Tooltechnic Systems GB Limited; and Ulmia GmbH.

For help with the sourcing, supply, and preparation of timbers and veneers, thanks go to the following merchants and individuals: Alan Curtis; Capital Crispin Veneer; Exotic Woods Incorporated; George Sykes Limited; Gilmer Wood; ITC Limited; Peter Kidman, Kidman Furniture; Mathews Timber; Ockendon Timbers; Thorogood Timber; Timbmet; Timberline; the Timber Research and Development Association (TRADA); Alan Ward; and Yandle and Sons.

Dorling Kindersley would like to thank: consultant Julian Cassell and writers Alan Bridgewater, Gill Bridgewater, Glyn Bridgewater, Colin Eden-Eadon, Sally Francis, John Lloyd, Jonathan Tibbs, and J. M. Wilkie. DK India: Senior Editor Nidhilekha Mathur; Editor Arani Sinha; Senior Art Editor Ira Sharma; Art Editors Aparajita Barai, Vikas Sachdeva; Assistant Art Editor Sourabh Challariya; Managing Editor Alicia Ingty; Managing Art Editor Navidita Thapa; Pre-production Manager Sunil Sharma; Senior DTP Designer Tarun Sharma; and DTP Designer Mohammad Usman. DK UK: Senior Designers Joanne Doran, Clare Marshall; Project Editor Shashwati Tia Sarkar; Managing Editor Penny Warren; Jacket Designer Rosie Levine; Pre-production Producer Andy Hilliard; Senior Producer Alex Bell; Creative Technical Support Sonia Charbonnier; Art Director Jane Bull; Publisher Mary Ling; Vicky Read for design assistance; and Sue Butterworth for indexing.

PICTURE CREDITS

The publisher would like to thank the following for their kind permission to reproduce their photographs:

(Key: a-above; b-below/bottom; c-center; f-far; l-left; r-right; t-top)

27 Dorling Kindersley: Fire Investigation Unit at Acton Police Station, London (tr).
35 Silverline Tools: (Forstner bit). **38 Dreamstime.com:** David Coleman (clb).
50 Courtesy of Axminster Tool Centre Ltd.: (cl). **142 Dorling Kindersley:** John Lloyd Furniture (cra). **143 Dorling Kindersley:** John Lloyd Furniture

All other images © Dorling Kindersley

For further information see: www.dkimages.com

ABOUT THE CONTRIBUTORS

Alan and Gill Bridgewater formed AG&G Books in 1998, and have gained an international reputation as producers of highly successful gardening and DIY books across a range of subjects, including garden design; ethnic woodwork; and, of course, household woodwork.

Glyn Bridgewater MA (RCA) studied furniture design at Loughborough College of Art and Design and at the Royal College of Art, London. He is co-author of *How to Make Simple Wooden Puzzles and Jigsaws* and *The Boxcart Bible*.

Colin Eden-Eadon has been involved with wood all of his working life. Having worked for the Forestry Commission in England, he trained as a furniture maker before moving into teaching and writing about woodworking after a period spent as a master craftsman with renowned furniture maker John Makepeace. He later became a contributor to and editor of *Furniture and Cabinetmaking*.

Sally Francis is a post-doctoral-qualified botanist working as a writer, journalist, and consultant specializing in crops, timber, and trees. Her articles and features have been published in *Furniture and Cabinetmaking*, *Woodturning*, the farming media, gardening magazines, and elsewhere. Sally is also a keen woodworker and enjoys turning and furniture making.

John Lloyd is trained in cabinet making and antique furniture restoration and conservation, and was awarded the City and Guilds of London Institute first prize for advanced studies in furniture for furniture making and antique restoration. His commissions include work from Sotheby's, Christie's, St. Paul's Cathedral, and numerous private clients, along with site work for the National Trust. He runs courses at his own workshops in Sussex and has lectured at West Dean College. John is a full member of The British Antique Furniture Restorers' Association.

Jonathan Tibbs studied fine art at Falmouth College of Arts and went on to specialize in furniture making at the Building Crafts College, London. Since graduating, he has exhibited internationally and picked up a number of awards for his work. He now runs his business designing and making bespoke and batch production furniture.

J. M. Wilkie has had a lifelong interest in working with wood. A chartered civil engineer, he retrained as a furniture maker, being awarded the City and Guilds Medal for Excellence on completion of his training. He now has his own commercial workshop, is a member of the Society of Designer-Craftsmen, and holds the Master Carpenter Certificate.

Neither the authors nor the publisher take any responsibility for any injury or damage resulting from the use of techniques shown or described in this book. The reader is advised to follow all safety instructions carefully, wear the correct protective clothing, and, where appropriate, follow all manufacturers' instructions. For more detailed information on Health and Safety, please see pages 11 and 52–53.

SECOND EDITION
Senior Editor Dawn Titmus
US Editor Kayla Dugger
Senior Art Editor Glenda Fisher
DTP Designers Manish Upreti, Satish Gaur, Rajdeep Singh, Anurag Trivedi
Manager, Pre-production Sunil Sharma
Senior Production Editor Tony Phipps
Senior Production Controller Stephanie McConnell
Jacket Designer Amy Cox
Jacket Coordinator Lucy Philpott
Managing Editor Ruth O'Rourke
Managing Art Editor Christine Keilty
Art Director Maxine Pedliham
Publishing Director Katie Cowan

Content previously published in the United States in *Woodwork: A Step-by-Step Photographic Guide to Successful Woodworking*, 2010.
This American Edition, 2021
First American Edition, 2014
Published in the United States by DK Publishing
1450 Broadway, Suite 801, New York, NY 10018

A catalog record for this book
is available from the Library of Congress.
ISBN 978-0-7440-2687-0

Printed in China

For the curious

www.dk.com

FSC
www.fsc.org
MIX
Paper from
responsible sources
FSC™ C018179

This book was made with Forest Stewardship Council ™ certified paper—one small step in DK's commitment to a sustainable future. For more information go to www.dk.com/our-green-pledge